GÁBOR VÉKONY

DACIANS-ROMANS-ROMANIANS

2000

MATTHIAS CORVINUS PUBLISHING

Original Hungarian title:

DÁKOK, RÓMAIAK, ROMÁNOK
Akadémiai Kiadó
1989, Budapest

****
Special thanks to Dr. László Jeney, who many years ago
gave us a good start with a substancial contribution
and is still one of our regular supporters.
Also heartfelt thanks to his family:
Dr. Piroska Jeney, Dr. Kriszta Jeney and her husband
T. S. Magyarody and Dr. Elisabeth Jeney,
who are all our faithfull contributors.
****

First English Edition

ISBN
1-882785-13-4

Library of Congress No.
00 130069

Printed in the United States of America

THE AUTHOR

Dr. Gábor Vékony was born in 1944 in Hungary. Received his degree in history and archeology from the Eötvös Loránd University of Budapest in 1968. With his dissertation on the Iranian connections to the Central European early Iron Age, obtained his Ph.d. in 1969.

Worked between 1968 and 1967 in a Museum, and has been lecturing at the Eötvös Loránd University since 1970.

His main area of research: The prehistory of Central and Eastern-Europe and also the ethnogenetic process of the same area. He led many archeological excavations and still does it in Hungary. Several of his books and over two hundred studies, essays had been published so far. He was also a major contributor to the **History of Transylvania**, published in 1994, by the Akadémiai Kiadó of Budapest.

Dr. Vékony was also engaged in an intensive study of Eastern-Europe in the early Middle Ages and wrote a major work on Hungarian ethnogenesis.

In his studies he elicited the truth regarding the Rumanian ethnogenesis, and the theory of Daco-Roman-Rumanian continuity.

In 1987 received the prize of the Academy and was among the first ones to receive the Széchenyi Professorial Scholarship. He is a Candidate of the Hungarian Academy of Sciences.

Among his works are:
The Prehistoric Transylvania, 1986
Inscriptiones runiformie medii aevi in Hungaria, 1987,
The Age of Anonymus and its Authenticity, 1991,
Ancient History of Mankind, 1993,
Prehistory, 1994
The Stages of the Hungarian Ethnogenesis,
From Scythia to Hungaria
The Ethno-Political Relations in the Carpathian Basin in he 9th Century

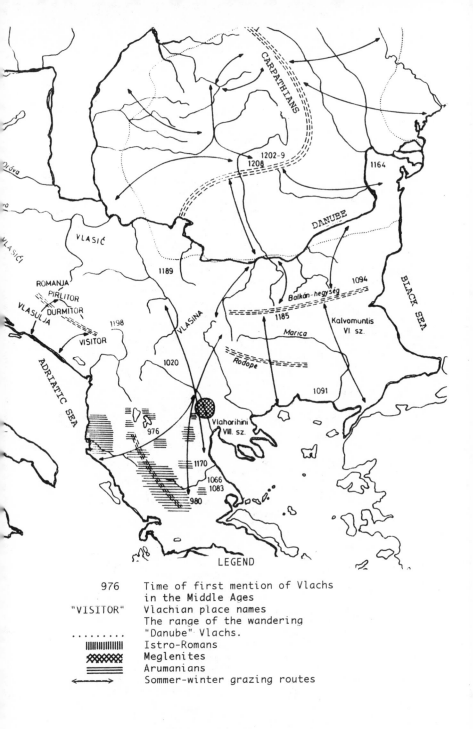

LEGEND

976	Time of first mention of Vlachs in the Middle Ages
"VISITOR"	Vlachian place names
....	The range of the wandering "Danube" Vlachs.
▦	Istro-Romans
✕✕✕✕	Meglenites
≡≡≡	Arumanians
←——→	Sommer-winter grazing routes

DISPERSAL OF THE VLACHS FROM
THEIR SOUTHERN-BALKAN HOMELAND

v

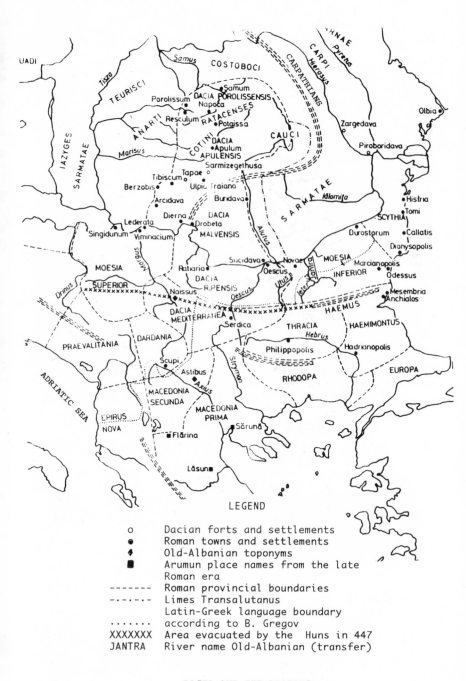

LEGEND

o	Dacian forts and settlements
●	Roman towns and settlements
♦	Old-Albanian toponyms
■	Arumun place names from the late Roman era
-------	Roman provincial boundaries
-..-..-	Limes Transalutanus
....	Latin-Greek language boundary according to B. Gregov
XXXXXXX	Area evacuated by the Huns in 447
JANTRA	River name Old-Albanian (transfer)

DACIA AND THE BALKANS
IN THE LATE-ROMAN PERIOD

vi

Chapter I

The development and history of the theory of Dacian-Roman-Rumanian continuity

Let us clarify for the reader - who may not necessarily be an expert on the subject - that first, we will only be discussing viewpoints pertaining to Rumanians who inhabit the former Roman province of Dacia (present day Oltenia and part of Transylvania). There is nothing unusual about the continuity and survival of Latin speaking ethnic groups from the region/era of Imperium Romanum. On the other hand, if the Rumanian language is heir to the language spoken by the inhabitants of the province of Dacia, then this language was spoken not only here but on most of the Balkan Peninsula; Rumanians inhabiting Romania today are not the only ones using this neo-Latin language. We know that Rumanians also reside beyond the borders of Romania. The 1977 Rumanian census counted 19,003,511 Rumanians within Rumania; 2,525,687 in Moldavia and also smaller entities in Yugoslavia, Bulgaria and Hungary. An estimated 1,200,000 Rumanians lived in the diaspora prior to World War II - mostly in the Americas and in Australia. By now this census data is no longer accurate, of course. It is less well known that, in addition to Rumanians who live outside Romania, national entities can be found in several areas of the Balkan Peninsula which speak a language or languages similar to Rumanian. Most significant among them are the Arumuns who live in Greece, Albania, Macedonia and Bulgaria.

Their estimated number varies between 300.000 and 600,000. The majority reside in Greece, in Thessaly and Epirus (the area of the Pindus Mountain), where an estimated 150 - 200,000 live. These peoples are frequently called Macedo-Rumanians but call themselves Ar(u)mân^u, Rumân^u or Râmân, while Greeks know them as Kutsovlach (lame or limping Vlachs). Their Albanian name is Rëmër or Çoban originating, respectively, from the Latin *romanus* and the Turkish word for shepherd. In Bulgaria, they are known as Belivlachs i.e. White Vlachs (while Rumanians in Romania are called Karavlasi, or Black Vlachs). The Serbs know them as Cincars which is a nickname, making fun of the frequent "c" (ts) sound in the Arumun language. The majority of the population are shepherds practicing transhumance, a form of herding characteristic of this population. Some have also become skilled merchants and craftsmen. Other than Rumanians living in Romania, only the Arumun have a written language among the Rumanian speaking nationalities in the Balkans. Their oldest linguistic relic is an Icon - inscription, dating from 1731, which was found in Albania.

The Arumun also had notable scholars, such as George Murnu who was exploring the history of his people. Also, Pericle Papahagi and Tache Papahagi; they compiled a collection of Arumun literature. Another nearly extinct group of Rumanians of the Balkan Peninsula are the Meglenoruman(ian)s. This name derives from the Moglena region of Macedonia, where this group of people lived along the right bank of the river Vardar. They call themselves Vlaşi: the only

Rumanian ethnic group in whose language we do not find "*romanus*" (in Meglenoruman[ian], this word could be "*Rumon*)". We have no exact data of their number. Various estimates range from 14,000 to 26,000. They became Mohammedans and a significant number of them resettled in Asia Minor after W.W.I.

The Istrorumanians are the smallest group of Rumanians, living on the Istrian Peninsula. Statistics from 1846 claim their number to be 6000; there were only 1200 -1500 by 1971. They call themselves Vlaş or Vlas. Earlier they also used the name Rumeri or Rumări, another version of Romanus. To the north the Žejanians call themselves "cici" and the Croatians and Italians call the Istrorumanians: "ciribiri". Both are names of derision, based on certain characteristics of these respective languages. That they themselves were willing to use these names suggests the extent of their assimilation. Without exception, they speak Croatian; sooner or later this bi-lingualism will make their assimilation complete.

There have been disputes pertaining to the origin and interrelationship of these four Rumanian groups, and they continue to this day. It should be noted that these languages have a common pre-history based on similarities of syntax, vocabulary, inflection and like absorption of new-word segments; they cannot be separated from each other. Theirs was a perpetual relationship up to the 11th century: *Common Rumanian*. Of the four Rumanian groups of common origin only the Arumuns and the contemporary (northern) Rumanians appear in early literature of Byzantine and western writers. Of the two, the Arumuns appear first; partly in the writings of Byzantine authors and partly in western accounts of the Crusades. The first unmistakable reference to Northern Rumanians in the Carpathian Basin is to be found at the beginning of the 13th century; among the armies sent by Joachim - the overlord of Nagyszeben (Sibiu) - to liberate Vidin, Rumanians (Olaci) are noted along with Saxons, Szeklers and Petchenegs. This event occurred between 1208 - 13; probably in 1208. Only much later do references appear pertaining to the origin of Northern Rumanians inhabiting the territory of the former Dacia.

Poggio Bracciolini, Florentine humanist (1380 - 1459) makes first mention of this topic in a work he wrote in 1451. According to him, in the western part of Eastern Europe *(apud superiores Sarmatas)* live the descendants of Emperor Trajan's settlers, who retained a great deal of the original Latin language. Among others, they used the Latin words *oculus* (Rum. *ochi* ´eye´), *digitus* (Rum. *deget* ´finger´), *manus* (Rum. *mînă* ´hand´), *panis* (Rum. *pîine* ´bread´). Poggio Bracciolini bases these observations on hearsay. While we know nothing about his sources, we can take it for granted that he is writing about Moldavian Rumanians; in those days Sarmatians were mentioned only in relation to areas east of the Carpathians and of the Vistula river. In all likelihood, it was a mercantile center along the Black Sea, which spread word about a language - similar to Italian - being spoken by Moldavian Rumanians. When this news reached Italy, local scholars well-versed in the history of Rome inferred a connection with the Dacian conquest of Trajan and specifically with the Romans who were resettled North of the Danube. Nevertheless, our author makes no mention of Dacia. From the end of the 14th century on, Moldavia lay east of Dacia during the reign of Rome, within the area east of the Carpathians, up to the river Dnestr and south to the Black Sea. Thus, the first statement as regards the similarity of Rumanians to Romans - as in the case of Rumanians in the Balkans - did not refer to those Rumanians who live in the area, which was once a province of Trajan.

If not Dacia itself, but Dacians are recognized by Flavio Biondo, noted secretary and scholar of the Clerical State (1392 - 1463). After the fall of Constantinople in 1453 he writes about Dacians or Valachs *(Ripenses Daci sive Valachi)* who are of Roman descent. In some of his letters he writes about *"Ulachos* of Roman Blood" but he identifies them not with Dacians, but with the Moes-es of antiquity, who lived along the banks of the Danube. (For good measure, he also includes Serbs and Bulgarians.) It is noteworthy that Flavio Biondo uses the designation *Ulach* for the Rumanians (Vlachs), whose sound pattern resembles their Hungarian name *(oláh)*. Even though Biondo knows of the Rumanian descent of János Hunyadi, he is familiar primarily with Rumanians South of the Danube and in Wallachia.

Northern Rumanians - as remnants of Trajan's Dacian settlers - first appear in concrete form in the writings of Aeneas Sylvius Piccolomini (1405 - 1464) who will become known as Pope Pius II (1458 -1464). This noted author of many scholarly works has a clear view of Rumanians north of the Danube who are supposedly descendants of Roman soldiers, sent to fight against the Dacians. The Roman legions were to have been commanded by a military leader named Flaccus (Pomponius Flaccus in Latin), Governor of Moesia. Rumanians were to have been named after him: *Flaccus* becoming *Valachus.* According to Aeneas Sylvius, Rumanians speak a notably flawed Latin - Italians can barely understand it. This intellectual exercise - along with Ovidius' story about Chief Flaccus -

took on a life of its own in the historiography of the origin of the Rumanians.

Subsequent to such prolegomena Antonio Bonfini attributes a level of scientific study to his essay pertaining to Rumanians' descent from Roman settlers in Dacia, i.e. from the legionnaires of Trajan. Bonfini (1427? - 1502) lived in Hungary from 1486 on; he had, in contrast to his compatriot Italian Humanists, local knowledge. He was familiar not only with Italian literature on the subject, but also with Latin inscriptions and ruins from Roman times in Hungary. Yet, the only - albeit incessantly repeated - proof of Rumanians' Roman origin is their language and, incidentally and implicitly, their habitation in the place where Dacians and Getas once lived. He has various explanations as to why these Roman - Rumanians are called Valachs. Bonfini disputes Aeneas Sylvius' theory that they were named after Flaccus. He links the origin of their name to their skill in archery (Greek *ballo* means 'to throw, to shoot') but it is also possible that their name is a flawed version (due to the poor pronunciation of Dalmatians) of Valeria, a province named after Diocletian's daughter. These are the explanations of a scholar of his times (and also that of subsequent historians of the 18th century.) The contemporary reader wonders whether Bonfini has ever seen anything of Dacia. It is here that this former Roman province became linked to the Rumanians, and in his text one may also find the seeds of the theory of Dacian-Rumanian continuity. Bonfini also showed interest in the genealogy of Mathias Hunyadi (King of Hungary 1458 - 90); he explored the background of the Corvin lineage: the Roman patrician Corvina-family, the ancestors of the Hunyadis. The Rumanian origin of King Mathias played a significant part in the interest generated in the Roman roots of Rumanians. This was already evident in the case of his father, János (John) Hunyadi (seen in the writings of Pietro Ransano, among others). Descriptions of the Rumanians' Roman origin and of Trajan's settlements by Ransano and in the popular works of Aeneas Sylvius became their scholastic legacy; future historians of the 16th and 17th centuries used this data as their major source, whether they were Hungarians, Transylvanian Saxons or other Europeans. As time goes by the Chieftain Flaccus is omitted as the source of the name: Vlach for Rumanians, but for a long time the view is prevalent that Rumanians are in reality Italians. In part, the reason for this view has to do with Italian scholars' belief that Rumanian is a "half-Italian" or "flawed Italian" language. Another reason: Poles used a similar name for Italians and Rumanians. The first reference to this factor can be found in the writings of G. Pomponio Leto (1425-1498). He was traveling in Eastern Europe, including Poland, around 1480. Leto states: "Dacia is a province extending in both directions beyond the Hister (Danube) which, in our day, was called Volochia and their inhabitants, Volochs. Volochia is Italy, since the Dacians (Rumanians) speak Italian."[1]

In the Polish language Italians were called Wloch, Rumanians were called Woloch. The latter is a word of Russian derivation. The combination of these two designations creates the image that Rumanians are of Italian origin and that they speak some kind of Italian. We can read in the biography of Zbigniew Oleşnicki, Bishop of

---

[1] A. Marcu: Riflessi di storia rumena in opere italiane dei secoli XIV. e XV. Ephemeris Dacoromana I (1923), p. 381.

Crakow (Written by Filippo Buonaccorsi Callimaco (1438-1496) who lived in the court of the Jagellos) that Poles considered Rumanians to be Italians (Italos) and called them by the same name (*Italiae indigenas*).

The views of humanist scholars about the origin of the Rumanians were conclusions based on the science of the Age of Humanism. The facts were: 1) An ethnic group resides in the Lower Danubian and East-Carpathian region whose language resembles Latin and Italian. 2) In the region this population is known by the same name as the Italians. 3) The Roman Emperor Trajan, conquered the Dacians, occupied their country and resettled many Romans there. 4) The Dacians' land, Dacia, was in the same area where the Vlachs lived, who spoke a language resembling Latin.

It is a natural consequence of these facts that the Vlachs (Rumanians) are the descendants of the Roman settlers, sent there by Trajan. The logic of this reasoning leads to the same conclusion and was used not only by Humanist scholars of the 15th and 16th Centuries, but by our contemporaries as well.   Possibly, another circumstance also added weight to this conclusion. The name by which the Rumanians call themselves - Rumîn - is similar to Romanus: Roman (this is its derivation), as well as Italian *romano* etc. An Italian, or speaker of Latin, discovers easily this similarity. For such an individual, nothing could be more natural than to identify *Rumîn* with *Romani* (the Romans). As logical as this supposition appears to be, the first mentioning in a written source of the fact that the Rumanians use a name for themselves, which would suggest Roman extraction appeared very late. The first two references to this circumstance derive from the same time-period and the same environment. Both Tranquillo Andronico (Dalmatian 1490-1571) and Francesco della Valle (from Padua, who died after 1545) belonged to the entourage of Alois Gritti, a governor under Hungarian King János Szapolyai. Tranquillo Adronico writes in a letter, dated Dec.16,1534, that the Rumanians *(Valachi)* now called themselves Romans *(Romani): (nunc se Romanos vocant)*. In 1532 Francesco della Valle accompanies Governor Gritti to Transylvania, Valachia and Moldavia. At this time he notes that they preserved the name of the Romans *(Romani)*.

From this time on we frequently come across mention of Roman for Rumanian in Latin texts; variations from this pattern start to occur from the 17th century on. Orichovius (Stanislaw Orzechowski, 1513-1566) notes as early as 1554 that in their own language, Rumanians are called Romîn (after the Romans) and Walachs in Polish (after the Italians), (qui eorum lingua Romini a Romanis, nostra Walachi, ab Italis appellantur). This version of the name recurs in this short sentence by Francesco della Valle: Sti Rominest? (Şti românеşte?) In the 17th century *Rumîn* appears as Rumun (Johann Tröster), Rumuny (Paul Kovács de Lisznyai), *Rumuin* (Laurentius Toppeltinus), and *Rumen* (Johannes Lucius and Martin Szentiványi).

Undoubtedly, all of them refer to names by which Rumanians refer to themselves. Nonetheless, we believe all this could not have effected the unfolding of the history of the origin of the Rumanians by the Humanist scholars. The first available reference regarding this name is made about a hundred years after we hear of the idea that they descended from Trajan's colonists. There may be several reasons why their name (as Rumîns) played no role originally in the perceived process entailing descent from Trajan's colonizing settlers. There may be several reasons why, as a designation (for Rumanians) Rumîn played no role in the picture, which suggested that the Rumanians derive from Dacian Romans. First and foremost Rumîn in the Middle Ages meant "serf". This may have been why in Rumanian texts and in the language a conversion took place, as a result of which the name evolved into Romîn. This is the usage we find in a 1582 foreword of a partial translation of the Bible (the name appears once as Rumîni and twice as *limba rumînească*). On the other hand, we assume Rumîn was not a frequently used term. Because in their small sheep-herding communities the names they used were frequently an altered form of the name of their leaders *(cneaz)*: Iacobeni, Bogdaneşti; and regarding larger areas, we find names which derive from geographical entities: Moldoveni, Ungureni.

The perceived descent of Rumanians from Roman Dacians, which Humanists propagated on the basis of information available to them, found its way into Rumanian scholastic thinking. Once again, it is Francesco della Valle in whose writings we find the first such reference. He was supposedly told by monks at the monastery of Dealu near Tîrgovişte that Rumanians were supposed to be descendants of colonists whom Trajan resettled. The Greek monks at the monastery in Dealu must have heard this from the Franciscan monastery of Tîrgovişte where many of the friars were Italians.

It is of interest that, originally, Rumanian sources held different descent-theories. The following legend came down to us from the annals of the Russian church in Voskresen; it was written in Old

Church Slavonic, but its Rumanian origin is certain. The chronicle was written around 1504 by an anonymous author. The quotes contain relevant passages. "In 6867 (1359 A.D.) two Christian brothers, Roman and Vlahata are fleeing persecution by heretics and leaving Venice, they come to a place called Old Rome. Here (they) built a castle and named it Roman, after (them)selves. They lived in it up 'til the time when Pope Formosus left the true, Pravoslav (i.e. Byzantine) church for Rome.

Following a division of the laws of Christ, the Latins built themselves a new castle and called it New Rome. They asked the Rumanians (Romanovci) to join them in the Latin church but (the latter) preferred to start a war, rather than forsake the Christian faith.... At the time of King Vladislav the Tartar (Mongolian)s came from the region of the rivers Prut and Moldva. With their Chieftain, Nejmet, they advanced against the Hungarians. King Vladislav got word of the Tartar (Mongolian)s' attack and turned to the Pope and the Emperor in Rome for help. He also sent emissaries to the Old-Romans and Rumanians (Romanovci). Thereupon, we (Romanovci) united with the Old-Romans and went to Hungary to help King Vladislav (László in Hungarian). Soon a decisive battle took place between King László - (Vladislav) and Nejmet, Tartar (Mongolian) Chieftain, along the banks of the river Tisza. The Old-Romans were at the forefront of the battle.... And they defeated the Tartar (Mongolian)s: first the Old-Romans, then the Hungarians and Rumanians (Romanovci); of the Old-Romans not many fell in battle.

László, the Hungarian King, was glad of God's help and highly appreciative of the Old-Romans, whom he rewarded for their fighting spirit..... and he urged them to join his forces and not to return to Old-Rome, because the New-Romans will do them harm... they did not believe the King and asked permission to send some men to their homeland who were to find out whether their women and their children were left alive in Old-Rome. The emissaries left and soon returned to report: our castle, Old-Rome, is in ruins and the New-Romans induced our women and children to adopt their faith. Then they asked King László not to force them into the Latin church and that they should be permitted to keep their Christian faith according to Greek rites. They also asked the King to give them a place to stay. The King was very pleased and gave them land in Mármaros, [at the time part of Hungary; became part of Rumania after W.W.I; translators remark] between the Rivers Tisza (Theiss) and Mores at the place called Krizs. That is where the Old-Romans settled. They started to marry Hungarian women and led them to their own Christian religion. Up to this day they have been living like this...[1] ".

This confusing and historically quite inaccurate story does not crop up anywhere else, but in the 17th century, *logofăt* Istratie, *dascăl* Simion and *călugăr* Misail also connect the settlement of Rumanians in that area with king László the Saint (King Ladislav). According to this version King László asked Rome for help against the Tartar (Mongolian)s, who sent him felons released from prison: these were to have been the ancestors of Rumanians in Máramaros and Moldavia.

It would be difficult to identify the sources of this "Chronicle Anonymous". As suggested by Gábor Lükő, the source could have

---

[1] I. Bogdan: Vechile cronici moldovenești până la Ureche. Bucharest 1891, p. 185-187. (Hungarian translation by G. Lükő: On the Legend about the Founding of Moldavia. *Ethnographia* 47 (1936).

been the Legend of St. László (Ladislav), which was well known in the age of the Anjous. In all likelihood the views of the Humanists during the reign of King Mathias in Hungary may also have given impetus to the legend. Reference to "New-Rome" in connection with the origin of the Rumanians can only be found with Pietro Ransano; he talks about Roma Nova, as well as Romanea. According to his narrative, Constantin the Great was to have brought people from Rome (and Italy) to settle (in Roma Nova) but they went instead to Thrace, Greece and adjoining areas; later Flaccus dux led settlers into Dacia. Ransano does not mention Trajan and his legionnaires, nor does the Anonymous Chronicle. However, he calls New Rome "Romanea", while in the Anonymous Chronicle Old Rome appears as Roman (which, by the way, is a well-known town in Moldavia: roughly translated as Roman Fair). Undoubtedly, the Anonymous Chronicle used Hungarian sources, as well and so did the Istiatie logofăt version! To be sure, these are "scholastic" theories and do not reflect the existence of an established "Roman identity" among Rumanians. On the other hand, there could have been historical basis for land in Máramaros being given to Rumanians by the Hungarian King "between the Rivers Mores and Tisza in a place called Krizs". The Rumanians might have had some reminiscence of such settlement. Geographical data accompanying this notation may be inaccurate (but no more than customary for the period) but we can deduce that Moldavian Rumanians had an awareness that they were newcomers, late settlers along in the territory framed by the Rivers Maros, Tisza and Kőrös-es. In the 15th century and about 1500 some memory must still have existed of settlements being founded in the 13th - 14th centuries. Let us remember: the narrative in the Anonymous Chronicle is typical of legends depicting the origin of nations (in this case the settlement in Moldavia) with sibling-ancestors and hunts, where one animal leads the people to a new land. These legends always contain a kernel of truth.

The Anonymous Chronicle left no traces in the writings about Rumanian history. The first significant Rumanian diarist, Grigore Ureche (1590 - approx. 1647) was a boyar of great learning and culture. When he writes about the origin of the Rumanians, he speaks only of descent from Rome (de la Rîm) and of Flaccus - as per Aeneas Sylvius - name-giver to the Vlachs, describing him (i.e.Flaccus) as "hetman rîmlenesc", i.e. Roman leader. He doesn't even mention Trajan or Dacia and Flaccus is said to have fought the Scythians, although the person whom Ureche used as a resource, Joachim Bielske, (Kronika Polska, 1597) knows about Trajan's wars. He quotes the Latin equivalent of Rumanian words (occasionally incorrectly: părinte = pater) but he is aware that the Rumanian language contains a melange of words.

Miron Costin, Chancellor of Moldavia (1633 -1691) is an even more important personage than Ureche in the annals of literature. Of this Moldavian boyar, who is a writer and poet (and writes in Polish as well) P. P. Panaitescu states: "he worked not as a compiler, but as a historian".[1] In the various works of Miron Costin the "historian's" opinion undergoes a number of changes. In his work dated 1673, Flaccus (Fliah) is the one who is leading the ancestors of Rumanians

---

[1] P.P. Panaitescu: Miron Costin, Contribuții la istoria culturii românești, București, 1871, p. 555.

out of Italy, but by 1675 only Trajan is mentioned. Writing about the Moldavians in his old age, he specifically denies the validity of the legend of Flaccus and his role in naming the Rumanians. Naturally, he reflects the then prevailing Polish expression (Wloch=Italian and Woloch=Rumanian) in pinpointing Italy as the place of origin for Rumanians. He is the first who writes about the Roman Dacians moving to the mountains tò escape Tartar (Mongolian)s during the Mongol invasion. He writes about the "second founding" of Moldavia and Muntenia (the first attaches to the name of Trajan and to the Voivode Negru of legend). The Rumanian word for embankments (troian), which is of Southern Slav etymology, recalls Trajan and he is right in stating that rumîn is the equivalent of romanus. M. Costin presents a well- developed, almost modern, theory of the origin of Rumanians; his views have been given weight up to this date. In this history the Dacians have no role as ancestors of Rumanians. Costin was familiar with Laurentius Toppeltinus, who published "Origines et occasus Transsylvanorum" (The Rise and Fall of Transylvanians) in 1667, wherein he attributes Dacian ancestry to the Transylvanian Saxons and Costin says that the Dacians are old time Saxons (*dachii, a saşilor moşii*). This continuity theory also has its antecedents. Miron Costin was aware of the fact that the Rumanians who live in three different countries - Moldavia, Valachia, and Hungary - are the same people; his remarks also have a political edge.

Miron Costin - whose study was copied by his son, Nicolae, in 1712 - has a contemporary in Wallachia, the Greek Constantin Cantacusino (1640 -1716). He is a political figure of stature and a well-informed scholar, as well. He is impressed by the might of the

Dacians. It is not accidental that he is among those who attribute to the Dacians a role in the origin of the Rumanians. In his arguments with István Szamosközy, [Hungarian historian (transl.)], he disputes that Dacia was completely evacuated under Emperor Gallienus, but allows that some Roman soldiers could have settled South of the Danube. The Arumun (*coțovlahi*) are to have been their descendants. Contacusino also writes about the Huns - and about Hungarians, as the Huns' descendants. Accordingly, Rumanians descend from Romans in Dacia and Hungarians from the Huns who devastated the Roman Empire; this is how the Age of Antiquity overlaps the New Age and brings change to what seems unchangeable.

Contacusino is among the first who, albeit indefinitely, seeks the ancestors of Rumanians among the Dacians. While he is a writer who has fallen into neglect, he must be acknowledged as the precursor of the Dacian-Roman theorists. The learned Moldavian Sovereign, Dimitrie Cantemir (1673 - 1723) had no doubt that the ancestors of the Rumanians were Trajan's colonists and settlers: they were citizens of Rome and soldiers who - without mixing with the population - constituted the ancestry of Rumanians. Cantemir's views were not unique. The theory of pure descent from the Romans is shared by every member of the so-called "Transylvanian School" (*școala ardeleană*). Nevertheless, Cantemir was the first who claimed the Rumanian language contained Dacian words; these he attributed to the Dacian servants or wives of Romans. The following were considered to be Dacian words: *stezar* = oak (*stejar* -Bulgarian origin), *padure* (*pădure* = forest from the Latin *palus, paludem*) *halesteu* (*heleșteu* = fishpond - from Hungarian:"*halastó*"); *carare* (*cărare* =

path -(Latin: = *carraria*); *graesk* (*grăiesc* =I speak - of Serbian origin); *privesk* (*privesc* = I look at - Slav word); *nemeresk* (I get to - Serb word). The errors noted above should not surprise us, as they date from the beginning of the 18th century. However, Cantemir is also comparing Rumanian words with their Latin and Italian equivalents in order to prove that his language has a greater resemblance to Latin than to Italian. Early Rumanian studies of their history present the prevailing view that Rumanians' origins can be traced to Italy - not a surprising conclusion, given available sources.

The history of research into the origin of the Rumanians reflects the different theories which are being considered up to this day: the late arrival of the Rumanians to the Carpathian Basin (in the earliest Anonymous Chronicle and in the Hungarian Annals, a source used by many scholars - *Letopisețul unguresc*); descent from Trajan's soldiers (Miron Costin, Dimitrie Cantemir); the Dacians' participant-role in Rumanian ethnogenesis (Constantin Cantacusino).

The latter could be viewed as an early formulation of the theory of Dacian-Roman continuity. As a precursor of this theory we find Andronico Tranquillo writing in 1534 that the soldiers from the legions of Flaccus married the "provincials" and became one nation (*unam gentem ex duabus faceret*). Therefore, there is nothing Roman about them (*nihil Romani habent*), except their mixture of a language. It is most interesting that Andronico Tranquillo's companion, Francesco della Valle (who was also Gritti's secretary) knows nothing about this - or perhaps he doesn't want to know anything about this theory. He is only considering colonization by Trajan. Should we assume that there were differences of opinion about the origin of the Rumanians (in the environment of Gritti) even in those days ? Whichever way it was - and we can only make assumptions on the basis of the data at our disposal - we must note that the Rumanian annalists and the authors of chronicles were all humanists from the 17th century. What they were familiar with were the first attempts in writing European history from a modern perspective but based on a classical (humanist) tradition. After all, Miron Costin quotes Toppeltinus (a.k.a. Lorenz Töppel), the same Toppeltinus who claims that Transylvanian Saxons descended from the Getae and Dacians. The same claim was made by David Herman and Johann Tröster who died in 1682 and 1670, respectively. From the mid-18th century on, an increasing number of references can be found pertaining to Rumanians - the Arumun - who reside in Greece, in the Southern part of the Balkan Peninsula. Naturally, Contacusino and Cantemir mention them, too (the latter attributes Dacian origin to the Arumun). In addition to some earlier sources, it is the knowledge of the Southern Rumanians, the Arumun, which enables us to explore the origin of the Rumanians meticulously and in great detail. - Toppeltinus is already familiar with the Vita Aureliani, the biography of the Roman Emperor, Aurelian. It contains information about the withdrawal of the army from Dacia and of those who were left behind in the Province but (with minor changes in the text) the Rumanians continue to be viewed as Trajan's colonists. Different conclusions are reached in relation to the Rumanians of the Southern Balkan Peninsula. We have not previously referred to early data pertaining to them, as that would belong to the history of the Rumanians, rather than Rumanian ethnogeny.

Awareness of the Arumun has intruded early on upon the legend of Northern Rumanians' descent from Trajan. A good example can be found in the writings of Laonikos Chalkokondylés, Byzantine historian (1432 - 1490):...the same language is being spoken by the Valachs (the Arumun), living in the Pindos Mountain-region, as by the Dacians (Northern Rumanians)..... The Dacian language resembles Italian, but it is flawed and so different that Italians have difficulty understanding it.... I was unable to find out from anyone how they could have made it to the areas where they currently live, given their language and customs....[1]

In the Byzantine manner Chalkolondylés uses archaic names (Hungarians are Pannons, Serbs are Triballs), calling Northern Rumanians Dacians. He is quite vague regarding their origin. Ioannes Lucius, who is the first doing in-depth research on this theme, questions the theory of Trajan's colonization in a 1666 work, which pertains to Dalmatia and Croatia. Lucias doubts that the residents of the Roman province, headed by Trajan, would have remained in the territory in which many different populations appeared. Furthermore, scholars of the classical period make no mention of Romans. He thinks the Rumanians were settled North of the Danube by the Bulgarians, when they also occupied this area (i.e. Dacia). Here Rumanians from the Balkan Peninsula mixed with Romans, who stayed on beyond the Aurelian era.

There is hardly any difference between Lucius and the level of knowledge possessed by 18th century historians. In 1774 J.

---

[1] Laonici Chalcocondylae *Historiarum demonstrationes*. Scriptores Byzantini II., Ed. V. Grecu, Bucureşti, 1958, p. 190.

Thunmann declares that the Vlachs of the Balkans do not originate from Dacia. He believes them to be descendants of Tracians. He considers the Northern Rumanians to be Romanized descendants of Getae and Dacians who were to have adopted the Roman name under Caracalla (in 212 the Emperor extended Roman citizenship-rights to all people who lived in the Empire and who fled to the hills from the hordes of the Great Migrations). There, they became nomads and this latter concept emerges already in the writings of M. Costin. In his work on the history of the Rumanians, Thunmann makes reference to Anonymus, Scribe of the Hungarian King Béla, who is to have confirmed the presence of Rumanians at the time of the Hungarian Conquest of the region (cc. 986). (Anonymus appears as one of the major references in Schwandtnar's much-used collection of sources, which he published in 1746).

While Thunmann does not go beyond the theories propagated by Lucius, Franz Joseph Sulzer does (Geschichte des transalpinischen Daciens. - Vienna, 1781-82) in his History of Trans-Alpine Dacians. He maintains that, given the Slav infusion of words in the Rumanian language, they cannot possibly be descendants of Emperor Trajan's Dacian Romans. He believes it is inconceivable that a nation would resist barbarian invasion for 700 years without adopting some of the invader's words. They must have lived as aliens in Dacia, lacking (equal) rights and of the Orthodox faith. On the other hand, if they had been present on Hungarian land St. Stephen (Hungarian King 1001 - 1038) would have converted them to Roman Catholicism. Therefore, alleges Sulzer, they must have come from Great Valachia (Arumun land) around the end of the 12th century and later in the aftermath of the Tartar (Mongolian) invasion (1241). Sulzer is the first to bring to light specific data pertaining to Rumanians from the Balkans during the Middle Ages. However, he is mistaken in assuming that they could not have been indigenous to the area because they lacked equal human rights - today we know that such analogies are incorrect. Let us remember that the era under discussion is already one in which Transylvanian Rumanians strive for equality. A milestone in this development was 1697 - the Union of the Orthodox Rumanians of Transylvania with Rome. By this time the Rumanians are, indeed, the most significant population in Transylvania but political rights adhere to the three dominant nations (Hungarians, Saxons and Seklers). Advocating for political rights, Bishop Inochentie Micu-Klein asserts in 1735: "We are the oldest residents of Transylvania, (we) date back to the era of Emperor Trajan".[1] The "Rumanian Appeal" (*Supplex libellus Valachorum*) made in 1791 with, clearly, a political intent, also refers to Rumanian ancestry from the colonists of Emperor Trajan. Political interests will thereafter determine for a long time (much too long, it seems) how individuals relate to Dacian-Roman continuity; it is difficult to find studies which are exempt from political considerations. To us it seems that this historical argument - between Rumanians, Hungarians and Germans - has been useful. Although burdened by passion, it clarified many aspects of the origin and history of the Rumanians. Be that as it may, we find no Hungarian study validating Rumanian descent from Dacians, following the publication of *Supplex libellus Valachorum* (excepting that of Balázs Orbán and a few insignificant

---

[1] See *Erdély története* (History of Transylvania), Editor in Chief: Köpeczi B. II., Budapest, 1986, p. 1016.

authors). However, we cannot find any Rumanian studies, in which the theory of Dacian origin is disputed, albeit the Rumanian authors, who disagree, are not insignificant. German studies reflect divergent opinions, frequent among them the theory - attributed to Thunmann - that Rumanians are Romanized Getae and Dacians. Following the publication of Sulzer's work, rejection of the concept of Dacian continuity became the rule.

On the history of "continuity" the three members of the *Şcoala ardeleană* had great impact. Also known as the "Transylvanian Triad", they were Samuil Micu-Klein (1745 - 1806 - he was the grandson of Bishop Inochentie Micu-Klein), Gheorghe Şincai (1753 - 1816) and Petru Maior (1754 - 1823). All three were Greek Catholic, educated in Vienna and Rome. Both Şincai and Maior edit Rumanian language material for the University Press at Buda (Hungary), both are familiar with Hungarian historical studies. Micu-Klein wrote: *Elementa linguae Daco-Romanae sive Valachicae* (1780) and *Historia Daco-Romanorum*. In his belief- system Daco-Romania does not denote the concept of such continuity; the "Transylvanian Triad" propagated information about survival of Romans in Dacia. According to Gh. Şincai (*Hronica Romînilor,* Iaşi 1853 -1854) Rumanians descended from colonists who came to Dacia from all areas of the Empire, but primarily from Rome and Italy; most of them remained in their places also after the evacuation process begun by Aurelian. - P. Maior (*Istoria pentru începutul Romînilor în Dacia*, [i.e. History of the Dacian Origin of Rumanians] Buda, 1812) also considers Rumanians to be descendants of Dacian colonists and emphasizes that Roman settlers did not intermingle with Dacians. In the days of Emperor Gallienus some of them settled on the right bank of the Danube; these are the ancestors of Balkan Rumanians. According to Maior's view the Comans (who had a close relationship with Rumanians) were descendants of Romans from Cumae but he also allows that they received their name from Coman, a Roman prince.

Moldavian and Vallachian historians of Greek descent were inclined to believe that the Rumanians descended from a Romanized population in Dacia (D. Philippide 1816, Dionysios Photinos 1818); the influence of the teaching of the "Transylvanian School" can be felt here, as well (M. Cogălniceanu 1837, A. Trebonius Laurianus 1840). In 1860, the Transylvanian Orthodox Bishop, A. Şaguna states without any hesitation that Rumanians are the descendants of Trajan's soldiers and settlers - from the River Tisza (Theiss) to the Black Sea. In literature originating from others than Rumanians, B. Kopitar (1780 - 1844) constitutes a rare exception. A Viennese Slavicist of Slovenian origin, he notices elements in the Rumanian language that are shared with Bulgarian and Albanian and sees a link between Rumanian and the languages spoken by the Illyrians and Thracians who spoke the Latin used by the indigenous population of the Balkan Peninsula.

Robert Roesler's work (*Romänische Studien*, i.e. Rumanian Studies), published in 1871, was a pivotal research study on the subject of the origin of Rumanians, due to the wealth and depth of its thesis, the factual basis for his arguments and, finally, because of the vehement arguments it generated. Those who dispute Dacian continuity can count on being called "Roeslerians" which had turned into a pejorative adjective. Nevertheless, two prominent scientists of the 19th century became "Roeslerians": F. Mikolosich, a Slavist and

24

W. Tomaschek, a philologist. Based on Roesler's work, they relinquished their previously held views on the subject and adopted Roesler's thesis.

According to Roesler, Dacian Romanism differs from the Romanism to be found in other provinces of the Empire. In the latter, the indigenous population changes its national character but Dacians remain free of contact with Romanism. After Rome relinquishes the Province, it is occupied by Goths and the Roman provincial culture (107 - 272) completely disappears. The Rumanians came into being in Thessalia, Macedonia, Illyricum, Moesia and Scythia (a province of Rome, near the estuary of the Danube). They will be moving North from these regions at the end of the 12th century, at the time of Assenid rule of the Bulgarian-Vlach-Cumanian state. Rumanians did not constitute the provincial population of Dacia, who stayed in the region, as evidenced by the absence of mention of Rumanians at the time of the Avar-Byzantine wars during the era of the Great Migration; the "*argumentum ex silentio*" is already known to Lucius. Other arguments: The Slavic elements of the Rumanian language are from Old Church Slavonic, i.e., Bulgarian, while the Slavic place names are Ruthenian, (i.e. Eastern -Slavic, definitely not Bulgarian) and the use of the Bulgarian language by Rumanians in the language of church and government, up to the 17th century.

Although I. I. Russu, the latest critique of Roesler, maintained that Roesler and his followers created merely the "appearance of scientific work", we must declare that his prominent and controversial book was the first piece of research based on scientific principles, which dealt with the origin of Rumanians - its errors notwithstanding. Let us also examine the changes in the thinking of Miklosich and Tomaschek, who became "Roeslerians". In 1862 - before Roesler - they write about the Rumanians as the descendants of Trajan's colonists, who intermarried in Dacia and Moesia with the native Geta population and who are dispersed upon the Slavs' intrusion into the Balkan region, becoming Arumuns, Istrorumanians and Northern Rumanians. Following the publication of the Roesler book in 1879, he assumes that the origin of the Rumanians is a much -discussed but unresolved question. In his opinion the ancient home of the Rumanians was south of the Danube; this is the only way which he can imagine the Rumanians of the Istrian Peninsula, the Istrorumanians. By 1882 he believes Rumanians are Romanized Illyrians, that is a population in the western part of the Balkans (again influenced by the existence of the Istrorumanians).

In 1868 W. Tomaschek still believes that the Rumanians are Romanized Dacians and Getae, who never left Dacia. He explains the absence of their mention in existing records by positing that those contain records of dominant populations only ; not "passive" Rumanian shepherds and mountain dwellers. (This line of reasoning was already used by D. Philippide who claimed that only those are given notice who bear arms and not those who carry a shepherd's staff or plow the land.) Tomaschek is not immediately convinced by Roesler's thesis. In an 1872 critique he is still supporting the theory of continuity and it is rather odd that he should be reversing his earlier opinion in the course of challenging Roesler. In 1877 he states publicly for the first time - in a critique of J. Jung, a supporter of the theory of continuity - that Rumanians are Romanized Bessi, a

Thracian Balkan hill-people, who migrated to the Pintos mountain area (Arumun) and settled on the left bank of the Danube during the 9th and 10th Centuries. He writes more on the subject in 1881 and presumes that Rumanians are descendants of the Bessi and the Illyrians, provincial residents of the Balkans, whose original home was to have been West - Dardania (the area of today's Skopje). He believes they migrated north from the right bank of the Danube between 1074 - 1144; the period coincides with the appearance of the Petchenegs (Patzinaks) and the Cumanians along both banks of the Danube. It is Tomaschek who first provides extensive linguistic data. He argues that the Romans who would have remained in Dacia would have preserved the Roman language spoken at the time of Trajan and Gallienus, while the Rumanian language continues the Latin spoken *within* the Roman Empire between 400 - 600 (this cannot be disregarded by serious linguists even in our day). Rumanian words, which have to do with Christianity also suggest that their forebears must have lived within the borders of the Roman Empire in the 4th Cent., while there are no place-names of Roman origin in Dacia. In 1893 Tomaschek published a comparative study about Thracians. Not one Dacian god or family name from Dacia is known to us, he writes; the only possible explanation for that is Trajan's extinction of Dacians for the most part. Those who remained were absorbed by the Romans. In the rest of this work he repeats what he said earlier about the origins of the Rumanians.

If not Roesler's book, then Tomaschek is - possessing reliable scientific credentials - could have brought to an end the recurring controversy pertaining to this issue. This did not happen. For one, the

Rumanian scientific community disregarded him; after all, he wrote about the Balkan Peninsula and Thracians. Furthermore, the argument continued to be impacted by emotionally charged political considerations. A.D. Xenopol and D. Onciul reviewed Roesler's work in detail and presented almost the same rationale in opposition which - up to this day - proponents of "Continuity" have been using to prove that the Rumanians can trace their origin to Dacians. Xenopol, whose beliefs reflect the Humanist thinking of his day, assumed Dacian colonists all came from Italy and that only the rich moved out when Dacia was evacuated. He also thought that Rumanians practice the Slav (Orthodox) rites because Bulgarian control extended to Moldavia, Valachia and Transylvania. He states their presence (preceding the coming of the Hungarians into the region) was noted by Anonymous, Nestor (chronicler from Kiev), the Niebelungen song from the time of Attila, King of the Huns, and Simon Kézai [chronicler in the court of Hungarian King László IV, 2nd half of 13th century - transl.].

Of these the only plausible proposition pertains to Rumanian Orthodoxy and its Bulgarian connection. It was 870 when Bulgarians completely accepted the Eastern church. This means that they had some 25 years in which to convert Rumanians before the Hungarians took possession of the area (895 - 896) (and the Rumanians held on to the faith even after Bulgarian influence and the church disappeared; what's more, they recognized the jurisdiction of the Ohrida Bishopry, which was founded in 1020 by Greek Emperor, Basileios II!)

The disputed arguments belong to the same category as those of Onciul, who thought that the circumstance that the Rumanian chronicles know about the descent from Trajan but make no mention of re-migration to Dacia, was based on popular tradition. We saw earlier that the idea of the origin from Trajan entered into Rumanian scholasticism from the thinking of the Humanists. But written legacy of national lore - what little there exists - (The Anonymous Chronicle, the *Letopiseţul unguresc*) gives an account of migration. We must, however, credit Onciul that, 14 years later (1899) he attributes less significance to Dacian Romanism and grants a much more significant role to migration from the south. Actually, it is about this time that the Rumanian research takes two different lines of inquiry into the matter of origin.

E. Hurmuzaki follows Roesler's reasoning; he states that Vlachs derive from the indigenous Moesian population, residents of the towns built along the banks of the Danube and those who were resettled from Dacia. He assumes (1878) that they moved to the region North of the Danube in the 9th (the time of Bulgarian hegemony) and 10th Centuries. As a result of the development of comparative Neo-Latin linguistics, O. Densusianu looks first to Balkan Romanism in analyzing the origin of the Rumanian language(s). With the occupation of Dacia this would cover an immense territory, from the Adriatic to the Black Sea and from the Northern Carpathians to the Pindus mountain range where Latin was to have been spoken. According to him, the Macedo-Rumanians (Arumuns) evolved through Illyrian-Latin cohabitation. He gives more weight to the Illyrian element in the Rumanian language than to Thracian; undoubtedly, because of the linguistic connection between Rumanian and Albanian. The latter were considered to be heirs of the Illyrians. We hold that O. Densusianu attributes much too great a significance in the history of the Rumanians to the shepherd way of life. What's more, he mentions sheep herding groups migrating between the Pyrenese and the Carpathians.

In Rumanian linguistics Al. Philippide (1859 - 1933) was an outstanding scholar. His writing is contained in two large volumes; up to this time it can be considered the book of reference on the subject, in spite of some errors which, by now, we can detect. (*Originea Romînilor*, 1925, 1927). According to Philippide, the Rumanian language is a legacy of Balkan-Romanism. As proof he cites its derivation from the Late-Latin of the 3rd and 4th Centuries. The connections of the Rumanian language with Albanian force us to put the area in which Rumanian developed to the region south of the Danube. Dalmatian and Rumanian are late vestiges of Balkan-Romanism. Dalmatian developed from an Illyrian-Pannonian base (it became extinct by the end of the last century) and Rumanian came from a varied substrata, with a common Thracian base. Philippide does not exclude the permeation of Dacian Romanism but claims it is impossible to know ("*nu se poate şti*") whether they ("*populaţie romană*") retained their language or were assimilated to the migrating, invading peoples. Nor do we know whether the Romans - who stayed on the left bank of the Danube - retained their language up to the in-migration of the Rumanians, or if they gave it up for one of the Barbarian languages. Philippide asserts that if Rumanians are Romanized Dacians, they would call themselves Dacian (Daci). They, instead retained Romanus as their name because they came from different provinces and used it as a differentiation from Slavs. This is also how the Dalmatians held on to Romanus. Philippide believes Rumanians migrated north of the Danube early on during the second half of the 6th century (given the data at our disposal, this thesis is unimaginable). He believed that the Illyrians descended from the Pannonians; a unique version of the Illyrian descent of Albanians - one of Philippide's hypotheses which later research (by others) did not reinforce. I.I. Russu deems it a "question to be re-examined" (*chestiunea va fi reluată*)[1] in another context, but mindful of the linkage to the Albanians (who are not an indigenous population at their present place of habitation).

Philippide's work became a milestone in Rumanian linguistics, but not in Rumania. A prominent linguist, A. Rosetti, challenges him by saying: "this theory does not correspond to currently known facts".[2] His remark alludes to the implausibility of Rumanians' northward migration in the 6th century because separation of various Rumanian dialects took place only between the 10th and 12th centuries. Northern Rumanians could have reached the region North of the Danube only at that time.

Among post-Philippide Rumanian linguists only I. Iordan and E. Petrovici gave serious consideration to the Balkan Peninsula, as the place of origin of Rumanian development. However, both maintain the possibility of the theory of continuity. From the start of the century none of the Rumanian scholars expressed any doubt about the development of the Rumanian language - and people - in Dacia Traiana and in neighboring areas. This thesis was given credence especially after the very influential work done by I. Iorga, an outstanding writer and historian. An assertive critic of his, C.C.

---

[1] I.I. Russu: *Etnogeneza românilor*. Bucureşti, 1981, p. 172/10.
[2] A. Rosetti: Les origines de la langue roumaine, in: *Mélanges linguistiques*. Bucureşti, 1977, p. 105.

Giurescu, also believed that Rumanians descended from Romanized Dacians. He thought that they had a continuous presence on their erstwhile land and they had continuity in maintaining some kind - or different kinds - of statehood. As we have seen in a different context and in different periods, historians had a greater impact on public opinion than did linguists. After all, the work of linguists is hard to read: one must speak several languages to be able to follow them and their strange abbreviations and technical jargon are difficult to understand. Linguists who were following research principles lost out to I. Iorga's version of history, of whom Al. Philippide stated that what Iorga wrote was not true history but a deliberately falsified pseudo-history!).

20th century research no longer belongs to the development and conditioning of the Dacian-Roman-Rumanian, Daco-Roman continuity theory. Scholars of Latin (popular late and neo-Latin) cannot conceive of the development of the Rumanian language anywhere but on the Balkan-Peninsula, South of the Danube (E. Gamillscheg is an exception). Yet, lately a certain reticence could be noted which expressed itself through the neglect of the issue. Joseph Herman explains: "...the hypothesis of the Dacian population's survival as a national entity and their exceptionally fast Romanisation constitutes one of the elements of the theory of continuity. A calm and open discourse of this question is hardly possible in view of the emotionally and politically charged aspects of the case.[1]

---

[1]   J. Herman: Új *eredmények, új kérdések a román nyelvek kialakulási folyamatának vizsgálatában* (New Results, New Questions in the Study of the Development of the Romance languages), Budapest , 1985. p.43

I would like to call attention to a recently published work. It is a detailed study of Dacian-Roman-Rumanian continuity. The author used a pen-name, André Du Nay, the work (*The Early History of the Rumanian Language,* 1977) has many printing errors and, at times, its conclusions seem to be based on inadequate information. Its style and structure suggest that it originates from Rumania. The author considers all the arguments for Dacian continuity put forward in recent times but he concludes that there was no such continuity. A. Du Nay is a linguist, thus he gives primary consideration to linguistic evidence. However, he does also pay attention to archeological data and to the historical arguments in favor of continuity. Perhaps, there is a reason why, lately, we have been hearing in professional literature mostly from those who deny the theory of continuity - they have no difficulty with the facts. Du Nay's book resolved the dispute for a long time to come. The emotional aspects of the dispute must be challenged by facts.

Chapter II

The Dacian kingdom.

Barbarian statehood in antiquity in the Carpathian region

The history of the Dacians of the Boirebistas era dates back to about 1,000 BC. This was the tail-end of the late Bronze-Age, the time of the development of a vast archeological/cultural entity, which extended to the eastern part of the Carpathian basin, Galicia and Bessarabia. In this area we find the peoples of the Gáva-Holihrad culture. They lived in wide-spread farming (peasant) settlements; their burial rites favored cremation - the ashes preserved in urns. Some of this population reached the Dnieper region and the environs of Kiev. As the yield increased from agriculture and animal husbandry, so did metal work; also, the development of bronze-crafts and the beginning of iron-works. The latter must be related to the appearance of an ethnic group which came from the East to the region inhabited by the peoples of the Gáva-Holihrad culture, who must have been horsemen. This assumption is based on the pieces and fragments of riding equipment which came to light. There may be a link between these findings and other traces, - such as fortified settlements or the burial mounds of the rich - which were kept separate from others. These suggest a social hierarchy, evident in the Kurgans of Lăpuş (Hungarian Oláhlápos) and Bobda (Hung. Bogda).

It is, of course, difficult to provide exact information about peoples and languages existing at a time when there were no written records. Nevertheless, the bases for the unity of the Gáva-Holihrad culture seem to be clear. This community has been growing since the turbulent period of the Great Migration of the 14th century BC, being shaped by a gradual fusion of the local population and the newcomers. In all likelihood, the center for this developmental process was the area bordered by the rivers Maros, Tisza (Theiss), Danube and the Southern Carpathians. It is from this area that the Gáva-Holihrad culture spread far and wide; a population-spread but also a cultural expansion. This archeological/cultural entity has unmistakable links with the contemporary population of the Lower-Danube region and with the Babadag culture of today's Bessarabia and the peoples of the North-Bulgarian Pšeničevo culture. It would be logical to infer that those who settled in the region were people related to one another and that there also was a similarity between the languages they spoke. Yet, we know from early sources - in this case from Herodotos, - that, in the 6th century BC., Getae lived North of the Balkan mountains. These were the same Getae of whom Augustus' scribe, Strabon notes that they speak the same language as the Dacians. Strabon also writes that Getae intermingled with the Moesians and Thracians. V. Georgiev was able to make it probable from linguistic data that Dacians and Moesians spoke a similar language. During the period between the end of the Bronze Age and the first century, there is no evidence of extensive changes in the population which would have brought radical change to the ethnic configuration. Thus, in all likelihood, the population constituting the Gáva-Holihrad culture - and other related ethnic groups - must be recognized as the forebears of the Dacians, the Getae (and the Moesians).

Obviously, the above does not mean that the population in this region has stayed put since the first century and that there was no migration during the time. Among others, Strabon writes that Getae are wandering along both shores of the Danube. In the 8th century BC, at the time of the late bronze-age, ethnic groups from the East appear in the region, upsetting local conditions and resettling in the area some of their groups. We have concrete information about them; they were horsemen and they spoke an Iranian language. It is unlikely that they would be Kimmers, who played a significant role in the Middle-East. The personal and community names they use - such as *Sigünna, Agathürs, Spargapeithes*, attest that their language must have been related to the Scythians' from Eastern Europe. It is no rarity for Iranian speaking peoples to settle in the area. We find large groups of them, in the period preceding the Gáva-Holihrad culture, in Transylvania and in the northeastern part of the Hungarian Plains (Noua-culture), and they are, beginning with the 7th century BC, also present in the Danube delta. The appearance of the Sigunnae and the Agathurs-es dating from the early Iron-Age creates fare-reaching changes; especially in Transylvania, the central region of the Dacian Kingdom. There, the original population disappears almost completely. Our legacy of objects from the culture of the new arrivals is predominantly of those, which are so well-known in Scythian culture: unique arrowheads, Scythian daggers, akinakes-es, bronze mirrors, etc. Such great impact and such changes cannot be found in other territories penetrated by the Gáva-Holihrad culture. On the contrary:

data at our disposal point to the continuity of the indigenous population in the region of the lower-Danube and the area of the Tisza (Theiss). Here migrant Scythians quickly begin a process of intermingling with the indigenous population. In cemeteries, cremation rites are taking precedence later when, in addition to a new Scythian influx, there came migrant groups from the central part of the Balkan Peninsula - from Moesian territory to settle along the Tisza river. Around 500 BC, on the turn of the early and late Iron Age, there emerged in the Carpathian Basin the Vekerzug - Hetény culture and beyond the Eastern and Southern Carpathians the Bîrseşti - Ferigile culture. All of these came about through an amalgamation of Scythian newcomers, Balkan settlers and the indigenous population. There will be diverse rates of acculturation and of specific characteristics: we rarely find burial mounds within the Carpathian basin but, outside the region, that will be the accepted form of interment. This evolutionary process will create a cultural entity by the late Iron-Age -similar to the Gáva-Holihrad period - but there will be local differences, some of them significant. Within this context, the (self)segregation of the Transylvanian Agathurs-es is noteworthy as is the unique conservatism of their burial rites. So far, we have no clues why they disappeared without a trace at the end of the 5th century, BC They will be replaced partially by the Dacian segments of the Vekerzug-Hetény culture from the Great Plains in the west. The cemetery at Băiţă (Hung. Szászbanyica) has vestiges of their early presence.

The history of the Wallachia region takes a very different turn in this era. The culture of the Getae - who inhabit the area of the Lower Danube - is increasingly being influenced by Greek colony settlements along the Black Sea; the most important among these cities is Histria, which was founded by settlers from Miletos in 657 B.C. The changes in the material culture of the Geta tribes is most evident near the Greek cities - such as Dobruja. However, similar traces of this cultural transformation can be found to the West, along the Lower Danube. For example, in Alexandria (Wallachia) in the 5th century, B.C. and even further north, albeit in an altered form. Much of Wallachia remained unpopulated in the 5th century, B.C. - and through most of the 4th century Our substantiation comes from an absence of archeological evidence, and also from Herodotos and Arrianos, who describe this area as barren land. It is part of a strip of deserted land reaching to present day western Hungary (Dunántúl). The area becomes populated in the 4th century, B.C., after the disappearance of the Transylvanian Agathurs-es. The settlers on the western part of this land are Celts; not only do they take over the uninhibited area, but they overrun the Great Plains of present day Hungary and penetrate also into Transylvania. By the third decade of the 4th century, B.C. the Celts have also emerged in the central region of the Balkan Peninsula; by the end of the century they settle in all of Transylvania. Among them there is a sizable number of Dacians from the Great Plains but it is the Celts who impact the history of the region up to the 1st century, B.C., as seen in the minting process of Eastern Celts. This minting is now often called "Dacian". The tetradrachmae of Philip II. and Alexander the Great were used as sample; the main area of these coins is the Carpathian Basin and also within the Dacian territory, most of them were discovered in Transylvania. Outside the Carpathians, they are much fewer. Around the middle of the 3rd century, B.C.

Barbarian minting takes hold but has little to do with the work of Dacians. Up to the First century, B.C. we have no data which would indicate that Dacians engaged in politics. They had no political role up to the 1st century, B.C., since Celts dominated Transylvania from the 4th century on. Living there were several Celtic tribes: *Anartoi*, *Teuriskoi* and *Kotinoi* (erroneously described as *Koténsioi* by Ptolemaios); the first of these must have inhabited the Szamos-river region, the latter settled in Central Transylvania and South-.East Transylvania, respectively. There is evidence that Celtic power extended beyond the Carpathians, as well.

Let us sketch a broad outline for the antecedents of the Kingdom (arkhé) of Burebista (a.k.a. Boirebistas). Dromikhaites (early 3rd century, B.C.), Oroles and Rubobostes (2nd century) are frequently thought to be Geta-Dacian kings. Those who believe so seem to forget that the former is known to be the ruler of the Thracian Odrus-es and the latter two constitute a misspelled version of the names of Burebostes and Rólés (1st century, B.C.). Burebostes was a great Dacian king and we know that it was during his reign that Dacian power expanded: the *incrementa Dacorum per Rubobostem regem* (Justinus, *Prolegomena* 32) can only refer to him.

The conditions which preceded the kingdom or realm of Boirebistas' coming into power, were as follows: within the Carpathian Basin power was in the hands of the Celts who gained mastery over the native population of Dacians and their culture. Along the Lower Danube there were Geta peasant villages; passing through are Greeks from Pontus, merchants from Thracia in the south and adventurers, as well. In the 1st century, B.C. the southern part of the

Balkan Peninsula is already under Roman rule (Macedonia became a Roman Province in 148, B.C.). The Greek towns along the Black Sea are the subjects or allies of Mithridates, King of Pontus. From the belt around what is today Belgrade Celt Scordisci threaten emerging Roman rule on the Peninsula. Finally, there are the Bastarnae, whom we have not mentioned before. Classical sources call them Germanic, Celtic, Getan or Scythian - a people which has its home near the rivers Dniester and Prut. It is from this region that they cross and re-cross the Danube. Boirebistas ruled in this environment (which included Iranian-speaking peoples from the Steppes - by then known as Sarmatians).

All of these diverse ethnic, political and cultural influences converged in the area which became the locus of Boirebistas' power: along the banks of the River Szeret (Rumanian Siret), among Dacians or the Getae or among related Dacian-Getae. They were living near the Celts, the Scythians and Sarmatians of the Steppes. The Greek towns of the Pontus (Black Sea) were more distant, but still within reach. The Romans were even further and so was Mithridates (who could no longer be considered Persian). Our records about the period are limited, but sufficient to reconstruct much of Boirebistas' background. An inscription was found in the Greek city of Dionysiopolis, in Pontus (Balčik, Bulgaria). From it we can learn that Akarnión, a citizen of this town, traveled to Zargidava, to meet the father of Boirebistas. Eventually, he became a trusted member of the court and was sent as envoy to Pompeius, with whom he met before the Battle of Pharsalos (in 48,B.C. on Aug. 8th). "Although we have only an incomplete document to rely on, we can be fairly certain that the aforementioned Zargidava was the seat of Boirebistas' court - after all, the record was written during his life and reign. Zargidava (Zargedaua on the inscription at Balčik). This Zargidava is also mentioned by Ptolemaios in cca. 170, B.C., as a town on the banks of the river Szeret, adjacent to Tamasidava and Piroboridava. According to N.Gostar's considered opinion the latter was Barboşi (today: a district of Galaţi) and Tamasidava must have been Mînăstioara. Zargidava - known from Ptolemaios (Ptolemy) and the inscription found in Dionysiopolis - must be identical with the most significant Moldavian settlement: Poiana. In the 1st century, B.C. a three meters high rampart was built around the settlement. Deep trenches around it further protected the castle from encroachment. Incidentally, it was the only Moldavian castle which contained such a large number of Greek goods from the colonies. Undoubtedly, Poiana - Zargidava was the seat of the court of Boirebistas. Other circumstances about his reign are uncertain. According to Iordanes, a historian from the 6th century, B.C. Boirebistas came to power at the same time as Sulla, in 82 B.C. However, other information suggests a later date. When Mithridates, King of Pontus, plans his campaign against Rome in 64 B.C., he has no knowledge as yet of the Dacians, but the Pannonians, whose emergence is concurrent with the increasing might of the Dacians, appear in his plans. In 59 B.C., the Roman senate named Julius Caesar Consul of Gallia and Illyricum. Neither the Pannonians, nor the Scordiscans were important enough to justify such an assignment, only the Dacians. Thus, in 60 B.C. Boirebistas had to have been in power. The following year a group of Boi-s flees to the Helvetians. These Boii, as well as Taurisci from the region of the

Upper Tisza (but not from Noricium) fought Boirebistas under the leadership of Kritasiros. They were defeated. The battle must have taken place in 60 B.C.

This was the only one of the battles or campaigns waged by Boirebistas, for which we have a date. But we do know that they were fought within a short time-span, "barely a few years". We also know that he subjugated the Scordiscans, forcing them to enter into an alliance with him and that he extended his domination to the Greek colonial cities along the Black Sea, up to Appolonia (today: Sozopol, Bulgaria). Olbia, at the estuary of the Bug river, has been razed by him 150 years before the end of the 1st Cent B.C., therefore, the conquest of the Greek cities is said to have occurred between 55 - 48 B.C. Given the political happenings at the time, it was most unlikely that this conquest would have occurred so late. The Greek-colonized cities were ruled by the King of Pontus, Eupatór Mithridates VI, until 63 B.C., as were the Bastarnae. After the King's death, the governor of Macedónia, C. Antonius Hybrida takes over; in 61 B.C. he is defeated by the Bastarnae in a battle near Histria. It is unlikely that Boirebistas would have abstained from responding to the power vacuum created by the death of Mithridates. Attempts to fill the vacuum were made by the Romans and also the one-time allies and subordinates of the King. In all likelihood, the Bastarnae later came under the jurisdiction of Boirebistas. We know of no wars against them and, therefore, we can safely presume that it was Boirebistas who was leading the Bastarnae into battle in 61 B.C. (on the side of Histria) against C. Antonius. This does not mean that Boirebistas subjugated the Bastarnae prior to 61 but may suggests close ties with them. Just as we cannot separate the second half (..*bista*) of Boirebistas' name from that of the Bastarnae, a similar connection comes to mind as we examine the Bastarna-relics of the Poianeşti-Lukaševka culture along the river Szeret, which came to light in the castles and settlements adjoining the river. Records pertaining to the battle at Histria speak only of the Bastarnae. This may mean that they made up most of Boriebistas' army, these late allies of Mithridates, known as "the bravest".

War against the Boii and Taurisci followed the occupation of the Greek cities. They were separated from the Dacians by the River *Parisos*, according to our sources. *Parisos* is frequently revised to read as *Pathissos*, i.e., Tisza (Theiss). However, the paleography of the Greek text tends to validate the use of *Marisos* or *Marissos*. The Taurisci are later to be found East, then South of the Tisza, giving support to the usage of Marisos/Marissos. If the Marisos River is, indeed, the boundary of Dacian and Celtic power in the sixties, then existing archeological finds become more intelligible: between the 4th and 1st centuries, B.C. we find Celt traces exclusively; the characteristics of Dacian culture do not show up prior to the 1st century. It must be emphasized, however, that Celtic culture is not restricted to Celtic ethnicity, because Dacians living on the Great Plains adopted this culture, although they must have retained their language and ethnic identity. This may be behind the Dacian's unusual declaration of war: "they asserted this land is theirs". The ethnic connection thus appears as the impetus for war, based on the premise that the population living in the region to be occupied speaks the same language as the attackers or one that is similar to theirs.

The defeat of the Scordisci is mentioned by Strabon prior to the Boius war, which would suggest that the campaigns of Boirebistas took place within a short period of time: the years 61 - 60 (or 59 if that was the date of his victory) - exact dates are hard to come by. After their defeat the Scordisci fought as allies of the Dacians: Boirebistas continued to wage war after his realm (arkhé) was established. We know about one of these campaigns. Iordanes reports on a campaign against the Germans residing in the Czech basin and Moravia, as a result of which Dacian jurisdiction extended to Carnuntum, opposite the Morva river. Dacian forces may have penetrated areas beyond that point. If, for instance, the City of Setidava on the Vistula river, did not represent an error made by Ptolemaios then this typical Dacian name for castles could point to a conquest in the North by Boirebistas. He also lead campaigns on the Balkan Peninsula. On the inscription in Balčik he is called Thracia's "first and greatest" king. We have no evidence pertaining to eastern conquests but we know the Bastarnae were his subjects and that he destroyed Olbia. His power extended to the Dnieper river, or beyond.

The expansion of governmental institutions across the realm occurred after the first conquests, in the fifties. This must also have been the time for the establishment of the Dacian sanctuary site and power-center in Southern Transylvania, in the mountains of Orăştie. These events must have taken place by 50 B.C. In the forties, Rome sees the Dacians as a threat once more (an emissary of Boirebistas proposes an alliance to Pompeii in 48, B.C.) and we have no evidence of a large Dacian campaign in the latter part of the fifties. Regrettably, we also have very little data pertaining to Dacian power structure and government systems and there are some inconsistencies between earlier and later sources. As Boirebistas was "the first and greatest" king in Thracia (*prótos kai megistos basileus*), we can be certain that, beside him, there were other kings. To quote Iordanes: the king gave his Counselor and High Priest "nearly royal power" (*pene regiam potestatem*, Iord.Get.XI, 67). Boirebistas accorded Akornion the title of *prótos (kai megistos) philos* , "first and foremost friend". Among the descendants of Alexander the Great this is a proverbial aulic title in Hellenic courts. Boirebistas is then like the "King of Kings", the Persian and Hellenic rulers of one-time Persian territories. We find among his titles some which were also used in the Court of Mithridates. Not unusual, inasmuch as Boirebistas emerges on the North West shores of the Black Sea as heir to the rule and power of Mithridates. Also, proof that Boirebistas and his retinue were well-informed about the organization of Mithridates' Kingdom of Pontus.

Other sources attest to the existence of two separate strata among the Dacians. The Dacian name for one of these groups was Tarabostes also known as Pileati (Pilophoroi in Greek) after the headpieces (pileus) they wore. The other sector was subordinate to the former. These were called capillati (Kométai in Greek), or long haired. On Trajan's column, which commemorates the Dacian war, a description of both groups can be found: the head-piece wearing Pileati and the long-haired, bare-headed Capillati. We know hardly anything about the latter, somewhat more about the Tarabostes. According to Iordanes, Dicineus (Dicaineos) ruled also over kings (*et regibus imperaret*), "selecting amongst them the noblest and wisest men, instructing them in theology ..... making priests of them and naming them Pileati" (Iord. Get.XI, 71). Kings and priests came from the ranks of Pileati. Other sources also describe them as the Dacian elite. The Dacian *pleistoi* (majority), whom Iosephus Flavius (Antiquitates Judaicae XVIII,22) compared to Jewish Essenes, may possibly have been a corrupted version of *Pileati* and the Tarabostes may have constituted a closely-knit egalitarian stratum. We have a reference from Kriton, Trajan's physician, alluding to the dual power-structure. "Some were entrusted with the supervision of those who work with oxen and others - belonging to the King's retinue - were responsible for the fortifications (Suid. Lex.II. 35,368). This report, dating from the 2nd century, is far removed from the age of Boirebistas. However, if we presume a continuity in Dacian statehood, then it must be evident that the roots of administrative structure go back to the time of Boirebistas, just as do the Pileati and Capillati. The two occupational strata described by Kritón would compare with the Tarabostes and Capillati. This would mean that the overseer of farmers (working with oxen) were comparable to the Capillati. The overlords of regions where "the castle" was in control (and who were responsible for the fortifications) were comparable to Tarabostes, Pileati. In other words: the Capillati were, in reality, village chiefs and the Pileati had jurisdiction over larger territories. There is evidence that in the Dacian Kingdom there were, indeed, administrative areas the control-locus of which was the castle ("*dava*") and which carried the names of tribes (*Predavensioi, Buridavensioi*). The administration of the territory was, undoubtedly, built around decentralized control, encompassing smaller communities and villages and free of ethnic constraints. Our sources list only Pileati and Capillati among Dacians;

in the Kingdom only members of the ruling class(es) were (true) Dacians. We can see that the realm of Boirebistas had a centralized state administration, partially modeled after Eastern, Hellenistic rule. It was built around regional units and had specific "Barbarian" characteristics, without regard to ethnicity, as was the case in the areas ruled by the Boius — they settled ethnic groups to protect borders. Religion provided additional assistance to the centrally controlled state. South of the Danube among the Getae the Zamolxis religion was known as early as the 6th and 5th centuries — it promotes belief in the immortal soul. This is the religion which Dekaineos propagated among the Dacians; he was to have assisted Boirebistas in "teaching the people obedience." We do not know much about this religion, only that Dekaineos studied in Egypt and passed on to the people what he learned there. We also know that they obeyed him unconditionally. Strabon (Geographica 7,3,11) reports that Dacians ate no meat and drank no wine. Iosephus Flavius (*Antiquitates Judaicae* XVII, 22) was apparently close to the mark when he wrote that Dacian Pileati live a life similar to the Essenes. Zamolxis means earth-god or earthly-god. He was a god who died and was resurrected and who gathered in all Dacians who died. As we are attempting to reconstruct this religion, it gives us much to contemplate. We lack sufficient factual data for reliable hypotheses; it cannot even be excluded with certainty that they were monotheistic, as postulated by Rohde and Pârvan. This religion must have been forcibly disseminated - as suggested by written records (Dekaineos was to have conveyed the orders of God) and by a certain object found in all places of former Dacian habitation. This is a cup, shaped as a truncated pyramid, with or without a handle. It must have been used as a lantern, a sacral object used in religious rites.

As personification of a centralized state apparatus and of a forcibly disseminated religion, the Dacians created impressive and unique edifices in their seat of power, in the mountains of Orăştie. East of Hátszeg (Rum. Haţeg), along the river Városvize (Rum. Apa Orăştii), which joins the Maros (Rum. Mureş) river at Szászváros (Rum. Orăştie), in an area almost uninhabited even today, we find castles and fortifications built of stone: unique in Europe for its time. The center of the defense-system is at an elevation of 1250 m (3700 feet) at Dealul Grădiştii, near Grădiştea Muncelului. The centrum is protected by fortifications; the castles were built in the valleys, along rivers. Walls of castles were adapted everywhere to the requirements of the local terrain - in this region their style is unique and quite unusual. Square stones are superimposed on the parapet, creating the effect of a mantle. Dirt and pulverized stone are embedded in the walls, the blocks of stones were braced by joints - a method of building used in the Greek cities of Pontus. Accordingly, we must assume this usage dates from the period which followed the conquest of Boirebista, i.e. after 61, B.C. There is a school of thought, which attributes an earlier date to the rampart of Costeşti - Cetăţuia - perhaps the end of the 2nd century, B.C. However, this is not supported by archeological findings; all of these are from the 1st century, B.C. The ramparts connect with the stone parapets. Even if they were not built at exactly the same time, the building style of both reflected a similar concept and they must have been built close to each other. Greek master-builders must have been on site at many places. In addition to the style, similar to the one used by Greeks in Pontus, we have other evidence, as well. The late edifices of Grădiştea Muncelului yielded carved stone fragments with Greek letters and letter-groupings. Unfortunately, none of these were found as part of the wall they came from. Consequently, all kinds of suppositions attach to them (Royal List, calendar, etc.) although the letters signify only the placement of the blocks in the wall, as was customary in Greek-style building, and as noted earlier by V. Pârvan.

Thus, it cannot be said that Dacians used writing (as a nation or in groups). This does not exclude the possibility that certain individuals may have been literate but Greek masons' inscriptions on building blocks do not attest to Dacians' ability to write. However, they do have significance: many of them were unearthed at Grădiştea Muncelului on the site (11th Terrace) where the older, larger shrine stood as did the smaller and larger round shrines as well. Greek master-builders must also have had a part in this building project, probably during the reign of Boirebistas - (or, based on archeological evidence, later). The spectacular sacral and secular edifices at the seat of the Dacian Kingdom must have been built at approximately the same time. These were magnificent symbols of its power, projecting evidence of ideology and the might which enabled this empire to exist for nearly 200 years. If we can believe what Iordanes wrote much later (550 A.D.), the High Priest under Boirebistas, Decaineus "taught the Dacians almost all the philosophy... he taught them ethics, moderating their Barbarian morals; he taught them physics which enabled them to live in accordance with nature and their own laws; he lectured on logic, thus, in matters of thinking, they rose above other nations.... he taught them the meaning of the twelve signs (of the Zodiac) and how to observe the orbit of the planets and position of the stars.... he explained how the sun's fiery mass dominates the earth... One could observe how one Dacian would be engaged in scanning the sky, another would study the nature of bushes and plants; one would examine the waning and waxing of the moon, the other would watch the solar eclipse....." (Iord. Get XI.69). The reconstructed, so-called Large and Round Shrine at Grădiştea Muncelului are relics of Dacian mentality, impacted by a combination of science and religion. The shrine's arch is segmented by blocks of stone - understandably in accordance with astronomical calculations. As to the Dacians' familiarity with botany: in addition to the writings of Iordanes, we have additional evidence. In a book by Dioscorides, the Greek physician of Emperors Claudius and Nero, a list of medicinal herbs also provides the Dacian name for many of these.

We have hardly any information regarding commercial life in the realm of Boirebistas. Through indirect sources (such as the Getae's grain production) we surmise that they engaged in agriculture along the Lower-Danube region to a significant degree. On the basis of the information that Boirebistas had the vineyards destroyed, we assume they also engaged in horticulture, although in those days vineyards existed only in areas South of the Danube. The drab village settlements had simple huts, the few household goods and dishes left for posterity which were often roughly, unevenly made. What a striking contrast between those and the "davas", the stone buildings behind the castle-walls and their imported wares from Greece. The Dacians had an army of 200,000 and while it was not a standing army, they had to have major supply capability. It would be hard to imagine that this could have been provided by village-settlements and without a concentration of economic proficiency emanating from the seat of power in the mountain region of Orăştie. Later sources make reference to the great treasure owned by Dacian kings - especially gold. Yet, hardly any gold had been found in course of archeological excavations. Whether gold was really amassed in the royal treasury or has left the country in the form of payment for Greek and Roman imports, we must assume there was significant utilization of mineral wealth. We know for instance that iron ore was being mined by the Celtic Kotinoi, one of the tribes in the Dacian Kingdom (the 2nd century geographer, Ptolemaios - *Geographia* III.,8,3 - names them Koténsioi, after commonly used tribal names). Their habitat was in the northern part of the Carpathian mountains; they mined iron, according to Tacitus, to their "shame". In tribal societies it is not infrequent that ethnic groups are associated with certain specializations. Ore-mining and metal work was done mostly by the Kotinoi; in the Dacian Kingdom ironmongering showed Celtic influence. From Ptolemaios we also know of a Dacian tribe, the *Saldénsioi*, named after a place called: *Salda* (place of salt); probably their livelihood was related to this function.

It appears that the economic base of Boirebistas' kingdom was composed of low-level agriculture and animal husbandry but, primarily, of mining. We must also take into account that there was no counter-trade for imported merchandise. Greek wares in the possession of the Central Power(s) were plentiful; these were provided by Greek towns under colonial rule as their tax-payments. This kind of taxation was also levied against other regions of the realm - not only Greek cities, although it was more apparent in the latter case. We do not know whether this type of taxation was random or regulated. Certain characteristics of tribal societies and extreme poverty of rural communities in the Dacian kingdom suggest the application of the systematic exaction of taxes. Foreign trade was conducted only with the Roman Empire. As a result, the realm of Boirebistas was inundated with the *denarius* of the Roman Republic. What is more, it soon became the sole currency of the Kingdom. Evidence can be found at the castle of Tilişca; punches - used in the minting of coins - were found there.

No small wonder that conflict – generated by multi-ethnicity, a labile economic base and harsh taxation – reached crisis proportions. In 45 B.C. Boirebistas is killed in an uprising. Julius Caesar wanted to take advantage of this opportunity; he prepared for war against the Dacians but he was killed (3/15/44,B.C.) before he could go into battle. Power in Dacia passed into the hands of the High Priest, Dekaineos; the kingdom broke up. Our sources once again refer to Bastarnae and the Getae of Dobruja also have their own sovereign. What used to be Dacian territory has diminished in size but there was still occasional evidence of their erstwhile power. It appears that they attempted to intervene in the internal conflicts of Rome as allies of Brutus; this assumption is based on gold coins minted for the royal dynasty of Dacia which are copies of the denaria, minted in 42 B.C. by Brutus. They bear the inscription *"Kosón"* (possessive case) after the *Koso* dynasty. Dacians also intervened when, prior to the battle of Actium (31 B.C.), they had offered their support first to Octavius, then to Antonius. Presumably, they attempted to forge an alliance to counteract Octavianus' earlier (35 B.C.) thrust to Siscia on the River Drava in the Japod War. Subsequently, it was this assault which was considered to be the major inroad in the offensive against Dacia. We know that their King was still Dekaineos at this time. (Plutarch calls him :*Dikomés*) In a paper mocking Octavian, Anthony derisively calls him *"Coso"* the King of the Getae.

Dacians were a topic of conversation in Rome in 30 B.C. Not because they intervened in Romans' internal squabbles; after all, Dacian prisoners of war - who were captured as allies of Anthony - were sent by Octavian to fight in the circus as gladiators. In all likelihood, interest in the Dacians was re-kindled by the emergence of a new ruler. He must have acceded to the throne, after Cotiso Dekaineos had died, some time around 31 B.C. That year he launched several assaults from the Dacian stronghold in Transylvania against areas to the south. The Regent of Macedonia, Licinius Crassus defeats Cotiso's army in 29 B.C. We hear no more about Cotiso or about forays into Dacia until the middle of the 2nd century. The information is contained in a poetic reference of uncertain date about Appulus of Dacia, who can easily reach the Black Sea, the Pontus. (.....*et Dacius orbe remoto Appulus huic hosti perbreve Pontus iter....*- Consolatio ad Liviam, Poetae Lat. min.l. 118). They make a foray into Pannonia during the Pannon War of 13 - 11 B.C. (in those days it meant the region along the Sava river and not the Trans-Danubian territory, later known as Pannonia; Hungarian *Dunántúl*). In reprisal M. Vinicius leads a campaign against them; it was he who conquered the Dacian and Bastarna armies (*Dacorum et Basternarum exercitum*). He also conquered and routed the Cotini, Cauci, Rataci, Teurisci and Anartii peoples and forced them to accept Roman sovereignty.

We were left with only a partial inscription attesting to Vinicius' actions. Therefore, we can be certain of only the Cotini and Anartii and that the second name on the list begins with a "C" or an "O". Every completion accounts for five names and a reference by Strabon, according to which the Dacians were divided into five (groups) when Emperor Augustus sent his army against them. In this campaign the Romans ferried military equipment over the Tisza and Maros rivers. Consequently, they first reached the Cotini in the area of the Munţii Apuseni (Hung.: Erdélyi Érchegység) (*Koténsioi* as per Ptolemaios), then the Cauci (Ptolemaios: *Kaukoénsioi*) in South-East Transylvania. Data from Roman times enable us to place the Anartii in the region of the springs of the Crişul Repede (Resculum vicus Anartorum - Bologa, Hung.: Sebesváralja). The names of the Rataci (Ptolemaios: *Rhatakénsioi*) and Teurisci on the inscription can be reconstructed. The former lived along the upper reaches of the Mureş river, the latter along the Someş river. Records of the Vinicius campaign help us picture the ethnic composition of Dacia at the beginning of the 1st century A.D. They reveal that of the five parts of the fragmented Dacian Kingdom three were Celtic. What is more, for reasons of geography the Dacian seat of power in the Orăştie mountain area was on Cotinus land. Another articraft pertaining to Celts is a sword from the castle in Piatra Roşie. It suggests that Celts were present in Boirebistas' time in the defensive belt around Sarmizegethusa, a center of religion as well as the seat of royalty. We cannot be certain as to what language and ethnic group they belonged but, since Vinicius conquered Dacian and Bastarna armies, we can link them to the Bastarnae. Finally, we may assume that the tribe of Racatae are Dacians; we base this assumption on records which tell us about relations of theirs in Southern Slovakia, who bear the same name. The diminished and fragmented Dacian Kingdom retained its ethnic composition even after half a century beyond the era of Boirebista's conquest. However, the ethnic distribution of the area will change during the next few decades. The change is the result of Sarmatian migration from the Steppes of Eastern Europe to the region of the Lower Danube. In 11 - 12 A.D., attacking Dacians from the right-bank of the Danube are defeated by Sex. Aelius Catus and Cn. Cornelius Lentulus in Pannonia and Moesia; Catus resettles 50,000 Getae on Roman territory from the left bank of the Danube. Such actions will be repeated in the future in the Roman Empire but this is the first occasion for such a large-scale relocation.

Dacians lose the territory along the Danube. Not much is left of the former conquest of Boirebitas. The only way to retain some control over the fragmented kingdom is to establish a theocracy. Iordanes writes, referring to Dio Chrysostomos, that Comosicus (ruling until 29 A.D.) was the first to perform the roles of High Priest and King simultaneously. Actually, his sovereignty extended to a small area only, probably no more than the seat of government in the mountains of Orăştie and most likely the ore-mining areas. This is suggested by an increase of imported wares from the Roman empire in the 1st century A.D. and since we know of the loss of territory by Dacia, an increase in imports must have coincided with the increase in the exporting of mineral wealth from Transylvania, i.e. the Carpathian region.

Rumanian scientists pointed out that the resettlement policy of Catus depopulated the left bank of the Danube. We believe this resettlement project is only partly related to Rome's desire to create Roman provinces of territories along the right bank of the Danube. We must also consider the migration of a large number of Sarmatians from Eastern Europe to the region of the Lower Danube. They were nomads, needing vast areas of pasture land. Having been driven out of Eastern Europe, the Lower-Danube region's topography of groves and steppe-like grassland met their needs. It is, therefore, not surprising that Ovid, who was exiled to Tomi (until 17 A.D.) often referred to the Jazigs and the Sarmatians.

Subsequent to these events Dacian power continues to decline. According to Pliny, Sarmatian Jazigs chased the Dacians from the Mureş river to the Pathissus (Tisza). Additional sources place the action between 20 and 50 A.D. In all probability this occurred after 29 and around 40, since Iordanes tells us in reference to the Dacian King Coryllus (Scorilo) who ruled 29 - 60 that the Jazigs are separated from the Roxolans by the Aluta (Olt) river. It is unlikely that they could have lived for long in as small an area as that between the Danube and the Olt. We believe Pliny's (hard to understand) text was misread, as his River Marus is customarily identified as the Moravian Morva river. Pliny claims that in the Hercynia forest between the Danube and Carnuntum (*usque ad Pannonica hiberna Carnunti*), on the plains, Jazigs are living, and in the hills and forests Dacians. These Dacians were by the Jazigs chased from the Marus river to the Pathissus (*inter*

Danuvium et Hercynium saltum..... campos et plana Iazyges Sarmatae montes vero et saltus pulsi ab iis Daci ad Pathissum amnem a Maro - Pliny, *Naturalis Historia* IV; 80-81). By Marus he must have meant the Maros (Rum. Mureş) and the lower part of the Tisza. In other words, the Jazigs took the Bánság (Rum. Banat) from the Dacians. It would not be logical to identify here the *Pathissus* with the Tisza River, as is frequently done, unless we consider the location of *Partiskon* (Ptolemy) and the river *Parthiscus* (Ammianus Marcellinus). In this case it might be identical with the Upper-Tisza, but it is more likely to be a Transylvanian river, such as the Kis- Szamos (Someşul Mic) or the Kőrös (Criş). After the Jazigs appear on the scene, the Dacians are compelled to retreat to Transylvania. (They are separated from the Svebes and the Kingdom of Vannius by the Duria river - which could very well be the Tisza below the Maros (Mureş) estuary. We hear no more about them until the end of the reign of Scorilo in 69 A.D. but we know that Scorilo did not permit them to intervene in the civil war following Nero's death. The reason for this may be found in an earlier time. Between 62 - 66 Plautius Silvanus Aelianus freed the brother of Dacia's King from captivity and allowed him to return home - a sign of the good relationship between Dacians and Romans. Dacians attack Moesia at the beginning of 69 and overrun several military installations; eventually Mucianus beats them off. Yet, the traditional relationship is not broken (there seems to be a continuous flow of Roman money into the Kingdom) and there is no repetition of Dacian forays into Roman territory. Friendship between the two countries flourishes until the mid-eighties. In the winter of 85 - 86 the Dacians unexpectedly attack Moesia. The assault scatters the armed forces of the province, the Viceroy, G. Oppius Sabinus also falls in battle. The Dacian attack threatened not only the borders of the Empire but also the legionnaires' encampments and the very survival of the province. The Emperor Domitianus appears in person as Commander-in-Chief; the Roman armies are led into battle by the Commander of the Praetorian Guard, Cornelius Fuscus. In 86 he routs the Dacians and retakes Moesia, the region south of the Danube.

We do not quite know why hostilities broke out. According to Iordanes the Dacians decided to break up their alliance (*foedus*) with Rome because of Domitian's greed. One assumes this meant that Dacians failed to receive their annual subsidy. However, it should be noted that Pannonian military capability has been systematically strengthened; the process began in 80 during the reign of Titus, with troop maneuvers in 80, 84 and 85. These could not have been directed against Dacia which was separated from the Province by the Jazigs who spread out along the Danube and up to the river-bend. In Dacia Scorilo was succeeded by Duras (a.k.a. Diurpaneus - 69 to 86). In the Dacian kingdom power may again have been consolidated in the hands of one ruler. Duras voluntarily relinquished his power to Decebal and does not appear to be the kind of person who would have wanted to undertake major military conquests. Thus, the Dacians' forays into the Roman province must have had to do with Domitian's greed, after all - although not for the reasons proposed. During the reign of Augustus waterways of the Empire constituted ideal borders. The first modification occurs under Domitian: he advances beyond existing boundaries in the war against the Germans living along the

Rhine. He occupies the area between the Rhine and the Danube and forces its resident to tithe (*agri decumates*). The concentration of army units in Pannonia may have been part of the strategy later to be used against the Markomans and Kvads. The campaign against the Dacians may very well have been part of overall military strategy. Caesar and Augustus were already planning to attack them - at least this is the word they spread; the Dacians must have retained the memory of this propaganda in their consciousness. Accordingly, the Dacian attack on Moesia could be viewed as a preventive maneuver, whatever Domitian's actual plans against them may have been.

The reorganization of Roman military forces made it possible to continue the war against the Dacians after they were forced to withdraw from Moesia. Cornelius Fuscus uses as his starting point the legionnaires' camp at Oescus (now Gigen, Bulgaria) near the Danube. He continues his campaign along the river Olt but suffers catastrophic losses at the Vöröstorony-pass (Rum: Turnu Roşu). The Dacians capture many Roman prisoners and military emblems; Fuscus is killed. By this time Decebal is the King of the Dacians, he succeeded Duras (Diurpaneus), who abdicated in his favor after the defeat suffered in Moesia. Our sources describe Decebal as a good diplomat and excellent military strategist, but the record only covers his peace overture to the Romans and the defensive military action in which he was engaged. Following the victory he won in 87 all his martial skills are insufficient to fend off military attacks against Dacia in 88. The newly appointed military commander of the Roman forces is Tettius Julianus, who marches against the Dacians by way of the Bánság (Rum. Banat) and claims decisive victory at Tapae in Transylvania.

He holds the key to the power-center of the Dacians but does not advance further. Decebal disguises fallen tree-trunks as soldiers to trick and scare the Romans.

Tettius Julianus halts the campaign. It is possible that events taking place in Pannonia played a part in the interruption of military action: Domitian decided to move against the Markomanns and the Kvads, angered by their failure to aid him in fighting the Dacians. However, the Markomanns defeat the Roman commander, who had refused Decebal's offer of peace in 89 but is now prepared to halt the fighting and reach a peace agreement with Decebal. This enables him to send part of the army, which had been fighting the Dacians, and can thus pass through Dacia to the battle front in Pannonia (*per regnum Decebali regis Dacorum*, ILS 9200) to fight the Kvads, Markomans and Sarmatians. The peace treaty turns Dacians into a client-state of Rome. To the commemorative ceremony of this event Decebal sends a man named Diegis, accompanied by a few Dacians. He also returns some of the Roman weapons and prisoners he was holding. Domitian places the diadem, given to client-Kings, on Diegis´ head and the Dacians take home a great deal of money, a significant amount of aid ("*Stipendium*") and many craftsmen whose skills can be used in peacetime, as well as in war.

A realistic analysis of these events is rather difficult in view of biased Roman historical reports, hostile to Domitian and influenced by Trajan's wars against the Dacians. These wars will also influence later historical writing, even though Trajan went to war against the Dacians without cause. (Dio Cassius writes that Trajan could not tolerate that Dacian's power and pride was increasing and that he had to pay them annual subsidies. Yet, all this is a natural adjunct of client-state status.) It should be noted that Domitian brought the Dacians under Roman rule as a client-state, although the Dacian Kingdom did not become an integral part of the Empire, as did the Territory (*agri decumates*) between the upper reaches of the Rhine and the Danube. There are no data to substantiate that Decebal would have demonstrated hostility against Rome between 88 - 101, when Trajan started his campaign against the Dacians. No "Dacian threat" existed; it was Dacia that was threatened from 98 on by Trajan's expansionist policies.

This is the ruler who wanted to follow in the footsteps of Alexander the Great and to advance to the Indian Ocean. While he did not achieve that goal, he did conquer the Kingdom of Dacia in a war he planned, just as Julius Caesar planned his campaign against the Galls. This planned conquest ran counter to rational political considerations and was quite senseless. His successor, Hadrian, wanted to relinquish already at the beginning of his rule the Dacian territory Rome occupied, just as he wanted to - and did relinquish - the lands in Asia which Trajan conquered.

Due to these circumstances it is almost impossible to validate data pertaining to the Dacian wars of Domitian. To wit: according to Iordanus, Domitian's adversary in this war is Dorpaneus (Diurpaneus = Duras) and it is Diegis who becomes his "client". At the same time, the only Roman inscription in Dacia referring to Decebal fails to describe him as a King (*Decebalus per Scorilo*). Nor does his title appear on the inscription pertaining to Ti. Claudius Maximus, the Roman soldier, who cut off Decebal's head.

Yet, there is a record of an officer of Tettius Julianus - C. Velius Rufus - who proceeds to the Pannonian battle lines in 88 from Tapae through the Kingdom of Decebal, King of Dacia (*per regnum Decebali regis Dacorum*; ILS 9200).

Notwithstanding the distortions of Roman historians regarding Domitian's rule, we can be certain that the Dacian Kingdom had twelve peaceful years as a client-state of Rome. Contributing to the prosperity of the Kingdom were the contributions of Roman craftsmen, as well as aid Dacia received from Rome. A great many of the edifices built in Boirebistas' time were reconstructed, such as the large, round shrine in Grădiştea Muncelului. Castles and other important structures were also being rebuilt. Even though the products of Roman craftsmen remind us of the Greek cities of the Pontus (roof-covering, plumbing), we can be certain that these were put to use during the Domitian - Decebal *foedus* and should not be attributed to the era of Boirebistas. Especially, since the roof tiles are to be found on buildings and in areas which could not have been erected in pre-Decebal times, such as in Costeşti, Blidaru, Piatra Roşie, Grădiştea Muncelului, Piatra Craivii, Barboşi and Popeşti.

The import - export link between Rome and Dacia are not substantiated by Roman coins only. In Grădiştea Muncelului a wagon-maker's tool was found, inscribed: HERENNI. The Herenni were a well known family of craftsmen from Aquileia in the 1st century A.D. This may be their only product which found its way into the Dacian Kingdom, although there were a great many nameless, unsigned implements made of iron that were unearthed.

In all likelihood the sources available to us today mirror the administrative structure of the Kingdom in its day. We assume these originated in Boirebistas' time. A substantiating reference might be the description of Kriton, physician to Trajan, of castles and the overseers of oxen, reflecting the two social classes known to us from the era of Boirebistas: the Pileati and Comati. What we know of the geography of the Dacian Kingdom and of its administrative units came to us from the Geography of Klaudios Ptolemaios. This geographer left to us many works written around 170 A.D. for which he used earlier works as reference, (basically: Marinos of Tyros) but he augmented these with current knowledge. This did not happen in the case of Dacia. Ptolemaios makes no mention of Roman colonies or legions, and he does not know the situation in the province - although he is familiar with the organization of every other province. He goes on to call Sarmizegethusa *basileion*, i.e. "Royal" which can't be possibly accurate, given the date of 105 - 106, after Trajan's 2nd Dacian war. Ptolemaios' description refers to the Kingdom of Dacia when it was a client-state - therefore, no later than 104. We cannot link Ptolemaios' data with Trajan's 1st Dacian war in 101/102 because of the Roman names to be found on his list of Dacian cities. These include Praetoria Augusta or Ulpianum. It is evident that both names are linked to Trajan (Marcus *Ulpius* Traianus). Roman place - names must date from the garrisons which Trajan left behind in 102 in the Kingdom of Decebal. Consequently, Ptolemaios' description of Dacia must refer to 103/104 and is a reliable reflection of the organization of the Dacian Kingdom.

Ptolemaios' writings reveal that one of the kingdom's border check-points is in the Carpathian Mountains where the Dniester (*Tyras*) winds its way east. This is the area of Hotin (today's Ukraine), i.e. the mountain region of Maramureş and Rodna. From the west along the Timiş (*Tibiskos*) river, the Jazigs' land abuts Dacia and from the south it is the Danube to Axiopolis or to the southwest corner of Dobruja, where the Danube winds north. Ptolemaios also identifies the Siret River as Dacia's Eastern border (*Hierasos*). This area differs from the later Dacian Province inasmuch that the latter did not include the region bordered by the Southern-Carpathians and the rivers Olt, Danube, and Siret. According to one source, this territory which was brought under Roman sovereignty by Trajan between 103 - 106.

This Dacia is populated by the following peoples - starting at the region's North-West border:

Anartoi Teuriskoi   Koistobókoi

Predauénsioi Rhatakénsioi Kaukoénsioi

Biéphoi Buridauénsioi Koténsioi

Albokénsioi Potulaténsioi Sénsioi

Sadénsioi Keiagisoi Piephigoi

Of the 15 names, nine are names of peoples or tribes formed from place names (*Predauénsioi*, etc.) Even if we assume that in some of the cases -*énsioi* (Lat.-*enses*) was analogous to foreign usage (such may have been: *Rhatakénsioi, Kaukoénsioi, Koténsioi*) the frequency of this type of name is noteworthy. These names must be older than the place names they resemble. Neither the city-lists of Ptolemy, nor do later records refer to them and we have no record in Dacia of Predosa, Alboca, Potulata or Salda - Buridava being the one exception. We can trace these names to the time of Boirebistas along with the organizational system, emanating from fort-centric settlements. We have additional references which attest to this kind of jurisdictional system. Sarmizegethusa retained its title as the capital of Dacia but - in reality- it is located some 37 km from Grădiştea Muncelului, which can only be reached from Sarmizegethusa by detour. The Roman Apulum lies a distance of 17 km from its Dacian predecessor, Piatra Craivii. Many Roman settlements are somewhat removed from the native communities which preceded them but none of them are as far removed as in Dacia. These distances are the direct consequence of castle or fort-centric communities, wherein whole large areas were named after the castle which dominated them. We can also take for granted that each castle or "*dava*" had one master; community names bearing the name of the castle (and his owner) attest to that. Markodaua must have gotten its name from Mark3 (Lat. *Marcus*?); we are familiar with the inscription on a pot from the age of Augustus, which came from the Dacian castle at Ocniţa and states: ....."by King Markos" (BAICΛEYC...ΘIA MARKON). Markodaua may have been named after him but its name-giver could also have been the Tarabostes who was the castle's "overseer". We can assume that, in the case of Ziridaua, Komidaua, etc. there was a similar situation. This territorial apportionment is quite similar to the county-jurisdictional system used in the period of Árpád in Hungary. We are also reminded of the Polish *"castellanatus"* and there are other analogous situations as well.

The Dacian state apparatus also had "early feudal" characteristics. The above-mentioned inscription from Ocniţa appeared on a 1st century B.C. dish fragment (naturally incomplete): BAICΛE .IAMAPKO. According to I.I. Russu: from these fragments one can reconstruct BACIΛEΩC ΘIAMAPKOY, which means ˊ Belonging to King Thiamarkos´. In the second group of works Θ could also be Δ. Thus, the text could also read: διά Μάρκον, which bears a remarkable resemblance to the inverted cone of the ritual dish from Sarmizegethusa, with DECEBALVS/PER SCORILO inscribed on it (this is on what Cassius Dio must have based his story about a letter written on a mushroom - it has the shape of a mushroom jar and there is an inscription on it!). Several people considered this inscription to be Dacian, meaning: "Decebal, son of Scorilo" (V. Georgiev, C. Daicoviciu). However, Decebal's name has the regular Latin ending in the text written in Latin characters, thus it must be a Latin inscription; in which the name of Scorilo is not declinable. Therefore, the inscription on the vessel from Sarmizegethusa should be read as "Decebal, by way of Scorilo". The findings from Ocniţa are similar: βασιλε [ύς...ος] δία Μάρκο[ν] - the reconstruction suggests: King by way of Marcos. For the missing name of the King we may substitute Comosicus. On these inscriptions one name is that of the King and the other the name of the Tarabostes. This we deduced in the case of Marcos from a similar-sounding castle (place) name. As for Scorilo: he has the same name as one of the Dacian Kings and those came from among the Tarabostes. Thus, this leaves us to understand that the Tarabostes could act only in the name of the Dacian King and that there was a strong, interdependent relationship between the King and the overseers of the areas under suzerainty of the castle(s). It is conceivable that there also existed a multi-level dependency - the inscription from Sarmizegethus suggests that. Next to Decebal's name the designation of Rex (king) is missing, which implies that he was not a king. Let us remember that, in 89 Emperor Domitian invites Diegis as King of the Dacians with the diadem bestowed upon the ruler of a client-state. Thus, it becomes evident that, behind King Diegis (and High Priest?) stood Decebal, who did not use the royal title but held actual power. The food-container with the inscription could not have been made prior to 89 for the simple reason that Roman craftsmen came to Dacia only after the peace-treaty and the etched inscription bears the mark of a Roman master-craftsman.

The inter-dependent relationship which existed between the King and the Tarabostes, i.e. the king, Decebal and the tarabostes, must have been similar to the one found between the Tarabostes and the village chiefs, or comati. It is possible that this hierarchical chain was extended with an additional link: Cassius Dio Vezina, one of the Dacian notables, from the Battle of Tapae, is designated as the second in command after Decebal (Cass. Dio.67,10). It is also possible that, in the text, we simply see the translation of the Dacian word: tarabostes; as we shall see the meaning is similar.

Ptolemy's list about different etnic groups suggests these conclusions regarding the Dacian government and power structure. There are many names on the list, which derive from place-names but we can also identify names of tribal origin. At least half of these are Celtic (*Anarto, Teurisko, Koténso, Koténo*) the other are definitely not Dacian. As I.I. Russu pointed out: there was no "*ph*" in the Dacian language, thus *Biephoi* and *Piephigo* could not be Dacian although it is possible that the Greek "*ph*" was in this instance, signifying "*f*". The "*au*" diphthong is also missing from the language - that eliminates the *Kaukoénsioi*. The many different writings of *Keiagisoi* make it extremely difficult to provide an explanation for this name. Yet, unless we wish to assume that we are talking about a few obscure and extinct groups we can assume that, excepting the *Kaukoénsio*, they are Iranian. We assume that both *Biéphoi* and *Piephigoi* derive from Old Iran, *pāpa* = father/*papaios* (Herodotos) Chief of the Gods. - *Ya*- and -*ya-ka* become suffixes. - Sensioi may also be of Iranian derivation (from *Senoi*; "King" in Old Iran. is *xšaya* (plur. = *xšay...n*). At the start of the 1st century B.C. "Royal Scythians" and "Royal Sarmatians" were frequently-used terms and, if the Scythians from Dacia are "like gods" that should not be surprising, either.

This would tell us that the "real" Dacian tribal names are not Dacian, but Celtic and Iranian. It must also be noted that these tribal names are to be found only in areas which, following the death of Boirebistas, drop out of the orbit of Dacian suzerainty in the Orăştie mountain region. The Anartoi and Teuriskoi settle in the area of the rivers Someş and Criş, the Sensioi, Keiagisoi and Piephigoi between the Southern Carpathians and the Danube, while the Biéphoi inhabit the Bánság (Rum. Banat). They could not have returned to the Dacian Kingdom prior to Domitian's Dacian wars. If so, we should have found in the writings of Ptolemy from 103/104 regional designations derived from place-names. As an exception to the above we want to call attention to the tribe of the Koistobókoi-s which was demonstrably Dacian. However, this was a small ethnic enclave in the area of Rodna, - at present part of the Ukraine (and Maramureş) (Kurgans with burial mound in the region constitute their archeological legacy) which was never part of Dacia: not in the post-Boirebistas era, nor in Roman times.

Thus, immediately preceding the Roman conquest when Dacia was a client-state of Rome, Celts lived there, along with Iranians (i.e. Scythians and Sarmatians) and Dacians. Kaukoénsiosi, who must have been related to the Bastarnae lived alongside, (it is unlikely that they were Germanic as their name is related to Gothic *hauhs*). It is almost impossible to tell how many Dacians there were in the Kingdom. The ethnic lineage of the population in Dava-ruled territories is indeterminate; we can find Celts even in the hill-country center of Orăştie. The Celtic sword from Piatra Roşie is only one of the artifacts found there; among the iron implements several others were unearthed. The Dava's archeological legacy became the legacy of the Dacian Kingdom. However, these objects cannot be viewed as ethnic identification, having come from a region which was a multi-cultural entity. We know very little about rural settlements but are aware of the existence of late-Celtic objects found even beyond the Carpathian Mountains. Poverty was a characteristic feature of the settlements within the Carpathians. We might even call this the "state-culture" of the Dacian Kingdom: hand shaped utensils, lacking individual character. The mass-migration from Moldavia and the Lower-Danube region to the Mountain region of Orăştie during the reign of Boirebistas, was almost totally absent from other parts of Transylvania. (One of the best pieces of the characteristic articrafts of these people - typically slender-shaped dishes adorned with knobs- was found in Costeşti). From Ptolemy's list of peoples and from archeological data we can deduce: the Dacian Kingdom had a population of diverse ethnicity and not even the area of their power-center was exempt from this diversity. Celts, Iranians, Dacians and Bastarnae lived side by side - among them were also Greek and Roman traders and probably others, too. The Pontifex (High Priest) of Sarmizegethusa may have been a unifying force, although we take this to be only superficial unity. We posit that true concord was not possible, given the economic and cultural disparity among the people in the land.

Not too many conclusions can be drawn from Ptolemy's list of Dacian city-names. 14 out of 44 end in *daua*. Yet, it would be a mistake to assume this meant extensive presence of ethnic Dacians, any more than other words with the same meaning of city: Hungarian - *város;* Rumanian - *oraş* and Serbo-Croatian - *varoš*, although it might reflect cultural or governmental influences. There is another reason for not attaching ethnic significance to the - *daua* suffix. The names to which they are attached are mostly derived from family names and none of them is certainly Dacian (though several can hardly be anything else.) There are two more original village names: *Porolisson* and *Patruissa* (misspelled version of *Potauissa*). They are definitely Dacian, the latter to be found on Dacian Rhataka territory, while — strangely — the former can be traced to a Celt habitat. (Names that are most definitely of Dacian origin do not end in *-on* or *-um* in Latin). The great number of Latin town-names is surprising: *Ulpianon, Salinai, Praitória, Augusta, Angustia, Pirum, Pinon* (cf. Latin - *pinus* - pinetree). There were also Greek names: *Triphulon, Hydata, Zeugma, Phrateria.* Among the latter *Triphulon* is unique because the name of this city of three tribes is not of the contemporary, regular Greek pattern, but is either transmitted by Latin or represents a very old Greek form. In case of the latter we can presume an old Greek settlement (from the time of Boirebistas) in the Dacian Kingdom - a reasonable presumption. However, in this case the Greek city-names pre-date Trajan's first Dacian War. Silver objects found in Sîncrăeni (Hung. Csík-Szentkirály) and Surcea (Hung. Szörcse) are links to a Greek presence; while the items suggest the craftsmanship of Hellenistic-Roman goldsmiths, they weren't likely to be imported objects - much too unique for that. One third of the city names listed by Ptolemy are thus ethnically undefinable names of the *–dava* type, another third is Latin and Greek and the final third would be Dacian. However, some of these cannot be identified and others can definitely not be considered Dacian (example: *Akmonia*).

What do we actually know about the language of the Dacians? The answer should be easy if we rely on writers from ancient times. According to Strabon, Dacians and Getae speak one language and Iustinius states that the Dacians are the descendents (*suboles*) of the Getae. Appianus believes Trans- Dunabian Getae are known as Dacians. Yet, some of these same writers claim that Getae are connected to the Thracians. Logically, then, the Dacian language had to be identical with Thracian, or one of its variants. Unfortunately, the sources which would validate these assumptions are limited and hard to interpret. Yet, this is what we have to rely on, trying to understand the Thracians' language. It is necessary to seek substantiation of the views of ancient writers; — they called the Bastarnae: Celts, Germanics, Getae, and Scythians — if this were accurate they would have to speak four distinct languages. We have other examples of misinformation: Hungarians, as late as the last century, were said to speak a Turkish language and Hungarian was considered a Slavic language before then. We know of no inscription or other text written in Dacian (the inscription on the dish at Sarmizegethusa was obviously in Latin). Ovid is to have written poems in the Geta language when he lived in Tomi as an exile, but these have not survived. The research material on which we rely for an understanding of the Dacian language is confined to personal names (*Boirebistas, Decebal*, etc.), geographical designations of places, rivers and mountains, and Dacian herbal names. The latter were included among the medicinal herbs, which Pedanios Dioskorides listed. He lived in Anazarba in the first century, A.D. His list gives the Greek and Latin names of herbs and in several instances records their equivalent in Egyptian, Punic, Syrian, Celtic and Dacian. Dioskorides' collection was drawn up in its final form toward the end of the 3rd century in alphabetical order. There is also a Latin version of this glossary. We know it as *Medicaminibus Herbarum* and it was complied by one Apuleius. The exact date of this work can not be determined since we know about six men named Apuleius who were botanists and who lived during the time spanning the 2nd - 4th Centuries. We do know for certain that at the turn of the 4th and 5th centuries this glossary was already in use. On both Diaskorides' and Apuleius' roster of herbs we find Greek and Latin names among those which were listed as Dacian. D. Dečev's explanation for this lies in Dacia Aureliana which was established South of the Danube after 271 and where, according to him, the herbal names were recorded. On the other hand, C. Váczy attributes the Greek/Latin names to merchants of like background. For reasons of chronology, Dečev's explanation is unlikely and Váczy's artificial. It is evident that the Greek and Latin names of Dacian herbs come from Dacia Traiana i.e. from Dacia between 106 and 271.

What we know of the Dacian language comes from sources of no real significance. It is barely worth noting that the glossary of herbs gives us a more realistic picture than family or place names. A description of the Dacian language had been attempted on the basis of the above a long time ago, but a more palpable knowledge of it we owe to W. Tomaschek whose definitive works on the subject (written in 1883 and 1884: *Die Alten Thraker*) earned him recognition as the Nestor of Thracology. As the title of his work (which is still valid) tells us, he linked Dacians, on the basis of the Antique sources, to the Thracians, as did all of those who wrote about the Dacian language after him (P. Kretschmer, D. Dečev). The publication of V. Georgiev's study in 1957 was a turning-point in this regard. Based on a voluminous research of facts, Dečev realized that, linguistically, the "Thracian" region could be divided into two larger units. He concluded that place-names ending in -*dava* were not characteristic of areas which were historically Thracian and place-names ending in -*para, -bria* are not found in areas populated by Dacians. He was also able to substantiate a sound shift in the Thracian language (similar to Germanic), while the same cannot be found in Dacian. Thracian is a so-called AMTA-language; Indo-European *bh, dh, gh* became *b, d, g; b, d, g* became *p, t, k* and *p, t, k* became *ph, th, kh*. Such a sound change also exists in Frisian and in Armenian - (but here the Germanic link is less likely because these are satem languages and Germanic is a centum language). These sound changes are not characteristic of Dacian, where *b, d, g* and *p, t, k* remained unchanged and *bh, dh* and *gh* became *b, d, g*. These differences are similar to those which separate Germanic from Celtic or the Italic languages. Even if Georgiev's interpretation were to be challenged on some points, it is clear that Thracians and Dacians (also Getae and Moesians) cannot belong to the same linguistic entity. No wonder Georgiev's theory was accepted by scholars of extinct Indo-European languages and of linguistic history.

Contrary to the beliefs held by our sources on antiquity, the Dacians' language was distinct from the Thracians'. This we propose to illustrate, although we cannot do so extensively, given our limitations of space.

Personal names

Boirebistas (Byrebistes, Byrbistas, Boirebistas, Beirebistas, Byrebista - indecl., Byrabeista - indecl., Byrebistas, Buruista, Rubobostes: Burobostes).

In contemporary sources, the first part of the name is *büre, büra*; the second *bista, beista*.

The name of Dacia's first king (62 - 45 B.C.) was given different interpretations (Tomaschek, Dečev, Georgiev, Russu). The explanations are not sufficient and it is unlikely that the name can be made to fit into a known or reconstructible Indo-European language. The second half of the name cannot be separated from the name of the *Bastarna* people and we suspect that *bista, beista* is a superlative form of an adjective with an *-st* affix - this equates the indicator: *prótos, megistos* in the inscription at Dionysiopolis. (Cf.Old Ind.- *ištha*,

Old Ir.- *išta*, Greek -ιστος (, Gothic -*ists*). Thus, the name of the first Dacian king derives probably from the language of the Bastarnae.

Decebalus (Decibalus, Decibalis)]

The first half of the name of the last Dacian king (87 - 106, A.D.) is attributed by Tomaschek and Russu to "-*dek*[1]-" take, receive, respect (Idg). The interpretation must be erroneous, though, if we consider that the second half of the name can scarcely be separated from Greek φαλλός (or Gaelic *ball* ´membrum, penis´. On the basis of similar names (such as *Triballi*), we have to consider (Idg) $dek^1 m^2$ ´horse´, as the basis of the first part of this name. This explanation assumes that the name comes from a kentum language (the same applies also to the theories put forward by Tomaschek and Russu); thus we must assume either that the word comes from an extinct language or from the language of the Celts, who were dwelling in the Dacian kingdom.

Dekaineos (Dicineus, Dikomıs)

Idg.-dek[1]- take, receive, respect, cf. Lat. *doceo*, Greek =δέκομαι (ref. Tomaschek, Russu). Once again, not satem language. Quoting Tomaschek: "schlägt dies die thrak, çatam Theorie über den Haufen". (It makes the Thracian - çatam theory a shamble), _ i.e., it negates the satem-theory. Yet, in this case this does not apply; reliably Dacian words leave no doubt that Dacian was a satem language.

Vezina

Idg. u^3edh = to lead, to carry - is a past participle with the affix -
nt, thus, it means "leader, commander". This explanation is supported
by Vezina's role: according to Cassius Dio, he was 2nd in command
to Decebal. The *di* > *zi* change is a characteristic feature of the
Dacian language.

Geographical terms:

Akmonia

It would be difficult to equate the term with Agnaviae mansio. Idg.
akhmen-/akhmen-; Lithuanian *akmuõ, akmueñs*; Old Slavic - *Kamy,*
Old Ind. - *aśman* ´stone´. The Baltic and Slavic equivalents prevent
its use as centum-specific, but it is an example of the Dacian - Baltic
connection.

Aizisis (Azizis)

Idg, *aiœ-* ´goat´ Armenian *ayc* etc. Satem type.

Alboka (Albokénsioi)

Idg. *albho-* ´white´. A typically European word.

Apo

A river (probably the Karas). Idg.: *ap-* = water. In this territory, we
cannot exclude the possibility of a Sarmatian origin, given the
extensive usa of the word in Iran.

Karpatés

Ptolemy used the name as we currently use it. Idg. *sqer-, - qer-* ´to cut?´, Alb. *karpë* ´rock´. The Indo-Germanic etymology (proposed by Dečev) is very dubious, but there is little doubt about the link with Albanian. The name is important because of the Dacian-Albanian relationship.

Dierna (Tierna, Zernés, Zernis, Tsierna, etc.).

The most frequently analyzed place name, because of its position at the mouth of the Cerna river. The word's Slavic meaning is "black" and an early Slavic connection has been assumed. However, Dierna is one of the "entrances" to Dacia. Therefore, cf. Idg. $dh^u er$-, Gothic *daúr,* Old English *dor,* Old French *tor,* Greek δυρα, Latin *fores* ´gate, door, entrance´. The sound changes *e > ie* and *d > z* are characteristic of Albanian. The place name then means "gate", "passageway" and has nothing to do with the later name: *Cerna* river, which is an independent Slavic word. The Dacian-Albanian line is apparent in *Dierna,* too.

Germizera (Germigera, Germisara, Germizirga, Zermizerga, Zermizirga)

Known today as Algyógy (Roman settlement, hot-springs, and stone quarry). The first part of the word means "heat" in Idg. ($gh^u er$-m), Old Ind. ved. (*gharmá*) "hot" Av. (*garäma*), Arm. ($j^4 erm$) and Greek (δερμός), "fire" in Alb. (*zjarr*), etc. - Regarding the second part of the word, cf. Armenian ezr (<*eĝhero*), meaning "bank". It is also compared with a Slavic word: Russ. *ozero.* The variations create some uncertainty but the meaning is likely to be "hot water". Cf. also Arm. *jur* ´water´. Independently from the proposed etymologies, this word is in agreement with the satem character of Dacian and shows also its Albanian connection.

Marisos (Maris, Marisos, Parissos: Marissos, Marus, Marisia)

Today the river Maros, (Rum. Mureş). Idg. *mari-*, Lat.- *mare* etc. A European Idg. word.   The affix is probably *–sk¹h-,* cf. *Tibiskos, Partiskon*, etc. Old Eng. - *merisc.* Mid.(lower)German - *marsch* and German - *Marsch* ´marsh, swamp´. (Idg.) *sk* becomes *sh (š)* in Alb. Dacian sound-characteristics are present here, as in the name of many other rivers in the Eastern part of the Carpathian Basin.   In Hungarian, the river is called *Maros*. Several hypotheses analyzed the Dacian context. - The only tenable one assumes an indirect transfer, as posited by Melich J., and G. Schramm. Of course, this does not permit us to conclude how long the Dacian language continued to exist in the region.

Salda (Saldénsioi)

Idg. sal- ´salt´ and its declination: *sal-d*, cf. German *Salz*. Its location is around the So. West Carpathians. It cannot be traced to Dacian since its Albanian links would necessitate an "h" or "Ÿ" as a starting letter.

Sarmizegethusa (Zarmesegethusa, Zermizegethusa, Sarmategte, Sarmazege)

Name of the capital and cultural center of the Dacian kingdom and of a nearby provincial seat. This place-name has successfully resisted analysis (despite by the Tabula Peutingeriana's or Geographus Ravennas' misperceived etimology). Yet, it can be parsed as *sar-mize-gethus(a)*   Sar means "head" in Idg. k^1her-, cf.Gr. κάρα, Hom.Gr. κάρη, Old.Ind. *śiras-*, Old.Icel. *hjarni* ´brain´; Lat. *cerebrum*, Arm. *sar* ´mountain´; *mize* means ´center´, cf. Idg. $medhi^5o$-, Old.Ind. *mádhya*; ´mid´ Arm. *mēj* - ´inside, amid´; *geth* means water: Idg. u^3ed-, cf. Arm. *get* ´river´. Thus, the meaning of Sarmizegethusa's name is simply ´Chief (summit) (among the two) rivers´.   Grădiştea Muncelulni is indeed between two rivers, the Valea Godeanului and the Valea Albă; Castle Hill (Dealul Grădiştei) is a mountain peak bordered by two waters. The name fits. Just the same, it is not congruent with our knowledge of the Dacian language, in spite of the ending of the name: (dual genitive (Idg. – ou^3s) this is to be expected from this structure. The -a is a designator, which we find in many Dacian names as *–e, -a;* probably – *Ä, Ä* [7] (G.Schramm). Our analysis is supported by the name of the *Sargetia* river, cited by Cassius Dio (Cass.Dio 68,14); it is the river - at the central seat of power - where the royal treasure is hidden. In all likelihood the word derives from a more original form: *sar-get.*   This   clarifies   that   here   *sar*   really   means "chief"(major):(Hauptort, Hauptsitz) and not "mountain" or "peak". Therefore, Sargetia really means "chief (city) river" and *Sarmizegethusa* is "chief (city) (between 2) rivers". The characteristics of the name point to an AMTA-type language, such as Thracian, Frisian or Armenian. It would be difficult to disregard the latter two: Frisian may be considered   as the forerunner of Armenian.   The equivalent of *sar* we find only in Armenian. (It is geg *krýe*, tosk *kríe* in Albanian but this is a foreign word, adopted from Latin). Once more, this is where we come across *get* and *mize* which cannot be Dacian either (cf. Alb. *mjet*). There are two possible explanations. Either we are misinterpreting Dacian language-data, or the name of the capital of Dacia (and the river which joins the Maros) are not in Dacian. We will adhere to the latter hypothesis. Our sources assert that the High Priest of Boirebistas came from a foreign land and that the spread of faith and language were concurrent. Archeological findings also reveal the existence of foreign elements in the Orăştie mountain region at the start of the reign of Boirebistas. We presume that the Dacian seat of power had a significant population from the eastern part of the Middle-East - this is what the name of the capital city conveys to us. In the end, we find a common thread which connects the death of Mithridates and the appearance of Boirebistas.

Tibiskos (Tibisis Her..? v_, Tibiskon, Tibiscum, Tiviscum)

The Temes River - on the Western border of the Dacian Kingdom at the beginning of the 2nd century. - Idg. *tibh-* cf.Gr. τῖ⁶φος (= marshlands) (Dečev, Georgiev, Russu). Use of affixes is likely to be the same as in the case of the Maros. The Hungarian name *Temes* (Old Hung. *Timis* >Serbian *Tamiš*) contains an *m* in the place of *b,* a sound change that existed in Dacian and exists in Albanian. This is one of the circumstances which indicate that the name was transferred directly from Dacian to Hungarian.

Names of Plants.

Seba - elderberry

Both Tomaschek and Georgiev base it on the Lith. *šeivà* 'tube, pipe'. (Idg. *keywā*). The similarity between the Dacian and Lithuanian words suggest that the Dacian is a compound word: *sew - ba*, cf. Lith. *šeiva -medis*.

Duódela (diodela, Ziodela) 'camomile'.

Dečev's interpretation for the first part is "shining" but one of the Greek names of the plant is *parthenion* "Jungfernkraut", i.e. "virgin's grass" and that leads us to consider the O.Slav. *děvā* (Idg. *dhei-wā, dhoi-wā*) 'virgin'. The second part of the word, *-dela*, appears in the Dacian names of many plants, as *-dela, -dila, - zila, -tila*. From Tomaschek on this word has been interpreted in re. to Idg. *ĝhel* = greening (flowering) and including O.Slav. *– zeľje* 'cabbage', Russ. *zel´e* '[herbal]grass, poison'. In view of the above it must mean 'grass, herb'. It is worth noting that we know of Armenian words, meaning "grass, plant, herb, medicine": Mid-Arm. - *delo-*, O.Arm. *del- oy* 'grass, plant, medicinal herb, medicine'. Could *dela* and *zila* be two separate words? The Armenian connection is, once again, apparent.

Amolusta (amalusta,amulusta) 'camomile (anthemis)'

We find it only in the writings of Pseudo-Apuleius, in addition to *thusci ambolicia, amolusta, amolacia, campani amolocia*. Thus, these names were used also in Etruria and Campania. Georgiev would associate it with Alb. *ambël, ëmbël* 'sweet' but - as Váczy states - this

does not apply to the plant. One of its Greek names is "dwarf - apple",
bringing it in line with the Idg. variants of apple.

mantia (manteia, mantua) 'blackberry'

Alb. *man* dialectally *mand, mën* 'strawberry'. Thomaschek has
already linked the two words, it would be hard to dismiss the Dacian -
Albanian tie.

kinuboila 'white grape'

Tomaschek called attention to its relationship with the Lith. *šùn-obuolas*. Georgiev calls it "dog-apple" (*kun- ãbõlo-s*. Idg. "dog" =
k¹huon/k¹hun) - this word doesn't fit into the satem character of
Dacian. - The second part of the word most resembles O.Iran. *ubull*
and Lith. *óbuolas, óbalas* 'apple' among the words for apple the Idg.
languages. The antecedent must have been the Celtic *ablu* (cf. Gallic
avallo). In looking at Celtic roots we note that *kin* for dog is unusual
(error or dissimilation? cf. O.Ir. *cu*). The name of this plant comes up
only with Dioskorides (we exclude Apuleius as he uses the word in
relation to the Bessae.) It must date from the time of the Dacian
Kingdom and can be seen as undisputed evidence of the Celts'
presence in the Kingdom - a people speaking a kentum language.

Skiaré (skithe) 'Dipsacus laciniatus, Teasel (Split - tear)'
Tomaschek pointed out the connection with Alb. *shqer* 'to cut'.
Georgiev reconstructed an original *skerã*. Yet, the equivalent of the
skher - root exists only in Germanic and Celtic languages (cf. O.Ir.
scara(im) 'I divide'). Therefore, we view the Albanian word as the
adaptation of a foreign word (*shq-* cannot be original). Thus, if there is
a connection between *skiaré* with Alb. *shqer,* Old German *sceran* ,

etc., it must originate from the Celtic languages of the Dacian Kingdom.

dielleina (dieleian, dielian, dielia, dieleia) ´henbane, stinking nightshade; Hyosciamus niger´

It must be related to "white", given the Celtic belenuntia and also the Slavic designation of the name. Dečev and Tomaschek explain this word from Idg. *dhel* ´shines, lights´. However, the word bears such strong resemblance to the Bulg. (etc) *blěn* and Celtic *belenuntia*, that it seems more realistic to assume a more original form of the word: *dibleina, dibeleina;* the *dielleina* version could be the result of an error in the writing or of mispronunciation. The word is *hyoskiamon* ´broad been; Vicia faba´ in Greek - compounded of *di - bleina, di-beleina. Di* should be compared to Alb. *thi* ´pig´ and the second part of the word can be related to Bulg. *blěn (*sū-bhēl-no-).*

dyn ´big nettle´

Idg. *du - nt* ´burning´. An old but valid explanation.

dakina

Its Greek name, among others is "wolf's leaf" and can clearly not be separated from the name of the Dacians, which can be linked to the Frizian δάος *(daos)* = wolf *dhāu³kino* as per Georgiev.

propodila (propedila, propedula, prepudula, procila, procedila, probedula, pempedula, pongaidula, pompedula) ´potentilla, garden valerian´.

This name may be related to Celtic Galii *pompedula*. In several languages this plant is called "5-leaf"; in the second half of the word "leaf" and not "grass" should be sought. (kymr *dail* ´leaves´, O.Cornwall *delen* ´leaf´, *procila, procedila* would permit us to conjure up the Dacian word for "five" *påk'e - Alb.- pésë) but it is more likely that the word stems from the Celts of the Dacian Kingdom. Other explanations are improbable.

diesema (diessachel, diasathel, diesapter) ´mullein; Verbascum´

In ancient times the plant was used as a torch; its name reflects this usage in several languages (cf. German *Himmelbrand*). The etimology proposed by Georgiev appears to be right (cf. Tomaschek, Dečev). Idg. *di(y)es- ews-mn*[8]: "celestial fire".

Mizela (mozula, mizola, mizula) ´thyme´

The plant has been used for the treatment of diseases in the urogenital system. The etimology proposed by Tomaschek seems to be right: *m(e)iûœhe-ûœhel(i)yo* - cf. *meyœh* - ´urinates´ (Georgiev).

salia (Trapogon? Hypochoeris)

This plant has several names (*tragon, tragokerós, cornulaca*), all of which allude to "horn". The root of the word is probably Idg. k^1her- or k^1her-u^3 ´horn, deer´, affixed by *–yā* cf. Av. *srū, srvā* ´horn´, etc. Because the sound change *–ry-* > *-l-* is characteristic also of certain Sarmatian dialects, we cannot exclude its origin from Iranian, but that would require **sala*. However, the *r>l* alteration is characteristic of Albanian, thus, this plant-name points to Dacian-Albanian links, conforming to existing data.

The words noted above characterize sufficiently the Dacian language and also a view of the lingustic circumstances and - to some extent - the peoples that existed in the Dacian Kingdom. Nevertheless, we need to mention additional words such as the Dacians' name: in Greek: *Dakos, Dakoi*, Lat. *Dacus, Daci*. We are also familiar with other versions: Gr. *Dauos, Daoi*, Lat. *Davus*. It is also logical for us to consider *daos* (Friz. - 'wolf'), as did Kretschmer. Words such as *dhāuo-s, dhāu-ko-s* mean 'predatory': O.Sl. *daviti* 'to strangle', Idg. *dheu-*. It is not unusual for animal names to be used as names for peoples. Especially the wolf, which frequently recurs in many nations' history of origin. In this case, however, we can be more specific: in the Indo-Iranian societies, communities of young men, associations of males played an important role, as described by Wikander and Widengren. These young warriors were called "wolves" (Ir.-*mairya*, Ind. - *marya*, Av. *vährka-*). Their symbol is a black flag (*drafša*) decorated with a dragon- emblem; or it is the symbol itself, which is dragon-shaped. They wear their hair long or braided (Ir. *gaēsu*, Ind. - *keśava*) and they fight naked or half-naked. These associations have provided the upper strata in several Indo-Iranian, i.e. Iranian states, where they were among the movers and shakers of society.

We know that the martial symbol of the Dacians was the *draco,* a dragon made of linen. It had a wolf-like head which was carried on a stick. The Iranian origin of this symbol has already been pointed out (we have descriptions of Sarmatian and Parthus martial symbols with dragons - the Romans took it from here). In contrast to the Romans, in the case of Dacians there is more to observe than the Parthus regimental symbol. It is not by chance that one of Dacia's social strata are called *kométai, comati, capillati* i.g. "hairy" or "long-haired", the same as the warriors of Iranian men's associations. The ruling class of the Dacian society (their Dacian name may have been *koso*, cf. O.Ind. *keśa* 'hair' came from Iranian male brotherhoods; this is why the Dacians had the name "wolf". We really do not know when, exactly, this occurred, but it was probably not before Boirebistas' time.

The name of the Dacians has been linked etymologically to the Dacian name for castle: *dava (deva)*. The meaning of this word is confirmed by local place-names and a Greek glossary. "City" should be *leba* (sic!) to the Thracians (Hesych.). We have a valid interpretation for the word: *dhē-u³-ā-,* cf. Idg. *dhē-* ´puts, places´. *Leba*, in the Greek glossary, is a misspelled form of the original *deba* (δεβα). - In addition to "dava", we have a word for another type of settlement: *vis*. This we find in Porolissum and Potaissa (Patavissa) *(-iss, -viss)*. The word refers to a village-type settlement (Lat *vicus*, Slov. *ves*, etc.) and roots in Idg. *(*ueikh)*.

Thus, according to the testimony of language, prior to the Roman conquest in Dacia there existed 3 types of settlements. One of them is *sar.* ´capital, (administrative) center´. It consisted of a castle, an adjoining ritual center and quarters for craftsmen. Second: *dava*, the castle or city and, finally, *vis*: the village-type settlement.

This triad corresponds to the stratification of (the Dacian) ruling class. The capital is the seat of the king and the High Priest, the "davas" are the power-base (centrum)for the Tarabostes; the comati are village-chiefs. Let us pay attention to this word: *tarabostes*. When we analyzed the name *Boirebistas*, we pointed out that the second half of the name is a superlative, meaning "grandest", or something similar. Presumably, the Dacians identified their king with this (non-Dacian) word. The second half of *tarabostes* must also have a meaning related to kingship. The Albanian *tara* is very close to *tër* "beyond, behind". *Tarabostes* would then mean: "behind the king".

The pileati, the tarabostes did actually rank just behind the king; their name accurately defines their position.

Finally, we need to look at the chief god of the Dacians. Several theories circulated about *Zamolksis* (or *Zalmoksis*). The most likely is Russu's; he assumes that *zamol* is related to the Frizian *zemelo* "earth", in which case it is of Idg. origin: *dh(e)ĝhom-el* (cf. O.Sl. *zemlja*, Latv. *zeme*, Lat. *humus*. The second part of the name has to do with Ir. *xšaya-* "king" and the name of Zamolksis would then mean ′king of earth′. This explanation presupposes that the first part of the word does not mean "man" (cf. Frizian: *zemelen* ′slave′). In any event, the name of the god would be of compound derivation, as the second half is of Iranian origin. The question becomes even more complex if we take into consideration the opinion of Herodotos (Historiae IV., 94). He states that the god's other name is *Gebeleizis* (or that many Getae believe in Gebeleizis). As in the case of Zamolxis, the first part of *Gebeleizis* has to do with the Idg. *dh(e)-ĝhom-el-*, but it does not show the feature of the satem languages and its construction is not clear. Also, it shows the alteration of *m* and *b,* characteristic of the Thracian (and Dacian) languages (cf., among others, *Tibiscos* > *Temes* [river-name]). Whether we presume the existence of centum folkgroups in the 5th century B.C. (the age of Herodotos) among the Getae, or consider the termination of palatality for specific reasons, in the case of *Gebeleizis* we can look for examples in satem languages. Here the explanation would focus on a variant with metathesis: *ĝhdhom-el*. In any event, we are faced with linguistic deviations which make understanding impossible.

We have outlined a linguistic profile - what findings does it present? It establishes, first of all, that Dacian belonged to the statem group of Indogermanic languages. In addition, there is a connection with Baltic and Slavic languages, as noted before (cf. for example *dela, zila*: "grass", *sebā* ´elderberry´, etc.) Quite noticeable are connections with Albanian. The identical or similar Dacian-Albanian sound changes have already been compiled by V.Georgiev, which are convincing, although several incorrect etymologies are included. We can find surprising similarities in Dacian and Albanian vocabulary - surely, no coincidence. Dacian *mantia* - "blackberry", Alb. *mand* "strawberry"; "pig" - Dacian *di*, Alb. *thi*, "rock" -Dacian *Karpatés*, Alb. *karpë*. We might add the name of some rivers, too. The - š at the end of *Maros, Temes* can only be explained from Albanian, in which Idg. *s* corresponds to *sh*. As these rivers are in the region where Dacian had been the dominant language we can be certain that the Dacian language was a factor as we consider the š at word's end. I. Popovič, et al. have also pointed this out. As we examine pertinent linguistic data, we note that many of the words do not belong to the satem group. We not only see this in personal and place names, but also in the names of plants - the vocabulary which is considered to be most rooted in Dacian. We disagree with C.Poghirc who believed that Dacian - being on the borderline of the satem and centum languages - is an amalgamate language. We are of the opinion that in the Dacian Kingdom there was a diverse group of nationalities and languages to be found. Some linguistic co-mingling cannot be excluded, (as we illustrated with *Zamolksis*), but it is no accident that centum words are frequent - especially in personal names (*Decebal, Dikaineos*). One could assume that this was merely the fashion of the day. However, we note the same phenomenon among place- and plant-names, i.e. a preponderance of centum (non-Dacian) words (*Salda, Akmonia, Kinuboila,* etc.). Words of unknown or uncertain etymology might also belong to this group as does the toponymy of the Dacian capital and their Religious Center (*Sarmizegethusa, Sargetia*). The Dacian Kingdom was host to a rich variety of languages - or so we assume from the data at our disposal. In this kaleidoscope Dacian stands out most vividly. Celtic is also very visible and we need to take into account one satem and one centum language. The former has a link to Armenian and the latter has possible ties to the unknown language of the Bastarnae.

If we are to analyze the picture shown above about the Dacians in the context of Dacian-Roman continuity, we may say the following. Up to the time that Boirebistas forged his realm, mostly Celts were found in the region, which later became a Roman province. Also, Celticized Dacians; it was the latter's material culture which absorbed the Celtic influence. After Boirebistas assumes power, the southern area of Transylvania is settled by peoples from Moldavia and from the region of the estuary of the Danube. We assume the settlers included Gatae, Dacians (broadly defined) and Bastarnae.

We also need to consider the presence of a sizable population from (the eastern part of) the Middle-East. However, Celts continue to predominate in the central part of the realm - as substantiated by artifacts found there. Subsequent to the death of Boirebistas many of the peoples in his late domain became autonomous and the sovereignty of the Dacian king was reduced to a small area. The kingdom retains Transylvania's southern and - partially - central area and the outer region of the South and South-East Carpatians. Even so, part of this territory remains theirs only for a short time. Around 10 B.C. the Kotini, Anartii, Teurisci, and the Bastarna-Caucus- people achieve independence. Later Decebal unifies the area. However, during his time it is not the Dacian element that dominates - among other things, his own non-Dacian name bears witness to this. As we can see, in Decebal's Dacian Kingdom the Dacians are a minority in relation to the Celts, Iranians and Bastarnae. We cannot tell what their ratio is in relation to the other ethnic groups, the names of dava-districts do not reflect ethnic realities. In this context not much can be deduced from the names of plants (which indeed, are frequently of Dacian origin); we assume these names were told by priests to merchants visiting the religious centrum and the local clergy naturally spoke Dacian. It may be more noteworthy that, even in this center of Dacian life, several herbs/plants had non-Dacian names. (This does not include the glossary, dating from Roman times). The Romans conquered Decebal's kingdom. If we observe the substratum of Romanization, we find that it was not predominantly Dacian - it was also Celtic, Bastarna and Iranian. Therefore if this population had really undergone Romanization, then we should not talk about Dacian-Roman continuity but continuity involving Dacians, Celts, Bastarnae, Iranians - and Romans. Furthermore, if the result of Romanization is a Neo-Latin language which preserves the languages of the substrata, then we should find Celtic, Iranian, etc. words. Yet, we know of no such Neo-Latin language (in Rumanian there is no such substratum). What is clear to us is this: if Romanization of the substratum did indeed occur under the Roman occupation of the erstwhile Dacian Kingdom - we do not know their descendants.

It may be said against the above reasoning that the Dacian and Albanian languages are related and that it is well known that a close relationship also exists between Albanian and Rumanian; in vocabulary, among others. We shall return to this question when we begin to analyze the Albanian-Rumanian connections. I only would like to point out that ethnic Dacians - and those who spoke a similar language - remained outside of Roman-occupied territory for the most part (such as the Costoboci who lived in the Dacian Kingdom). Furthermore, the areas encompassed in the Roman Province did not have a Dacian majority (in all truth only the Ratakae can be genuinely considered as Dacian). On the other hand, the Getae (related to the Dacians) living in the area of the lower Danube and in Dobruja, may have been Romanized, as also the Moesae, who were also related to the Dacians and who lived in the region of the border-area which Gwould now correspond to the contemporary frontier-area between Serbia - Bulgaria. In the context of history and the ethnic relations of the Dacian Kingdom, a Dacian-Albanian, i.e. Albanian-Rumanian linguistic connection suggests that the locus of the latter was not the Roman province of Dacia. There, the linguistic substratum was much too complex and therefore, a Neo-Latin language originating from that territory would not show *only* Albanian connections.

NOTES:

[1] - denotes the letter k with a '$\wedge$' over it

[2] - denotes the letter m with a '$_0$'under it

[3] – denotes the letter *u* with a '∧' under it

[4] - denotes the letter *j* with a '∨' replacing the dot over it

[5] - denotes the letter *i* with a '∧' replacing the dot under it

[6] - denotes the letter *i* with a '~' replacing the dot over it

[7] - denotes the character *ä* with a '∧' over it

8[88] - denotes the letter *n* with a '∘' under it

8(These symbols could not be created by any Font set at the editor's disposal)

Chapter III
PROVINCIA DACIA AUGUSTI:
165 years of Roman rule on the left bank of the Danube.

At the beginning of the 2nd century, in the Spring of 101AD, Roman Forces marched against the Kingdom of Decebal. We already know what the Roman's rationale was for starting this war and we also know that the real reason was likely to have been the personal ambition of the first Provincial Emperor, Trajan (he was born in Hispania — a man of Macedonian background among Greeks). The Roman armies marched against a client-state of Rome, which was a subordinate ally of Rome. Decebal did not want to wage war against Rome and his recurring peace offers confirm this. It is unlikely that Trajan would only have decided on the total conquest of the Dacian Kingdom after he waged his first campaign in 101-102. After this, Roman garrisons were established in the Province - their ongoing presence is reflected by the Latin names of towns (as recorded by Ptolemy). At Dobreta they begin to build the stone bridge which will span the Danube. It was built in accordance with plans made by Apollodorus of Damascus to promote continuous traffic - it was an accomplishment unmatched - even by Rome. This vast project portends that Trajan began the expedition against Dacia in 101 with the intention of incorporating the Kingdom into the Roman Empire. The Emperor, who founded a city (Nicopolis) to commemorate his victory over Dacia, has embarked on this campaign not only for reasons of personal ambition. The economic situation of the Empire was dismal at the beginning of Trajan's reign; by the end of the second Dacian War it has vastly improved. The writings of Kriton, the Emperor's physician, constituted the basis of a report by Johannes Lydus in the   6th century: he describes the amount as taken from the plunder as 5 million litra gold and 10 million litra silver (=1,637,500 and 3,275.000 kilograms respectively). If we assume that they overestimated the booty by 90 % - as is customary - the quantity is still tremendous. This phenomenal Dacian booty causes the value of gold to plunge on the markets of the Empire. The Emperor could afford to bestow lavish gifts upon his people and to finance games in the circus, which lasted 123 days. The guilded statues in the forum - which he had built along with other edifices - bear the inscription 'ex manubiis', or 'derived from the booty.' As we can see, there were many economic reasons for the expedition. Indirectly, Trajan alluded to this in the 'official' Roman explanation for the war; he felt offended by the Dacian's annual demand for money. The Emperor, who had been the Dacians' debtor, became their tax collector. The late-Roman Lactantius reports that Trajan taxed the Dacians (*censui subiugati fuerant*, Lactantius: *De mortibus persecutorum*, 23,5). This tax - census - could hardly be anything but a reference to Trajan's pillage of war.

Roman forces numbered about 50,000 men. The divisions took up their position along the Olt, Zsil and Karas rivers. Starting out at Viminacium, Trajan proceeds along the Karas river on his approach to Tapae, the Transylvanian Iron Gate. Only one sentence was left to posterity from his writing about the war: *inde Berzobim, deinde Aizi processimus* (from here to Berzobis, then on to Aizi). This leads us to believe that this war was not meant to be a sudden attack, but rather a slow procession of troops. After all, the distance between Berzobis and Aizi is a mere 25 km-s and, as far as is known, there was no Dacian resistance. Decebal sent off several emissaries to ask for peace. So did the Burs and other allies of Decebal; according to Cassius Dio, the latter carried a message to the emperor, which was written in Latin - on a large mushroom. The lines are blurred between this story and the report of the vessel found at Sarmizegethusa which looked like a mushroomshaped headpiece which bore a Latin inscription.

Following failed attempts to secure peace Decebal's armies took a stand against the Romans at Tapae - and suffered bloody defeat. However, Trajan does not press forward. Winter is approaching and he reached the limit of his resources.

In 102 Decebal's army was defeated in several battles; the Dacians were unable to defend themselves against the Roman onslaught which threatened them from many sides. The Romans occupy Costeşti Castle, which guarded the road leading to the capital and regain the martial emblems which the Dacians took from Cornelius Fuscus in 87. Decebal surrenders to Trajan as his army is at the point of total collapse. Trajan's terms are merciless: Decebal must surrender all arms and military equipment, all prisoners and all Roman master craftsmen residing in Dacia. Decebal must also dismantle his fortifications, evacuate all territory occupied by the Romans and relinquish his own, independent foreign policy. Dio Cassius records that Trajan leaves garrisons in Sarmizegethusa and in other places before returning to Rome to celebrate his victory.

The Dacian Kingdom, which had been a client-state of Rome, becomes a country which lost its independence and which has become the prisoner of Rome. It is forced to dismantle its military installations in the Bánság (Rum. Banat) and in its small Trans-Carpathian territories. What is more, it also has to evacuate the population from those regions. Trajan's Column, which depicts the Dacian wars, shows in one scene (LXXVI) the migration of men, women, children and domestic animals from Roman-occupied territory toward the mountain region, over which Decebal retained sovereignty. The Romans have begun to cultivate the land which they won. We know that auxiliary Roman troops, the 'Cohors I. Hispana Veterana' were entrusted with protecting from 103-106 the fields of wheat which they tended in Piroboridava (Barboşi - today: a suburb of Galaţi) and in Buridava (Ocniţa i.e. Stolniceni, along the Olt); on Trajan's Column one can make out the picture of soldiers harvesting grain. The occupation of the Bánság was even tougher. The area is held by the IV. Flavia legion, which took part in the campaign and stayed on in Berzobis (Zsidovin) to oversee the occupation and, no doubt, to provide security for the troops which were stationed in Decebal's Kingdom. The latter were to be found in at least 12 locations: based on Greek and Latin place names listed by Ptolemy which must have come from the soldiers of the garrisons. We presume there was a larger contingent - perhaps a legion - stationed at the site of what later became the capital of the Province (Várhely). According to Cassius Dio, Trajan left a garrison also in Sarmizegethusa but we have no evidence of this at Újvárhely, the centrum of the Dacians and, therefore, we must attribute these data to the Sarmizegethusa of Roman times. The settlement became a 'colonia' around 110 and there is a presumption that it once was a military post.

Dacia has been utterly humiliated. Basically, they have only one option left: to fight the occupying power to the death. Decebal rearms, has his castle-fortifications repaired and overruns part of the land of the Jazigs in the Great Plains (today's Hungary). This conquest is usually placed in today's Bánság but, as we could see, this was an area occupied by the Romans and, probably, annexed to Moesia Superior. Therefore to pinpoint the area which Decebal took from the Sarmatians we need to look for the summer grazing-land of this population of ranchers, namely the region of springs between the Kraszna and Kőrös rivers. A confirmation of the above could also be found in the Jazig war of 117-119, after which a new province was established: Dacia Porolissensis; it was to have performed a defensive role. Let us note that one of the reasons for the outbreak of the war had to do with a territorial claim as the Romans did not return to the Jazigs the territory occupied by Decebal.

When news of preparations for war in Dacia reached the Roman Senate they dubbed Decebal an 'enemy of the State'. We cannot assess the accuracy of the rumors. They must have been exaggerated though. Trajan stated repeatedly that he intended to make Dacia into a Roman province (*Sic in provinciarum speciem redactam videam Daciam*, -Amm. Marc. 24, 3. 9). Besides, how intensive could these war preparations have been when all of this would have had to happen under the noses of the Roman garrisons? The emperor must have decided already earlier that he will make a province out of the Dacian Kingdom. And the rumors about Dacian activities gave him a good pretext. He comes to Moesia at the end of 104 to prepare his campaign and during the next 1 1/2 years, from the Spring of 105 to the end of 106 he manages to break all resistance. We have few details about this war. Written sources have provided only scant information and depictions on Trajan's Column are hard to decipher; conclusions reached are frequently ambiguous and controversial. We do however, know that Decebal again asks for peace. His efforts fail, as do those of the assassins whom he sent to kill Trajan. Roman forces keep advancing and the Dacians suffer one defeat after another. Fleeing troops set fire to their own fortifications. One of the strongholds throws itself at Trajan's mercy, another's choice of a way out is suicide. Following the loss of all his citadels Decebal kills himself with his dagger before pursuing Roman mounted soldiers could reach him. The Dacian Kingdom has ceased to exist. The last two frames of Trajan's Column (CLIV-CLV) show men, women and children herding their domestic animals through a forest. We could observe a similar scene (LXXVI) in the representation of the end of the first Dacian war. There, people were leaving Roman occupied territories. At the end there was mass migration; crowds of people opting for the unknown (which held freedom) in lien of certain captivity.

Universa Dacia devicta est - all of Dacia has been conquered. D. Terentius Scaurianus is the first governor of the province; its total annexation is beginning in 106. "Colonia Dacica", the first colony is, established around 110. Road-building begins and the first road, which leads to Potaissa (present day Hung. Torda, Rum. Turda) and

Napoca (present day Hung. Kolozsvár, Rum. Cluj) is completed in 109-110. We presume that the building of most of the network of roads began simultaneously. Along the new borders garrisons and guard towers are put in place which are connected by roads. Of course all this - as well as several additional developments - did not happen in a year or two. In 118-119 Hadrian assigns to Q. Marcius Turbo the governance of both Pannonia and Dacia. While this was wartime, it also suggests that Dacia's borders were still not finalized. The final organization of the Province (Dacia Inferior, Dacia Superior, Dacia Porolissensis) will take place after the conclusion of the Roxolan and Jazig wars (117-119). Following the Dacian war, IV. Flavia -a Roman Legion- was stationed in Berzobis (Zsidovin) until 118-119 when it was reassigned to Singidunum (Belgrade) in Moesia Superior. Dacia becomes a one-legion province up to the Markomann wars, i.e. 167. The Roman cantonment in Berzobis reflects not only the absence of well defined borders, but it shows us that, at the time, Roman forces also controlled a fairly large territory west of what later became Dacia's borders. (At the same time an auxiliary division is stationed at Versec - the Cohors II. Hispana.) Control extended to all of the Bánság, possibly including the southern area of the territory between the Danube and Theiss (Tisza) rivers, up to the Danubian border-region in Pannonia. This helps explain Marcius Turbo's dual governorship. In those days the reorganization of the province was in its beginning stages and we are told that Emperor Hadrian considered relinquishing Dacia. His friends cautioned against it fearing for the safety of the Roman citizens in the Province. The Emperor did not want them to fall into the hands of Barbarians and decided to forego the plan (*ne multi cives Romani barbaris traderentur* - Entr. Brev. 8, 6, 2).

In addition to the occupation of today's Bánság and the southern area of the Great Plains, the question arises whether the territory South of the Carpathians and between the Danube and Siret (Hung. Szeret) rivers was under Roman jurisdiction before 119. If so, we have no proof. Military records reveal that mounted soldiers (Cohors I. Hispana Veterana) were stationed in Pirobaridava and Buridava. One of these (Buridava-Ocniţa) is located next to the Olt river and the other at the Danube- Szeret delta (Piroboridava-Barboşi). This negates the likelihood that the Romans also occupied the territory south and south-east of the Carpathians and that they may have annexed it to Moesia Inferior. Besides, the above mentioned record pertains to the years 102-106 when Trajan placed garrisons all over the Dacian Kingdom. We know that Pirobaridava was a Roman bulwark on the left bank of the Danube and an inscription found in Novae (Svištov, Bulgaria) also makes reference to a native of the locality, Aurelius Victor Perburdavensis et Buricodavensis. Even though we lack substantiating data we cannot exclude the possibility that Rome exercised some lax control over the territory between the Danube and the Carpathian Mountains. We refer to the period between 102-119 and before final adjustments were made regarding Dacia's borders. Control was guaranteed by the Roman troops stationed on the border of the Province but, to a significant extent, also by the annual stipend which Rome provided to the Barbarians. It was the reduction of such a stipend which led to the outbreak of the

117-119 Sarmatian war (with the Jazigs of the Great Plains and the Roxolans of the Lower Danube region).

Thus, it was only in - or after - 119 that Dacia's final borders and internal structure came into being. Peace was made with the Jazigs but their summer pasture land - in the region of the upper Kraszna and Kőrös rivers - was not returned to them. As compensation they were given the Southern Plain (Hungary), after the Romans withdrew from the area. From here on, the borders of the Province run from the Karas-Danube delta up north through the western slope of the Bihar and Meszes mountains. The borders takes a turn along the bend of the Someş (Szamos) and follows the Someş-valley to the Carpathians. Along the inner slope of the Carpathians the border proceeds to the upper Olt and along the Olt, to the Danube. The Háromszék basin was part of the province for only a while - we do not have an exact time frame. However, we can tentatively identify the period: the era of Septimus Severus (193-211) at the end of the 2nd and beginning of the 3rd centuries, inasmuch as this border modification took place at the time of the *Limes Transalutanus*. This was a limes (line) which was built about 30 km from the Olt and extends along the Olt to the Danube.

The Roman province by and large corresponds to pre - World War I. - Transylvania supplemented by Oltenia, bordered by the So. Carpathians, the Danube and the Olt (known in the Middle Ages as the Szörénység. The internal organization of the Province largely corresponds to the geographic setting. There was North-Transylvania, Dacia Porolissensis, with Napoca (Cluj, Hungarian Kolozsvár): South-Transylvania, Dacia Superior with the Trajan-colonia, Sarmizegethusa and also, Apulum: the site of the garrison of XIII. Gemina, the only legion stationed in the province. Finally, Dacia Inferior with a portion of Oltenia and Capped by Drobeta (Turnu Severin) which was also one of Hadrian's municipia. A Hungarian writer, András Alföldi (1), wrote some 50 years ago. 'As a hydrocephalus wobbling on a thread-like neck, so swims this province in the sea of Barbarians'. In reality the territory of Dacia resembles a square, as do most provinces of the Empire. (Oh, but for the Roman passion for surveying land!) The Sarmatian Plain between Dacia and Pannonia was secured by roads, including those connecting Baja to Szeged (Hungary) which followed the Maros river, and which led from Aquincum to Porolissum (Mojgrád). The area differed from other provinces primarily in its absence of a waterway, which would serve as a border.'

This was the reason that prompted Hadrian to consider relinquishing this territory (in Asia he withdrew behind the Eufrates) and he had the bridge demolished which spanned the Danube at Drobeta. This was to have been the first step in re-shaping the borders of the Empire along the banks of the Danube. The reason he did not carry out this plan was due to his reluctance to abandon a large number of Roman citizens to the Barbarians. Barely ten years after Dacia became a Roman province a multitude of Romans could be found there (*multi cives Romani*) which does not frequently happen in new provinces. It is customary to create administrative entities under whose jurisdiction the natives are placed (*civitas peregrina*) and Roman citizens are normally found mainly in the settlements (*canabae*) established in the vicinity of the legionnaires' encampments. Also, of course, in the 'colonias' created for migrants. At the time of Trajan's death in 117, Dacia already had a 'colonia' of Romans at Sarmizegethusa and, we can also find budding Roman settlements (of civilians) at Berzobis and Apulum. Their total number would be around 10,000 (excluding Roman troops - it was easy to eliminate them from the count). Was this the *multi cives Romani* whose fate could not be entrusted to the Barbarians? Especially, since those civilians who lived in the vicinity of Roman encampments could have been as easily evacuated as the newly resettled veterans (who still had military tasks to perform). To sum up: within a remarkably short time, a great many settlers took up residence in the newly established province. The reasons for this are substantiated by a source from antiquity: "...after conquering Dacia, Trajan resettled there a multitude from all over the Empire, who were to populate the cities and the countryside (*propterea quia Traianus victa Dacia ex toto orbe Romano infinitas eo copias hominum transtulerat ad agros et urbes colendas*, Eutr. Brev. 8, 6, 2). In other words, this was the result of a conscious and perhaps forcible resettlement policy, aimed at having a sizable Roman population within 10 years - *multi cives Romani* - in Dacia. Another clue to the involuntary aspects of resettlement has to do with names. We find many citizens called Ulpius and Aelius. These must have been new citizens, such as veterans of auxiliary troops who, according to custom, adopted the name of the emperor who granted them citizenship (M. Ulpius Traianus, P. Aelius Hadrianus). Thus, Trajan resettled in Dacia newly created citizens from many parts of the Empire and Hadrian continued the practice after he decided not to give up Dacia. We believe that another group belonging to this category came from the ranks of *tribus Papiria* (Trajans tribe); A. Alföldi pointed this out a long time ago. Our above mentioned source also indicates why this resettlement policy was necessary. 'As a result of Decebal's lengthy wars there was a shortage of males in Dacia'. (*Dacia enim diuturno bello Decibali viris fuerat exhausta*, Eutr. Brev. 8, 6, 2). This leads us to one of the most important questions of Daco-Roman continuity: what happened to the indigenous population? Eutropius, an early resource, provides us with a rather clear answer although it is odd that he talks only about the dearth of males. A. Alföldi was of the opinion that Eutropius mentioned only men because he slightly altered his source data (the emperor-biographies which had been thought lost and which were discovered by Enman). The original sources recounted the extermination of Dacians. In his satire about apostate emperors, Iulianus has Trajan say: "I annihilated the Dacians". His information comes from the same source as Eutropius (Julianus Ceasares 327: τό Γετων έδνος έξειλον) Iulianus' words, given to Trajan, were considered an exaggeration, or satirical fiction. (C. Patsch, C. Daicoviciu). I. I. Russu assumes that Trajan could merely boast of having ground the population into the dust, i.e. having conquered the Dacians. First, we should note that Alföldi proved the common origin of Eutropius' and Iulianus' text (the more surprising the contradiction between the two) and that, even during Trajan's lifetime, the news has spread about the Dacians' destruction. Trajan's physician, Kriton, commented (Lucianus, Icaromenippos 16, scholion) that Trajan was to have spared the life of only 40 men (Russu notes with sarcasm Alföldi's failure to make use of this information). We have another source of reference in Pliny the Younger. He was encouraging Caninius Rufus to work on the epic poem about the Dacian war which he had in the planning stage. Pliny writes:.... "You will speak of new rivers crossing the plains and of new bridges spanning them, (you will speak of) two triumphant marches, one of them over a never-before-conquered people and the second which was the final one" (Plinius minor, Epistolae VIII, 4). It is apparent that Pliny also believed the Dacians had been annihilated if he considered the triumphant march of the Romans to be the final one in Dacia. Thus, there was a frame of reference in Roman literature about Dacia's destruction and, therefore, we do not have to discard or re-interpret Iulianus' text. However, there is still a contradiction to be cleared up between the text of Iulianus and Eutropius. Actually, there may never have been a divergence between the two because the critical sentence in Eutropius also exists in a different version: *Daciae (Dacia) enim diuturno bello Decebali res fuerant exhaustae* (Eutr. Brev. 8, 6, 2, comm. Santini). In other words: "the wealth of Dacia was plundered due to Decebal's long lasting wars". "Res" has a much more comprehensive meaning than we can translate; we can consider it to mean destruction and that Dacia became a "desertum", a barren wasteland, subsequent to Trajan's onslaught. This image would correspond with the words Iulianus makes Trajan say in his play: "I annihilated the people of Dacia".

Even if this did happen, we know the statement to be an exaggeration. We have scores of historical examples of reports on the destruction and extermination of nations which turn out to be untrue. What happened in these cases was mostly the cessation of a tribal entity of a nation-state or of the status quo - nothing more. Therefore, we do not have to take ancient reports about the destruction of the Dacians at face value, although there are many who do - especially among those who belong to the camp which disputes the theory of Daco-Roman continuity. Oddly enough, the earliest proponents of this belief (in modern times) were the members of the "Transylvanian School" (S. Micu-Klein, P.Maior) professing Transylvanian Roman continuity. They could only perceive the survival of pure Romanism.

Let us consider the reasons behind the resettlement effort which brought large numbers of people into the new Dacian province from other parts of the Empire. We know Eutropius' explanation: Dacia became a wasteland. We also know of the representations of the Dacian war on Trajan's Column, where Roman soldiers are portrayed as killing masses of Dacians. However, we should remember that these images were born of triumph and, naturally, depict murdered and dying Dacians. Undoubtedly, there were many suicides among the upper strata of Dacian society, the pileati-tarabostes, but it is doubtful that there would have been mass-suicide - although, some think so. The scene of Trajan's Column which depicts the suicides (CXL) shows men who kill themselves with a weapon and also a group dipping liquid from a bowl and drinking it. According to one theory: they are drinking poison. It is, however, more probable that we see a water-distribution system in action in a castle under siege. (The castles in the mountains of Szászváros [Orăştie] must, indeed, have been short of water during the siege.) There are scenes on the column which portray surrendering Dacians. These do not establish the survival of the Dacian population. Prisoners of war, who are carried away as slaves diminish the population just as do those who are killed in battle. Earlier we have spoken about the last scene on the Trajan Column: men, women and children marching off with their domestic animals. One could argue about - but not establish - their destination. There is a parallel scene on the column which depicts the end of the first war (LXXVI) eliminating the possibility that these would be Dacians returning to their abandoned homes. Nor can we assume that this would be the population from the central region of the Kingdom which was being resettled, because we do not see anyone in charge of carrying out the resettlement process. These are then emigrating Dacians, whose departure contributes to the depopulation of Dacia. Another reason why they could not have been returning emigrants: it was public knowledge in Rome that Trajan "annihilated" the Dacians. Under these circumstances they could not have been portrayed on the column as returnees.

There is no written text accompanying the representations on the Trajan Column; our analysis of the story-line will be supported by what literary parallel we can find. Data from another source can help us define the fate of the indigenous Dacian population after the conquest. One of these has to do with Dacians recruited to serve as Roman soldiers. According to Roman custom, when the natives of a province rose up, their warriors were made to join auxiliary units. These were ale and cohorts of 500 to 1000 men, respectively, whose ranks were supplemented by men from local tribes. In post-Trajan times it became more frequent and - eventually - the rule that the replacement came from the same province where the auxiliary troops were stationed (this was also the situation in Dacia where local men were serving in the ala Gallium, Illyricorum and Hispanorum Campagonum). Dacian auxiliary units were called Ulpia, Aelia and Aurelia. This would suggest that auxiliary troops were being organized from Trajan to Commodus in 192, because their name corresponds to the names of emperors during this period. Since only peregrines (aliens, i.e. natives of the province) were recruited in the auxiliary troops, there had to be a significant native population left, otherwise it could not be explained how Hadrian, Antonius Pius (Aelii) and Marcus Aurelius Commodus (Aurelii) could have manned the auxiliary troops in the province. On closer examination we find that these auxiliary troops do not provide unequivocal proof of the survival of Dacia's native population. We know of only two auxiliary troops which were created during Trajan's reign: the ala I. Ulpia Dacorum and the cohors I. Ulpia Dacorum. Both are stationed in the east; in Cappadochia, i.e. Syria. The existence of the ala, the Dacian cavalry, is open to question because Dacians were infantrymen. On Trajan's Column we see only one portrayal of a Dacian on horseback (and that in fording a river!). Ala I. Ulpia Dacorum was probably an ala which Arrianos called a Geta - in the 2nd century there were Geta units next to Dacians (Hyginus Gromaticus, *De munitione castrorum* 9) and we may be looking at auxiliary troops made up of Getae from Dobruja. (Romans frequently used Dacus - Dacia - interchangeably with Geta). There was nothing unusual during Trajan's reign about the creation of auxiliary units. First, because this was in accordance with Roman custom. Second, because we know from Johannes Lydus - whose information came from Kriton - that Rome 'took' 500,000 Dacians and their weapons. In other words: 500,000 Dacians were pressed into Roman service. This number must have been overstated (Russu maintains there were only a few thousand). Still, a substantial number of Dacians were taken prisoner and the two Dacian auxiliary units established by Trajan could not have absorbed them all. We surmise that the majority were attached to Roman forces as *symmachiarii* (as allies); we find Dacians listed among the "nationes" (Cantabri, Gaetali, Palmyreni, Daci, Brittones) in Ps. Hyginus' listing. After these 'nations' became more trustworthy - and somewhat Romanized - they achieved the status of regular troops. This is the explanation for the existence of Dacian auxiliaries under Hadrian (*cohors I. Aelia Dacorum miliaria*) - naturally, they came from among the symmachiarii. The largest number of relics we have came from this cohors, stationed in Britain. One inscription portrays the 'sica', a unique Dacian weapon.

There is some uncertainty regarding auxiliaries under Marcus Aurelius' rule. A mosaic inscription from Poetovio (Ptuj, Slovenia) reads: *Iustus optio cohortis II. Aur Dacorum.* This is the only reference on which we can rely and is not sufficient to give serious consideration to cohors II. Aurelia Dacorum troops. On these inscriptions we frequently come across missing letters; here only the modifier, Aurelia, appears to have been shortened. Dacian troops were, without exception, sent to distant provinces (Cappadocia, Syria,

Brittania). We know of only one Dacian unit in Pannonia: cohors II. Augusta Dacorum - it is most unlikely that there would have been more. I. Russu also brought up the matter of the two cohors' (reversed) identity. His reading of the inscription in Poetovio would read Aug instead of Aur and it would become unlikely that Dacian auxiliaries would have been established under Marcus Aurelius. Nevertheless had they been in existence, they would have been recruited during the Markomann wars from among local peregrines - only as a last resort and whether or not they were Dacians. Let us remember that at the time, the inhabitants of Dacia were called Daci whatever their ethnicity and that we have countless examples of the same process in other provinces. 'The Dacian Battalion' (*Vexillatio Dacorum Parthica*) which participated in the Parthus-campaign of Septimius Severus, belongs to the same category. C. Iulius took part in the campaign with this "Dacian Battalion". He was the tribune of cohors I. Brittonum which was stationed in Samum (Alsókosály), Dacia. Thus, the Dacian Battalion- the Vexillatio Dacorum- was made up of Dacian regulars and not of new Dacian recruits. We must also note that, in this context, Dacus does not denote Dacian nationality but residence in the Roman province of Dacia.

Those Dacians who were attached to Roman troops had been carried off by Trajan's army at an earlier time (thus contributing to the extermination of their peoples). We have no evidence to show that these troops were recruited in their place of residence. In truth, beginning with Hadrian's era, the custom was to do recruiting wherever the troops were stationed. It is remarkable that none of the veterans of the auxiliary troops returned to their native habitation, as was customary. Was there none to whom to return? In short: the Dacian soldiers of the Roman army do not substantiate the survival of the native population. The only thing certain is that Trajan carried off young warriors from Dacia and that soldiers from the Roman province of Dacia ended up in other parts of the Empire, as well.

One of the most weighty counter-arguments against the survival of Dacian natives is the lack of *civitates peregrinae*: native communities organized by the Romans. We do not have sufficient data to dispute the issue. Another possibility inherent in the discussion: there were simply not enough native communities to organize into civitae. This premise is sometimes countered by the theory that the Dacian tribes described by Ptolemy were a "particular type of civitas" (Russu: *un fel de "civitates peregrinae"*). However, the Ptolemy-narration from 103-104 cannot be applied to the first decade of the province (106-117); the designation of the occupying legions is missing, Sarmizegethusa is still the 'Royal seat', etc. Under Roman rule we should also be coming across the nation-names listed by Ptolemy - but we do not see them. The only exception is a milestone which was found at Nagyalmás near Bánffyhunyad. The inscription reads: R [ESC]VL(o) VICO AN[ARtorum]. Based on this, we assume that the name of nearby Sebesváralja was Resculum Vicus Anartorum. This place-name holds the seat of the "civitas" of the Celt Anartii - at any rate, an independent peregrinus area. This tells us there was evidence of the survival of the native population in the border-area of Dacia - even if the indigenous population was Celtic and not Dacian.

Following in the steps of A. Domaszewski and V. Pârvan, one additional area along the northern border of Dacia needs to be mentioned. During the era of Severus Alexander (222-235) a military post has been established at the delta of the two Szamos rivers at Samum. The commander of the post (the beneficiarus consularis) has a new assignment under Gordianus (238-244). He will become *agens sub signis Samum cum regione Ans*, as is revealed by inscriptions attributed to the years 239 and 243. We learn that the commander of the guard post also becomes the constable of a town (Samum) and of a territory (regio Ans.). This area was to have been the territory of Ansamenses, a Dacian tribe. Well, we know of no such Dacian tribe. In any event, their appearance would have come too late to be viewed as an original Dacian tribe, given the migration patterns of the intermediate period. Besides, the abbreviated Ans. can be given different meanings. The Latin name   regio Ansamensium may be a variant of Assamensium - Asamensium, from an earlier Ad-samensium. Here the - n - is a phenomenon of over-correction; in Latin the - n - is lost from the - ns - consonant group, resulting in "n" preceding "s" in "correct spelling" (thensaurus - thesaurus, etc.). Thus, the expression might simply mean "a territory in the Samum region" in which case the region is a border-area under the military jurisdiction of Ansamensium. (This is the theory of Á. Dobó). If we wish to read a tribal or national designation into the expression, we can posit two theories. Either of these will have greater plausibility than the sudden appearance of an unknown, Dacian Ansamenses tribe. The inscription we have been discussing was thought by K. Torma to read ANSVAL... M. Domaszewski modified it to: ANS V S L M. The deviation between the two versions is much too pronounced to be credible. (Domaszewski's is more in line with epigraphic history - but he may have been influenced by this very fact). Unfortunately, the (mile) stone from Kaplyon no longer exists and the ancient inscription on it cannot be verified. However, if we contemplate Torma's reading it is possible to assume that the original epigraph was ANSALORVM since the v.s.l.m. abbreviation would not have been an integral part of it. Ancient Ansalorum would be the territory of a well-known Pannonian tribe, the Azali (or Asali). (Their coins bear the ANSALI inscription). This tribe migrated to or was made to resettle in Dacia which would be understandable in view of the Pannonian connection; archeological material from Roman times reveals that the Porolissum region had close links with Pannonia.

There is another possible explanation, as well. When S. Cornelius Clemens was governor (170-172 - the period of the Markomann Wars), the Asdings attack Dacia, i.e. they request "receptio" -permission to resettle within the Empire. They hand over their families to the governor who sends them against the Kostoboks. After they are defeated he instigates an attack upon them by way of the Lakringos. Again they are subjugated and they ask the Empire for money and asylum. The historian of the Goths, Iordanes, assumes that they continued to live in the region of the Mureş and Samos rivers (Miliare, Gilpil) but this area is actually Gepida territory from way back. The Asdings must have been living in the valley of the Samos, near Samum. Inscriptions from this region were found, with epigraphs showing Regio Ans. - in this case regio Ans(dingorum). An additional piece of reference: the tombstone of Julius Crescens (a typical soldier's name). He was portrayed in a sheepskin cape; this was considered to be suggestive of native influence. Yet, we have never seen Dacians portrayed in this fashion. However, the Germans, Getae, Celts and Illyrians did wear such cloaks - there is plenty of evidence to substantiate this. If Julius Crescens cloak had been a typical local garment, then this could have been German. It may have been what the Asdings wore - we have already come across their name as Ansdingi. The Roman commander of Samum must have been overseeing an area in the Szamos valley which was tribal territory. In all probability it was the territory of a German people who found admission there. (Possibly, vicus Ansdingorum was also inscribed on the milestone of Nagyalmás, as well. We lack data in Roman Dacia about the regional native infrastructure and, perhaps, natives did not live there in large numbers. We can substantiate this further. As we have mentioned earlier, it was the Celtic Catini in the Dacian Kingdom who did the mining and metal-work. (Tacitus writes about their relatives who lived in the Gömör mining-area: "to their shame, they dig for iron ore...") We do not lack data about the mining areas of Ampelum and the vicinity of Alburnus Maior in the days of Roman hegemony. Without exception, the miners were relocated from Dalmacia: Pirustae, Baridustae, Sardeasi - along with people from Asia-Minor and those who did forced-labor. The Dalmatians lived in tribal communities under a ruling prince and a tribal chief. (Vicus Pirustarum, etc.). There are no Celt Kotini among them. After Trajan's war, not only do all Dacian miners and smiths disappear but, so do the other nationalities as well. In order to sustain the mining operation, different nationality groups - with specialized skills in mining - had to be brought in. It seems very clear that the Dacia of Roman antiquity lacks the regional structures which native populations are maintaining elsewhere. Yet, a system of self-government can be found among resettled Dalmatian miners or immigrant Germanic Asdings. This points to the absences of a native population in Dacia which could have been organized into a 'civitas' and from whose ranks a 'princeps' could have been elected.

The survival of the indigenous Dacian population is substantiated by the existence of a Dacian toponymy in the Roman province; the Romans must have had contact with this population - why else would they have continued to use Dacian place names? Without going into the rules of the adoption of toponyms and for the benefit of those who would attach importance to this premise, we would like to mention an example of a situation which occurred within much he same time-frame. In his geographical studies Ptolemy mentions many names of towns outside the Roman Empire's borders. In order to be familiar with the toponyms of a given locality, there did not have to be communication with its population, following occupation of the territory. Actually, Romans must have had contact with Dacians for an extended time period, starting with the war of 85-86 through the peace of 89, when Dacia was a client-kingdom. Let us further recall that Roman garrisons are stationed in the Kingdom from 102 on. Given the extent of contact between the two nations and the opportunity of borrowing of names, it is surprising that we have so little data about Dacian localities in later times in the region (Tapae, Boutae, Ranisstorum, Darnithith).

Our awareness of the ethnic relations in Roman Dacia also brings into question the survival of the local Dacian population. We can define those relationships by way of surnames on inscriptions; the etymology or geographical characteristics of these names connects them with specific natives or territories of the Roman Empire. We need to remember that the custom of inscribing objects (altars, tombstones, etc.) is already a sign of Romanization. For that reason Roman citizens (with three names) are a lot more evident than peregrini (aliens) with one or two names. In the case of Roman citizens the third name (cognomen) indicates the origin of the individual, although not always; veterans who served 25 years or more and who were given Roman citizenship, usually changed their cognomen. A Dacian reference exemplifies this process: Aurelius Vales qui et Esbenus (CIL III. 80-40); (the Thracian name of this individual is Esbenus.) Marcus Aurelius Eptacentus is the cognomen of a legionnaire from Aquincum. His third name is a typical Thracian name, which identifies his pre-Romanization nationality. The number of personal names in Roman Dacia, known by 1977, was around 3000. Out of these 2000 (73%) are Latin, 420 (14%) Greek, 120 (4%) Illyrian, 70 Celtic (2,3%), 60 (2%) so-called Daco-Moesian-Thracian and 70 (2,3%) from the middle East and/or Eastern Semi. Let us note that there is no Daco-Moesian-Thraco language. We have seen earlier that Dacian and Thracian are two separate languages. These names are actually Thracian. Therefore, they cannot be the names of the native population. There is much uncertainty here. In looking at I. I. Russu's statistics C. Daicoviciu notes that, at best, no more than 38 names can be attributed to the Daco-Moesian-Thraco grouping. A. Mócsy is right in claiming: "no names that are local - and definitely not Thracian or Moesian-Thracian - can be identified..." If Dacian and Thracian were not the same languages then the bearers of (these) names must have come here as soldiers - with their families - from Thrace or Moesia... If the two languages are basically the same, it would still be odd to find analogous names only South of the Danube (2). However, we know that the two languages are not the same and we can only conclude that, to the best of our knowledge, there are - statistically and numerically - 0(%) Dacian surnames in Roman-Dacia's roster of names.

K140

For additional analyses let us examine the last 50 years' statistics on Dacian surname data. In 1944 there were 2600 Dacian surnames known to us. Latin-1836 (70%), Greek-350 (13%), Illyrian-120 (4.6%), Celtic-60 (2,4%). Dacian, i.e. Thracian-67 (2,5%), Semi-60 (2,4%). Numerically, Illyrian and Dacian, i.e. Thracian names remained unchanged - the others increased. There was not much change statistically; the Illyrian and the Daco-Thraco group diminished by 1/2 %. In the case of the Illyrians there is a logical explanation: a significant number of these names (43) came to light on a wax tablet found at Alburnus Maior creating a statistical imbalance as early as 1944.

Another figure worth noting is the low ratio of Celtic names, especially since Celts in Dacia came from the west; from Pannonia, Noricum and from even further away. We have no reliable data on Celtic names in Dacia, although we know the Celts played a significant role in the Dacian Kingdom. To quote A. Mócsy: the presence of Dacian Celtic names approach - 0 - as do the Dacians. It is also noticeable, that there is no trace on the inscriptions of the Iranian-speaking nationality in the Dacian Kingdom. This suggests that all ethnic groups within the Kingdom: Dacians, Celtics and Iranians, were effected the same way during Roman rule; they became invisible. This really means that they are simply not there. Proponents of large-scale survival of the natives use a unique type of reasoning. Their theory assumes that Dacians feared Roman revenge and persecution and immediately adopted Roman names, which accounts for these names recurring: Ulpius, Aelius, Aurelianus. True, the roster of Dacian surnames looks nearly monochromatic; compared to other provinces there are a great many empire-bestowed 'gentilicia'. The number of Ulpii exceeds 100, Aelii: 250 and Aurelii: 300. In a way, the Aurelii should not be part of the list, in view of Caracalla's (212) edict. This gave citizenship to the provincials. Additionally, the right to be called Aurelius - if not belonging to the clan - could be claimed by anyone after 161, when Marcus Aurelius took power. If we adopt the above-mentioned survival theory, we have to explain why there would have been Dacians who began to fear Rome's revenge 50 years later? However, if we stick to facts we shall conclude that the large number of Ulpii and Aelii were in the province on account of Trajan's and Hadrian's policy of forced resettlement - as we had seen earlier.

Another part of the theory under dispute attributes the absence of Dacian names on the inscriptions to social and economic causes. Accordingly, Dacians were to have continued their patriarchal, peasant-sheepherding lifestyle, and lacked the means of rich city-folk to erect stone tablets and leave inscriptions behind. Besides, these forms of expression would be uncharacteristic. Prior to the Roman conquest they were not in the habit of erecting monuments(!) and would be even less likely to do so subsequently, as they have been living under greater duress than natives in the other provinces, etc. Such an illusory explanation does not require a response but there are some discrepancies here which merit further clarification. - On one hand, Dacians are rushing to adopt Roman names with "lightning speed", on the other: their socio-economic status prevents them from erecting tombstones or altars. These actions are not congruent and would require a determination: which of the two types are the truly Dacian? It is true that inscriptions are not reflective of the whole the population of the province, but erecting markers was a sign of Romanization in every province - perhaps this becomes clear even if we do not present a list of examples. As to oppression: the duress suffered by Dacian natives could not have been so much greater than that of others who were natives of different provinces. After all, native presence in Noricum accounted for 24 % and 33 % in Pannonia, while in Dacia - Zero. If Dacian natives do not make inscriptions on altars, reliefs, then we should be allowed to conclude that they did not conform, learn Latin, adopt Roman customs and that they retained a Dacian lifestyle. However, if they remained Dacians, then we cannot promote the concept of Daco-Roman continuity.

The surname-data we have regarding Roman Dacia provides visible proof that there was no numerically significant native population. Had there been such natives, nevertheless, their language would not have been Latin but Dacian and they would not have had a "cultural, linguistic and ethnic symbiosis" with the Romans. We find further validation of this premise if we study Roman sculpture of the period. They do not portray native symbols. This corresponds to the absence of native gods in Dacia. This has been an accepted line of reasoning dating back to Hirschfeld - but it should not be taken at face value. On the basis of data we have about the Dacian religion it is apparent it had no feature which could be equated with the Roman religious belief-system. (Of course, it was not a polytheistic khtonic religion as Russu believes). It would be futile for us to search for Dacian gods in the context of "*interpretatio Romana*" — because there were none, although N. Gostar has lately been proposing that Dea Placida, Diana Mellifica or Liber-Libera, etc. are Dacian gods.

Those who support a Daco-Roman continuity theory have insisted that "archeological research of the last 2-3 decades has proven - without question - Dacian survival under the Romans". Were this true, then we could not doubt the survival of the indiginous population, a population which did not assimilite, did not 'Romanize'. And if native cemeteries in Dacia differ from those of the Romans - the former lacking tombstones and memorial objects with inscriptions (D. Protase) - then this could only have been a non-Romanized population which retained its language, its customs. Once we give it a close look, however, this 'archeological proof' is nowhere near as self-evident. In reference, it is customary to present a long list of sites where findings were made. While we cannot examine each, let us name at least a few.

In Soporu de Cîmpie, Obreja and Locuşteni (in Oltenia) cemeteries were found with crematoria. We also know of a cemetery connected to a settlement at Obreja. Those who reported the findings believe them to be cemeteries of the indigenous population. Instead of detailed analyses and response we refer to K. Horedt, who writes: 'There is such great similarity between Karp cemeteries and the cemetery at Soporu de Cîmpie in their rites (graves with urns and a scattering of ashes, children's graves and skeletons), accessories (Dacian ceramics and silver jewelry), and the similarities so far-reaching, that in the Soporu de Cîmpie cemetery 'Karps must have been buried'. (3) The same would apply to Obreja and Locuşteni. All three cemeteries were burial grounds for the Karps who migrated to the area from Moldavia (and who were speaking a language related to Dacian). They were known for their repeated forays into the territory from 240 AD on. The mother of the later Emperor Galerius fled Dacia during the reign of Philippus (244-249) on account of Karps attacks. The three cemeteries mentioned above date from the middle of the 3rd century to the beginning of the 4th; (written) sources attest that Dacia was lost to the Empire during the reign of the late Gallienus (253-268). (*Dacia... amissa est* Eutr. Brev. 9, 8, 2). This period coincides with the timing of the Karps' in-migration. There were other sporadic discoveries which fit the picture, such as the grave for cremated remains at Medgyes, with its characteristic amphora - shaped Karp vessels, because "there were no Dacian graves in the province in the 2nd century." (K.Horedt, *Siebenbürgen in spätrömischer Zeit*, 1982, 55.)

Findings of other "native Dacian" cemeteries are also based on error. In Hermány (Caşolţ) a great many burial mounds were excavated. Even A. Alföldi was inclined to attribute them to Dacians. Three-legged urns came to light and lids which bore the characteristics of late Celtic pottery. The perpetuation of the characteristics of these urns leaves no doubt that we are contemplating the relics of a particular ethnic group. In this case they are most likely to have migrated from - or been resettled from - Noricum or Pannonia. A cemetery of an indigenous population was also reported from   Segesvár. However, here there are tombstones with inscriptions and the names on it are not Dacian but Illyrian. To repeat the earlier observation of Horedt: if there are no 2nd century Dacian graves in Dacia, then we cannot claim the existence of Dacian continuity.

We have pretty much the same situation with regard to village-settlements presumed to be Dacian (provided, we utilize reliable data). The cemetery at Obreja substantiates that this was a settlement of Karps' as further shown by the platter with a tubal base and the large, egg-shaped utensils found there. The Caşolţ settlement was also the habitation of the community interred in its cemetery, as archeological findings revealed. As we have seen, that points to settlers from Noricum — Pannonia. In the Roman settlements of antiquity, there were several which had once been Dacian; these Roman habitations naturally incorporate earlier Dacian shards - as we have seen at Szelindek or Maroslekence.

We find it even more incomprehensible that ceramics not made on a wheel which were unearthed at Roman camps at Sebesváralja and Vérmező are claimed as evidence of native survival. As long as the Roman fortifications stood - with Roman soldiers or auxiliary troops guarding them - under no circumstances could there have been natives, except when the Roman fortifications were overrun by Barbarians, who came from outside the province. (Among these there might have been Dacians). For now we must conclude that there is no archeological evidence of Dacian continuity (the allegedly Dacian shards of the *castrum* at Vérmező cannot be linked to any known Dacian artifact). Now, there may be some settlements with a Dacian legacy as a result of 12,000 "free" Dacians being brought to the province by Sabinianus around 180. These do not, of course, prove the continued existence of the indigenous population in the province.

There is nothing ambiguous about the above; we hold to our references from antiquity. Following Trajan's Wars, writes Eutropius and we paraphrase: *Dacia... res fuerat exhausta* (Eutr. Brev. 8, 6, 2, comm. Santini). This writer worked hard and without success to find evidence of a surviving Dacian population. In spite of the lack of evidence we found it is hard to believe that at least a segment of the Dacian population would not have remained in the Roman province. However, facts are facts. Therefore, we must emphasize that, within the borders of the Roman province of Dacia, we cannot account for a surviving indigenous population - and this applies not only to Dacians, but to Celts, Scythians, Sarmatae and Bastarnae, as well. We simply cannot identify any data to support the theory of Daco-Roman continuity. This theory has its place only in a work about the history of science, in the same way as the theory about Scythian-Hungarian and Hun-Hungarian Kinship.

Lack of substantiation of the Daco-Roman theory, (*continuitatea daco-romană*) does not mean that we should discard the existence of a Romanized, Roman, Latin speaking population in the region. In Dacia, Latin was the language used. Both Trajan and Hadrian impelled tens of thousands to resettle in the Province. The number of Roman citizens called Ulpii and Aelii who left a legacy of inscriptions is approximately (100+250) 400, perhaps as high as 500. Let us remember, that a majority of these newly-made Roman citizens had earlier been members of the auxiliary troops, and that they spoke a native language in addition to Latin. However, side by side, we can find also the Latin-speaking Apulum Legion (XIII. Gemina). Under ideal circumstances they would number 6000 soldiers, but we cannot rely on this figure as it was not constant. We must also take into consideration the civilian population residing in settlements next to military camps. They, too, spoke Latin. The population of Apulum (there were two of this town, - more about this later) was said to have been around 40,000 in its hey day. We cannot count on more than 10,000 during the middle of the 2nd century in the civilian settlements near the Legion's camp. Dacia's first city, colonia Dacica, (Sarmitzegethusa) was a community of veterans. Its amphiteather seated 5-6000 people, on the basis of which (as is customary) we can project a population of 20,000. Accordingly, around the middle of the 2nd century - and including Napoca and Drobeta -(two municipalities founded by Hadrian whose population must have been close to Sarmizegethusa's) - there must have been at least 100,000 people there whose everyday language was Latin. We can be certain that the language of communication was Latin for the peregrini settlers (Dalmatians, Pannonians, those from Noricum). It is surprising that even Greeks posted Latin inscriptions in Dacia and in an environment on which no resident peoples and languages impacted, Latin being the exclusive means of communication. Next to Italy, Dacia was one of those province in the Roman Empire during the 2nd century in which the Latin language was spoken by almost the entire population. In this context A. Mócsy's statistics are worthy of note. He found that 66 % of East-Dacian family names are so-called 'general' Latin names. We have to consider this a unique Dacian characteristic; in other parts of the Empire such names do not appear at such a high percentage. The uniqueness of these features is further demonstrated by a 57 % ratio of the Roman names being that of one of the emperors. This means that the majority who bear these names are provincials who where granted Roman citizenship. What is especially noteworthy here is language - the mother tongue, independent of tribal background. Thus, we cannot speak about 'semi-Romanization' as applicable to Dacia's whole history about some type of Greek Dacia (*Dacia graeca*) nor possibly about 'Dacia peregrina' (inhabited by non Latin population).

Dacia's history can be divided into two, sharply different eras, similar to the development of other Roman provinces in the Danubian region. The tremendous destruction brought on by the Markomann Wars (167-180) did not vanish without trace. The invading Barbarians carried away a large number of people from Dacia - just as they did in Pannonia. The situation was critical. V. Macedonia, the Legion stationed earlier in Troesmis, is sent to Potaissa; in 168 M. Claudius Fronto, the governor of Moesia Superior, was also entrusted with the governance of Dacia Apulensis (the former Dacia Superior). Soon, he will take charge of all three Dacias (Apulensis, Porolissensis and Malvensiss). Fronto's armies are defeated by "Germanics and Jazigs", he is also killed in battle. Thereupon Moesia Superior is annexed to Dacia. The interior of the province is also being affected by the fighting. In Alburnus Maior (Verespatak) their owners hid the wax-tablets with the written contracts. The last date which came to light was May 29, 167. Sarmitzegethusa was also in danger. In the East, Moesia Inferior was devastated by the Costoboci and Sarmatians; the invasion extended to the Greek peninsula. We have already made reference to the forays of the Asdings who attack Dacia after defeating the Costoboci. This occurred during Cornelius Clemen's governorship (170-172). The Asdings were led by Rhaos and Rhaptos into Dacia - they were eventually chased out by the Lacrings, who had been in the province earlier. Tarbus, the chief of an unknown tribe, also threatened with war unless he was given annual compensation. Around 180 Commodus, son of Marcus Aurelius, was fighting against the Burs on Dacia's northern border. After they were defeated, they were bound - by contract - not to graze their herds within 7.5 km (40 stadions) of the border and would not settle there. At the same time, Sabinianus settled some 12,000 Dacians from across the border. The devastation of war and the insecure conditions of their immediate environment became catalysts for an uprising around 180 by the provincials in Dacia. The legions involved in defeating the uprising were rewarded by the titles "loyal" and "steadfast" - most likely not only for having been faithful but for their cruel suppression of the uprising.

As it happened in Pannonia, the population of the Province might have been diminished by the Barbarians' destructive raids and in the aftermath of the defeat of the provincial's uprising. Those who hid their wax-tablets in Alburnus Maior never returned to their homes and Sabinianus' large-scale resettlement effort also suggests that the original population had perished. On the northern border of Dacia, inscriptions pertaining to the Amartii and Asdings date from the 3rd century (those from Samum are dated 239 and 243). It was during Septimius Severus' rule (193-211) that normalcy returned to the province. During his reign the number of cities in Dacia doubled: Dierna, Tibiscum, Apulum II., Potaissa and Porolissum become municipalities during this period. Five other towns are granted '*ius Italicum*' - exemption from paying property tax in the province. These privileges and other opportunities in Dacia must have served as a magnet. It follows that, by the beginning of the 3rd century, we find an unusual rise in the prosperity of the ruling class. Huge tracts of land are being leased to individuals and they become *conductores pascui et salinarum*, leasing all the grazing land or all the mines in the province. - The tax benefits and the opportunities for acquiring wealth brought a large number of new settlers to the province; this influx changes the ethnic and linguistic composition of the province. The change is evident: this is the era of the decline of Latin and the advance of the Greek language. During the reign of Alexander Severus (222-235), the last Emperor of the Severus-dynasty, Sarmizegethusa bears the Greek designation of metropolis, M. Antonius Valestinus (238-244) high priest of the province, had the title *coronatus Daciarum trium*, ´the crowned one of the three Dacias´, a word not used in Latin at the time, a calque of Greek *stephanéphoros*. New migrants from Asia Minor may have helped Greek to forge ahead; in 235 there existed in Napoca a *collegium Asianorum* - an Asian burial society.

It will be quite interesting to observe in this context the case of the two Apula which is such a unique phenomenon in the Roman Empire that even A. Alföldi was doubtful about it. The *canabae* (settlement near a military camp) of XIII. Gemina was stationed there. Apulum becomes a township under Marcus Aurelius (*municipium Aurelium Apulense* - first reference dates from 180; Gyulafehérvár-Portus) and a *colonia* under Commodus. Septimius Severus creates a new municipium near the camp and next to the existing *colonia (municipium Septimium Apulense* - Gyulafehérvár-Lumea-Nouă). In 250 Decius grants *colonia* status to this municipality or - as P. Király and B. Kuzsinszky believe - he unifies the two towns creating a new city (Colonia Nova Apulensis). It was most unusual to have two towns on the same land-grant right next to each other. Perhaps less so, once we realize that the colonia Aurelia Apulensis was called (251-253) 'the golden city' (Chrysopolis) and that five Greek inscriptions - one fifth of all in the province - were found in Apulum. It seems that in Apulum there were Greek and Roman town-sections and this may signal a near-equal use of the two languages in the province following the Markomann Wars.

We also have other indications of the increased importance of the Greek language in the region. Earlier, as we reviewed the Dacian language, there was mention of the Dacian herbal glossary of Dioskorides and Pseudo-Apuleius. These sources list some herbal names as Dacian when they were actually Latin and Greek! D. Dečev had an explanation: the Dacian names of herbs were listed after 271, in the two new Dacian provinces south of the Danube (Ripensis and Mediterranea). As we have seen earlier, Dečev's explanation does not hold up, we can take it for granted that Latin and Greek words were intermixed with Dacian herbal names, simply because the listing was generated in the Roman province. In terms of the chronology of

Dioskorides' and Pseudo-Apuleius' glossary (2nd and 3rd, 4th centuries, respectively) we find that the Latin or Greek names of herbs which Dioskorides attributed to Dacian were probably generated in the 2nd century. However, Pseudo-Apuleus' list was apparently compiled in the 3rd century. If so, a comparison of the words on the two lists must mirror the changes in the language-ratio of Latin and Greek after the Markomann Wars. Dečev's statistics reflect this. Before we look at them, it is worth noting that the names of herbs include many hapaxes (erroneous writings) which only appear once. Consequently, their explanation frequently lacks clarity. Therefore, these statistics give us only an approximate understanding of the issue. (I cannot give serious consideration to C. Váczy's statistics as they were developed without sufficient proficiency in linguistics.)

According to Dečev, the herbal names listed by Dioskorides read as follows:

Dacian (26 words) 62 %

Latin   (10   "   ) 24 %

Greek (7   "   ) 14 %

In this survey, the ratio of Latin to Greek names is 5/8 to 3/8. However, if we look only at the relationship of Latin to Greek, we find a ratio of 59% to 41%. In contrast to the situation of family names in all of Dacia, the list of Dioskorides are more similar to the situation in Dacia Inferior or Malvensis, where there are 69.5% Latin and 20.6% Greek personal names.

Dečevs' statistics on Pseudo-Apuleius's collection of names give us the following:

Dacian (14 names) 45 %

Latin   (9 names) 29 %

Greek (8 names) 26 %

Here the ratio is 6/11 Latin to 5/11 Greek; a significant shift from the ratio calculated from Dioskorides' list. If we compare the Latin-Greek components, then we find (rounding up) 53 % vs. 47 %: a strong increase of the Greek names. In reality, we could consider the ratio of Greek to Latin names as 1:1, partly, on account of an uncertain etymology, partly due to the chance-factor in the name-selection process. The result reflects what we have seen earlier; after the Markomann wars, Latin and Greek usage in Dacia reached equal levels. Another way of putting it: this part of the empire became half-Latin, half-Greek. Accordingly, prior to the Markomann wars there was the possibility that a Neo-Latin language would emerge. After the Markomman wars (from 180) - at best - a semi-Grecian, Neo-Latin language could have developed.   Possibly, its opposite: a middle-Grecian language, enriched by Latin words. This process does not support a theory of Roman continuity on Dacian territory. Based on the laws of linguistics the Rumanian language(s) cannot be successor to the Grecianized-Latin which was spoken in Dacia.

It would be difficult to describe the Latin which was used in Dacia, although the question is by no means insignificant. It is no longer a matter of understanding Daco-Roman continuity; as we look at the continuity of Romanism in Dacia we have to ask ourselves whether or not the Rumanian language could have developed in Roman Dacia. This writer concurs with the eminent Rumanian Latinist, H. Mihăescu, who pointed out that the Rumanian vocabulary (and the Latin borrowings in Albanian) are mostly concrete and primitive (peasant-like), while the written, inscriptive legacy from the Roman times of South-Eastern Europe reflects an urban, literate and abstract language. Contrary to linguists of Latin, he holds with the Romanists (specializing in the new, Neo-Latin languages) that the modification of Latin must have begun during the existence of the Imperium Romanum. In spite of the paucity of sources in this regard, he is inclined to believe that this linguistic differentiation began with the first year of the Provinces's annexation to the Empire. Mihăescu has compiled a formidable amount of data (based on textual samples). However, the inscriptive material known to us does not reflect this theory. In Dacia there could really be no such reflection: the population came *ex toto orbe Romano*, - from the whole Empire - and it would have been very difficult to retain dialectal characteristics they may have brought with them. - We can find no validation for Romanist efforts attempting to prove that the Latin language in Dacia was inseparable; this premise fails to take into consideration that Dacia cannot be compared to the other provinces of the Roman Empire, due to a relatively short period of occupation (106-271). During this period the development of dialectal differentiation was much weaker than in later years.

In spite of these difficulties, we can still access the Latin spoken in Dacia. Not from inscriptions, of course, but due to the fortunate circumstance that the Dacian names of medicinal herbs had been recorded - at times in Latin or Greek. In the glossaries of Dioskorides and Pseudo-Apuleius there are herbs attributed to the Dacians, but given Latin names; others require no explanation. Pseudo-Apuleius lists *aurimetellum,* which is identical with Latin *aurimetallum* ('gold coin' this is what the petals resemble). There are names which are given in "vulgar" - instead of classical - Latin. One of these is the Dacian word for gladiolus. Dioskorides writes it as ἀπρους (*haprus*) and it can be identified in its vulgar-Latin form as *aprus,* which derives from the Latin *aper* "wild boar" (*aper non aprus* - says the book of correct Latin from the 3rd century - *Appendix Probi* 139). Gladiolus means 'little sword', examplifying the pointed leaves. This is also where 'wild boar' must be coming from, its tusks being associated with the shape of the leaf. However, there are those Dacian herbal names which can only be described in local (ergo: Dacian) Latin. Example: Dioskorides' *sikupnux* (σικουπνούζ). One of its Greek names is Κάρυον i.e. 'nut'. The 'nux' of the "Dacian" (here, Dacian Latin) word means of course ΄nut΄ (Rumanian *nucă*). The *sikup-*syllables are an unidentifiable hapax, but we may be close to the mark in assuming that it is a misspelling of one of the words for *sicca* (Lat. ΄dry΄).

The following two names should take their place among local Dacian herbal names: βουδάδλα (*budathla*), *budama, budalla, buclama* (Carduus spec.?). According to V. Pisani this plant would be βούγλωσσον in Greek, *lingua bovum* in Latin and probably of Idg. derivation: g^u*ou-dngh (u-e) la*; V. Georgiev concurs. We believe this to be erroneous. The equivalent of Idg. g^u is a g in Dacian (and Albanian). The first part of the word suggests bos- "ox" in Latin. (cf. this plant's Lat. name: *lingua bubula*). If so, the second part of the name can only be a variation on the Lat. *lingua,* the misspelling of which makes it appear as *lama, (budama).* The Neo-Latin forms of *lingua* (Lat.) are *limbă* (Rum.), *langa* (Dalm.) *lingua* (Italian), *limba* (Sard) *leungua* (Rheto-Romance Engadin), *lenge* (Friauli), *langue* (lengue) (French), *lenga* (Prov.), *llengua* (Catalan), *lengua* (Span.), *lingoa* (Port.). Vowel-transformation occurs only in Dalmatian - i> -a -, (the French version is a later development). The Latin - *ngu* turns into - *ng* - in Dalmatian. We have examples of the - *g* - being dropped: *sanguisuga* (leech - Lat.) becomes *sansoike* (plural). *Bu-lama* (Greek) may be the equivalent of the Dacian-Latin *bu-laŋa* (perhaps *bu-lĕŋa*) which could derive from the Latin *bu-lingua.* Given the Dalmatian *langa* (tongue) the word can be traced to its Dalmatian origins; -*ŋ* - becoming - *m* - is not uncommon (- *ŋ* - *n* - *m*).

'Laŋa' (?lĕŋa) can also be found in another Dacian - i.e. Dacian Latin - herbal name: κοαλάμα (koalama), *koadama* ´water-spike´. One of the Greek names of this aquatic plant means "dog's tongue". It is more likely that the word's original meaning was *aquā-lingua* or water-(tongue). Thus, Dioskorides' description would mirror *kuā -laŋa.* When there is no stress on - *a* - at the beginning of a word, the dropped - *a* - is not uncommon in the eastern part of Neo-Latin territory: Latin *apicula*, Italian *pecchia* ´little bee´; it does not appear in Rumanian, (but it is characteristic of Albanian which was closely related to Dalmatian), in which water is called *apă,* systematically

evolving from *aqua*. The second part of the word is undisputedly Dalmatian-related (*laŋa*, cf. Dalmatian *langa*).

The following, Dacian Latin herbal name from the 3rd century is less clear in its origin: *Sipoax, scinpoax, scinplax, simpotax* ´plantain´: one of its Latin names is *septenervia* and one of its Greek names means 'seven-ribbed. This word is an almost unrecognizable compound of the Latin *septem* (seven) and *axis*. Its regular form would be *septem-axes*. Notable Neo-Latin variants of *septem* are: *şapte* (Rum.), *sapto* (Dalm.), *sette* (Italian), etc., while *axis* left no trace in either Rumanian or Dalmatian. When the word is reconstructed into *siptoax*, it suggests Dalmatian roots, to - *ks*- (*x*) - corresponds Rumanian -*ps*-, while in Dalmatian, it would has two representations: -*is*- and -*ps*. - In the case of the Dacian Latin name - *χs* - is more likely; there is no evidence of -*ks*->-*ps*- in the word. *Sipto* is irregular, having processed from the Dalmatian *sapto siepto> siapto*.

These are meager pickings of the provincial Daco-Latin language and burdened by quite a few hypotheses. Still, we can state unequivocally that Rumanian did not originate from this (provincial) Latin. Let us compare *laŋa* with the Dalmatian *langa* in contrast to the Rumanian *limbă* < *lęngua*. It could be considered a precursor of Dalmatian and, thus, in linguistic kinship with it. In provincial Daco-Latin this was to be expected. There was a large number of Dalmatian settlers, who must have been speaking this type of Latin, as did the numerically significant Pannonians (for example the settlement and cemetery of Hermány). The Latin spoken in Dalmatia and in Pannonia were closely linked under the Empire, as demonstrated by J. Herman. If we were to expect to see a continuity of Dacian Romanism (and not in its 3rd. century semi-Greek form, following the Markomann wars), then we would have to identify in the region a Neo-Latin language related to Dalmatian. We have no such data.

The last half-century in the history of the province is marked by evidences of intermittent prosperity, but what dominates the era are the repeated attacks by Barbarians. Concurrently, the population declines; first by way of individual and sporadic emigration and, later, through a mass exodus. The peaceful conditions, enjoyed during Severus' reign become rare exceptions to the rule after his death in 235. Emperor Maximius (235-238), who came from Thracian peasant-stock, takes the title of *Dacicus Maximus* in 236. Lacking additional information, we surmise the title alludes to the successful outcome (for Rome) of battles waged against Dacians who lived outside Dacia and the borders of the Empire. In 238 Karps and Goths ravage Moesia Inferior, the Imperial province at the lower-Danube, and raze Histria at the Danube-Delta. The raids were wide-ranging and resulted in strengthened fortifications at Marcianopolis (Devnja, Bulgaria). A citizen of Durostorum (Silistra, Bulgaria) gives thanks to the gods, having escaped Barbarian imprisonment. Karp attacks are renewed a few years later, or so we assume, knowing that, during Gordianus' era the enemies of the Empire (*hostes*) are devastating Thracia and Moesia. While Dacia was not untouched by the fighting, during Gordianus' reign (238-244) there is peace and calm in the

province (and inscriptions dedicated the Emperor). The above
suggests the population experienced no violent disturbance.
(160)

All this constituted a period of only transitory peace. After the
Markomann wars the artificial European border of the Imperium
Romanum managed to block for more than half a century the flow of
migration of tribes living beyond its borders. However, the
mechanisms employed to prevent the incursion repeatedly proved to
be inadequate. These included diplomatic manipulation, punitive
military action or periodic settlement of various groups of Barbarians
within the Empire. At the same time, there was a marked increase
among populations living beyond the borders of the Empire —
attributed in part to contacts with the Empire. Not only did they create
overpopulation in the territory they were inhabiting, the area became
densely settled and their desire for material possessions has also
increased. Subsequent to the Markomann wars (turn of the 2nd/3rd
Century) a large number of Goths settled along the northern banks of
the Black Sea. They established farms and villages which cut off the
movement of the nomadic shepherds of the steppes. Their constant -
and natural - movements could not be curbed for long. Thus, so the
Goths were forced to keep moving in search of other arable lands,
shifting others in the process. Their neighbors along the eastern
borders of Dacia were the Karps; they tried again (245-247) to take
possession of Roman territory. The effect of this fighting was felt all
over Dacia as we can see from coins (which were hidden at the time)
and which were later found in many localities (Săpată de Jos in
Muntenia; Dobridor, Vîrtopu, etc. in Oltenia. Ecel, Vízakna, etc. in

Transylvania. The Karps' attacks forced the Romans to relinquish a line of defense established under Septimius Severus, east of the Olt, the *limes Transalutanus*. They also gave up so.- east Transylvania which must have depended on this defense-line. We believe they gave up other areas, as well. 120 years after K. Torma wrote about the period we can only reiterate that, at the northern border of Dacia, during the reign of Philippus Arabs (244-249) and at the encampment of Alsó-Ilosva, the usage of Roman medals has ceased. The emperor adopts the title of *Carpicus Maximus* and defeats the Karps but the province beyond the water-border of the Roman Empire cannot escape destruction. Equally vulnerable is the territory beyond the Rhine and the Danube (annexed during the reign of Domitian (by Traianus, the *agri decumates*), which frees itself from the grasp of the Empire, although - at this time - not permanently. Emperor Trajan Decius (249-251) is shown on an inscription in Apulum as *restitutor Daciarum* i.e. the "restorer of Dacia", but takes the title of *Dacicus Maximus* in 250, which indicates another war. In retrospect the gains he has achieved must have been minuscule.

These gains consisted of the ability of larger garrisons to continue and maintain Romanism. The Roman border-defense of Dacia along the Lower-Danube is in its last throes. A new mint had to be established in Viminacium (Kostolac, Serbia) to pay the military; it ceases to operate between 257-258. There must be a connection between this event and Emperor Gallienus becoming *Dacicus Maximus*. Accepting the title and the discontinuity of minting operations suggest that rewards (propaganda) and reality were not always congruent. A large segment of the population fled the province during the reign of Philippus Arabs (244-249). G. Val. Sarapio, (an Egyptian!), builds a shrine in Apulum to Jupiter, "the mightiest", in gratitude for having been saved from the Karps (*a Carpis liberatus*). The mother of a later Emperor, Galerius, flees during this period to the area of today's Sofia and it wasn't even from the Transylvanian part of Dacia, but from Dacia Malvensis, which is currently Oltenia. Some of the refugees - perhaps most - did not flee south to Moesia but, probably, to Pannonia. Our assumption is based on the inscription made in Intercisa (today Dunaújváros, in Hungary), to the memory of Publius Aelius Proculinus, which tells us that he was killed at the "castle of the Karps" (*castellum Carporum*).

Contrary to most opinions expressed on the subject, we believe that Dacia was lost to the Roman Empire already at the time Philippus Arabs gave himself a decoration for his victory over the Karps in 247. Archeological evidence seems to corroborate this; it cannot be coincidental that, dating from the middle of the 3rd century, we are finding Karp relics all over Transylvania. What is more, they are different. The cemeteries at Septér, Medgyes, Sepsiszentgyörgy are unlike those in Soporul de Câmpie, Obreja and Locuşteni (the latter in Dacia Malvensis, Oltenia). The relics from the cemeteries in Septér and Soporul de Câmpie cannot be dated "post - 250"; there is a correlation between the appearance of Karp relics and the collapse of the North-Dacian line of defense (re. Alsó-Ilosva, Vármező). In Apulum and Potaissa only garrisons and the camps of legionaries remained and Decus' title - *restitutor Daciarum* - implies that Dacia was lost prior to 249-251 - otherwise, there would have been no need for restoration. The exodus, which took place during Philippus' reign is conclusive - the flights occurred neither before, nor after. Yet the province still exists - even if only through the continued presence of its garrisons and city-renovation efforts. Our sources from antiquity imply that Dacia was lost during the reign of Emperor Dacius Gallienus (253-268). Reports on this question are unanimous: *Dacia amissa est* (Eutr. Brev. 9, 8, 2) *et amissa trans Istrum, quae Traianus quaesiverat* (Aur. Vict. Caes. 22-23), *sub Gallieno amissa est.* (Ruf. Festus Brev. 8). Thus: Dacia was lost in the Gallienus era. The loss of Dacia is commonly attributed to Emperor Aurelian. It is true that it was he who also *officially* relinquished Dacia. Sources dating from antiquity (Eutropius etc.) inform us that Dacia was lost under and because of Gallienus (*Dacia, quae a Traiano ultra Danubium fuerat adiecta, tum amissa est*, Eutr. Brev. 9, 8, 2) but they also report that it was Aurelian who put an end to Dacia, transferring it to Moesia (*provinciam Daciam.... intermisit...* Eutr. Brev. 9, 15, 1). In the 260's (from 262?) Dacian legions (XIII. Gemina, V. Macedonia) are stationed in Poetovio, Pannonia. Although, one of the officers leaves an inscription in 260 Mehadia (Herkulesfürdő), this may very well be a memento of the effort to recover Dacia at the time of Aurelianus - or before him. The same effort is also reflected by the coins bearing the inscription of DACIA FELIX (as stated by A. Alföldi). To claim the "*Dacia felix*" coins belong to the founding of the Dacia south of the Danube remains unsubstantiated; Aurelianus only took his legions there: XIII. Gemina into Ratiaria and I. Macedonia into Oescus. Residents being taken from cities and the countryside (*ex urbibus et ex agris* - Eutr. Brev. 9, 15, 1) annotates only the end result, otherwise it has little substance, as our Rumanian colleagues often note.

We believe that the analysis of this chain of events in the matter of Daco- Roman, i.e. Daco-Roman-Rumanian continuity is not essential; although many, who deal with this question, consider it important. It is not essential, because the history of a 20 - year period has little significance within the context of centuries, but the withdrawal of Roman forces from this territory is substantiated by Karp cemeteries and graves (the latter evidenced by an accidental burial find) in the area. The history of the Roman Empire provides us with extensive data pertaining to the settlement of Barbarians but nothing to show that, in any one province, there should only be immigrating Barbarians. Besides, all specialists who have studied this period know that the immigrating barbarians are usually impossible to detect by archaeological methods. The Barbarians are unrecognizable due to their diverse legacy of objects. If the Karps are recognizable on Dacian territory, that means that the Romans are no longer there and, by the middle of the 3rd century, we can take this for granted. Thus, we may point to the era of Philippus Arabs, i.e. 247-248 as the time when Roman presence in Dacia ceased to exist. This was the time when they withdrew from the *limes Transalutanus*, their line of defense and the northern defense positions relinquish in the province as the immigration of the Karps begins. The process is given an additional impetus during the wars under Trajan Decius. The death of the Emperor - the "*restitutor Daciarum*" - in a battle against the Goths at Arbittus (Razgrad, Bulgaria) has an effect on the future fate of the province. We can infer there was a continuing exodus on the part of the provincial population; the probability of their staying put was most likely in areas where the military was stationed. We know of no Roman inscriptions dated after 258 and, after 260, no more large contingent of troops are stationed here. By 271, prior to his eastern wars, Emperor Aurelianus had to withdraw only the remnants of his troops. The evacuation was done under military auspices (*abductosque Romanos ex urbibus et agris Daciae*), "and the Romans who were displaced from Dacia's cities and land", Eur. Brev. 9, 15, 1) makes it evident that Aurelianus removed everybody from Dacia still under Roman rule. (At the time Dacia's eastern border flanked the Olt river the road led across Apulum, Napoca to Porolissum, as reflected by the Tabula Peutingeriana. The evacuation is further substantiated by the establishment of these new provinces for the displaced population: Dacia Ripensis and Mediterranea. Nevertheless, it is sometimes claimed that, in the evacuated areas, there were Latin-speaking, Romanized groups left behind. However, none of our sources identify a Romanized population that would have remained in Dacia and it explains why D. Protase would write: "... antique writers speak of only migrating peoples in Dacia and do not pay attention to the local population. We have direct sources of information: archeology, numismatics and (in the 4th Century) epigraphy which indicate that our written sources may not be accurate". Accordingly, there would have to be findings to establish the survival of the local population during the period following the surrender of the Province. If this were so, then this population would continue to use the buildings in the Roman cities and there would have to be burials in local cemeteries - even if not on the same scale as when the territory was part of the Roman Empire. Let us then examine what traces of survival we might find.

There are supposed to be many late-Roman findings in Sarmizegethusa, the former capital of the province dating from the 4th and 5th centuries. These would include the walled-in entrance of the amphitheatrum, roof tiles, bricks, statues and stones with inscriptions - re-used after the Roman era - and dwellings which were reconstructed with Barbarian-technique. Also, a small fibula (onion-shaped and decorated with buttons), the initials of Christ etched into a shard and a candlestick. The survival of the population would be further substantiated by the finding of medals, the last pieces of which date from the time of Valentianus I. (Valens) and another 9 misc. pieces spanning the eras of Diocletian to Gratianus.

The above would constitute the evidence, which, in contrast to written sources, would serve to prove the survival of the local population. In regard to Roman continuity Sarmizegethusa is, indeed, important. In the Middle Ages towns sprung up in the place of Roman cities (Apulum, Potaissa, Napoca, today's Alba Iulia, Turda and Cluj) but only an insignificant village developed in the place of Sarmizegethusa. If we were to look for sites that remained undisturbed and, therefore, survived the post-Aurelian evacuation without being scattered - this was the place. Yet, findings from the late capitol of the province are "still sporadic", as K. Horedt remarks. We cannot attribute the paucity of findings to the absence of urban-type construction which would have excavated buried relics. The "late-Roman" findings from Alba Iulia, Turda and Cluj - including those in the possession of collectors - are often of indeterminate origin. Thus, the situation is the opposite of what K. Horedt would assume with hard-to-follow logic. Let us take another look at the "traces" in Sarmizegethusa, which would be evidence of the presence of the then-local population. The entrance of the amphitheatrum is, indeed, obstructed - with pebbles from the river. This could not have been the work of Romans - neither the earlier, nor the "survivor"-kind. We have a clear indication of that in the fortification of camp-entrances, from the period immediately preceding the abandonment of the province (the Dacia-Felix era during the reign of Aurelian when - temporarily - East-Transylvania had been regained.) We can deduce from the erection of fortified twin-castles that the Romans were also attempting to rebuild the "limes Transalutanus" - their defense line. In erecting walls, they employ always Roman masonry-techniques and they make use of earlier stone remnants (tablets with inscriptions, columns, etc.) as could be seen in Porolissum (Mojgrad), Marosvécs and Énlaka. The entrance of the *amphitheatrum* in Sarmitzegethusa was walled in with large pebbles. This could have happened at any time but has probably occurred during the Middle Ages when Roman amphitheatres have been used as castles (defenses) in the Carpathian basin. Such was also the case with the military amphitheatrum in Old-Buda (Castrum Kurchan). In the absence of other chronological data we cannot deduce Roman continuity from the use of Roman relics (bricks, statues, etc.) in subsequent (building) construction. If we were to make this deduction we would have to attribute Roman continuity to any edifice - including those built in modern times - which incorporate such items (i.e. bricks, statues, etc.). The dry wall of the western wing of Aedes Augustalium, (which was not built with Roman technique) could be the work of any nation. During the Great Migration settlers in territories which had earlier been Roman, frequently made use of Roman edifices which were left standing (Sopron, Aquincum). The small button-embellished, onionhead - topped fibula must have been made in mid-third century, in view of the medals which paralleled the find. This is also what K. Horedt believes. In other words: it is not a relic from continuing Romanism. The monogram of Christ on the shard to which we referred earlier, could well be a Christian relic post-dating the surrender of Dacia (we have no specific information of Christianity in Dacia prior to 271). Even so, it would not be an identifier of a Romanized population, because it could just as well be Gothic, Gepida or Christian from Avar times. (There is an Avar-age relic from Sarmizegethusa, the so-called 'Slav-fibula'. It is more likely, however, that the inscription is a characteristic example of the kind of forgery of which we have seen several. The candlestick is not a Christian relic. It has the customary cross-shaped embellishment which dates it as prior to 271. We do not understand how the treasure of bronze-coins from the age of Valentian I, could be considered to be a vestige of a surviving population. After all, the owner of these coins came into their possession during the reign of the Emperor, (364-375) and not in the era of Gallienus or Aurelian. Besides, it is peculiar that these coins would be used as proof of continuity in the Dacia of late; after 271, traffic in Roman coins show similarities to the Eastern

Great Plains and contemporary Slovakia. The above reasoning would suggest Roman continuity in Slovakia, too. The little treasure from Sarmitzegethusa can easily be evaluated. Athanaric and his Goths are defeated by Huns at the Dniester; in 376 he withdraws to the hilly Caucalanda region and he gives chase to the Sarmatians. The treasure of Sarmitzegethusa is connected to this event geographically and chronologically; it also reveals who the inhabitants of the region were at the time. The eight coins spanning the eras from Diocletian (284-305) to Gratianus (367-383), do not indicate that there was a Romanized population at Sarmizegethusa in close connection with the Roman Empire, but it does point to the one-time provincial capital being overrun by the Barbarians. After the appearance of the Huns, a period begins during which the site remains uninhabited for a long period.

Three additional brick-graves were identified in the era subsequent to the surrender of the Province. One of the graves found among the ruins of a villa East of the city must, however, be attributed to the period falling between the reign of Philippus Arabs and Aurelian. Also, we possess data regarding both 2nd and 3rd century brick graves from Dacia; thus they do not have to have originated subsequent to 271. The same holds true for the brown-glazed shard of a vessel found in a brick-grave near the amphitheatrum. We do not have to assume a late date, as glazed vessels go back to the 2nd century - although they were rare in Dacia.

These then would be the "direct sources" telling us about the survival of Romanism, following the surrender of the Province. They speak for themselves - even if they do not substantiate that a Roman population stayed on in Sarmizegethusa. By and large, late relics found in other areas are similar. An undoubtedly Christian gemma has been found (but the circumstances of the find are murky) in Potaissa (Turda); also two clay candlesticks. These cannot prove the survival of the Roman population and the golden ring with the inscription: UTERE FELIX is not a Christian relic; the inscription is a good luck wish which was in general use. One of the difficulties with the Christian relics is that they belong to collections; several pieces attributed to finds at Mojgrád were actually purchased from antique dealers. In Turda bricks were found out of which a sarcophagus was reconstructed. That can also not be dated post-271; graves unearthed near the garrison (and hydraulic works) are accurately dated - mid-3rd century - by the onion-shaped, silverbutton - embellished fibula and a Commodus-coin. A similar fibula came to light during bridge-construction at the Aranyos river. Once again: dating from no later than mid-3rd century.

Most of the findings at Porolissum (Mojgrád), attributed to the 4th century, are of unknown origin. The graves found here are from the period of Árpád (Magyar Chieftain - 9th century - Transl.) and, therefore, cannot prove the survival of Romanism. A Roman platter from the same area is especially noteworthy. On the bottom there are the initials of Christ and this partial inscription: *EGO ... VIUS VOTum Posui*. We believe the engraving was made subsequently and is a forgery: it copies the donarium at Berethalom, which was re-discovered in 1941. A. Mócsy and E. Tóth reached the same conclusion. It is not unusual to find inscriptions etched into shards at a later date; we know of this practice in Rumania outside the province, too (ex. Socetu in Muntenia). Many findings and memorabilia presented as proof of survival fall into this category; we have to give up the attempt to prove that a more significant segment of the Roman population stayed put after the province was relinquished. In Dacia, there is no evidence of continuity of the settlements, such as the characteristic burial sites of the 4th century, even though they could be found close by, along the banks of the Danube. This is easy to substantiate, as Roman rule remains continuous in certain areas of Southern Dacia for some time. After they withdrew, Roman bridgeheads were left behind on the left bank of the Danube, as in Sucidava (Celei, opposite the encampment of the Legion V. Macedonia at Oescus), in Drobeta (Turnu Severin), and at Desa (opposite Ratiaria, the camp of the Legion XIII. Gemina). The characteristic of the cemetery at Sucidava helped us in identifying the findings of the period. Coins found here are from 324-361. There are simple earthen graves - no trace of burials in brick graves or sarcophagi. The graves contain large numbers of utensils, jewelry, glasses, iron knives, etc. These are relics which were not found in other areas of the Province. There is a hiatus even in Sucidava as shown by the coins found at the cemetery. At the end of the 3rd and beginning of the 4th century, the citizens apparently did not inhabit the town. At any rate, the history of the Danubian Plain differs from other areas of the former province. Constantin the Great (306-337) has a bridge built across the Danube in 328 between Oescus and Sucidava and rebuilds the Roman bridgeheads along the left bank of the Danube (Dierna, Drobeta, Sucidava, Turris, Constantiniana-Daphne, Dinogetia-Barboşi). After 332 his Goth allies construct trenches from Turnu Severin to Brăila, known as the *Brazda lui Novac de Nord*, or the "Wallachian Devils Trench". These provide for the defense of Rome's Barbarian allies in the same manner as its equivalent on the Hungarian Plain. Along the trenches, there are also Roman encampments (ex. Pietroasele); the troops are mostly allied, "foederati" soldiers. There are also Roman posts further away from the Danube; thus, a road is being built between Sucidava and Romula (Reşca). There are references to building going on in Romula, as well. These are transitory activities, as is the rebuilding of the castle at Mehadia. There are only sporadic signs of the Roman life-style and population we found prior to 271. We can no longer speak of Neo-Romanization of the territory; the findings in Sucidava seem to establish that this "Romanism" was mostly Greek by then. If so, it could not have supported the survival of Latin-speaking groups.

In spite of the above, in the late territory of Dacia there can be found vestiges of the Roman presence beyond the 3rd century. Moreover: not only near the bridge-heads along the Danube or on the Plain of the Lower-Danube which was under the supervision of Constantin the Great. Traces could also be found in Transylvania. We are not referring to pieces of chain on the bronze candlesticks, embossed with a monogram of Christ and the good wishes of Zenovius (found at Berethalom). It features similar findings from

Aquileia, Emona, Poetovio, Bonyhád and Sziszek. There is a strong likelihood, this artifact originated in Southern Pannonia and reached the region of the Nagy-Küküllő (Tărnava Mare) river in the 4th century, or later. This is seen as a relic of Gothic settlers of the Christian faith of the time; other memorabilia which were used to substantiate 'continuity' are probably also theirs (such as onion-shaped fibulae). During excavations of spas at Gyulafehérvár (Alba Iulia) at the beginning of the century, graves were found embedded in the Roman edifices. A significant number dated from the 10th century (Árpád-period), but among these there must have been Roman graves, as well. Out of these came nine bracelets with the charactéristic late-Roman design of a snake´s head. We cannot attribute them to a pre-4th century period - given the many similarities to Pannonia- the brick grave unearthed here also suggests Roman burial rites.

In 1927 a sarcophagus came to light in the so-called south-east cemetery in Cluj (Kolozsvár) which was reconstructed from a "cippus" (gravestone). It became the subject of an ongoing dispute: the earlier inscription had an O with a cross-shaped etching. This prompted P. Protase to assume that the marker was erected by a 'secret Christian' of the 3th century. We maintain that the cross or 'X', which was chiseled into the bottom of the coffin, preceded the - O - and we reject the supposition that the inscription was belatedly 'Christianized'. It is more likely that the etching may have chiseled out a supportive line scratched in earlier - we find other misapplied lines. However, the grave is important beyond its inscription: it revealed four

Roman hairpins neither of which could pre-date the 4th century. Based on this finding, we can attribute other graves to Roman times which were found in Cluj. These were graves incorporating Roman stone tablets which post-date the surrender of the province.

However, these Romans were not successors of the Roman population once living in Dacia. Their legacy - burial rites and bracelets - parallel Pannonian relics and suggest a connection with Pannonia. It is probably no coincidence that they resettled on the site of former Roman towns. If so, then we must consider the new residents of Apulum and Napoca as a voluntary (or planned) settlement. The projected chronology: the second half of the 4th, or the first half of the 5th century - this is what we glimpse from archeological finds. Actually, it is more appropriate to consider the 5th century. As it can be established that a large number of Roman provincials lived in Hun-controlled territory, such as Orestes of Pannonia, (the best-known example) who was Attila's scribe! It would be a mistake to assume that this Roman provincial population (which must have been resettled in Transylvania to work at salt and ore-mining) was the formulator of some kind of Romanism in the territory. No geographical names survived in Dacia in a form which would indicate the continuity of their use in Latin; and no trace is left of the names of towns or other localities. Romanism left no trace in Pannonia either, but we know of quite a few Roman towns (Sirmium-Szerém, Srijem, Siscia-Sziszek, Sisak, Poetovio-Ptuj, Pettau etc.). In Dacia, on the other hand, no vestige is found of the names of Apulum, Napoca, Potaissa. They could have been known to the

Pannonian provincials who were resettled here at the time of the Huns. It is also possible that they simply called these localities *civitas* or 'town'. Neither one, left any trace. It is quite remarkable that the rivers which do not penetrate the mountain-range encircling Transylvania bear late Slavic, Hungarian and Turkish names. The most characteristic example of this is the name of the river *Küküllő*, which derives from Turkish in the 10th century, and its Rumanian name, *Tîrnava*, is of Slavic origin. The possibility has been raised that the Ompoly river, which joins the Maros at Gyulafehérvár, would be derived from Roman Ampelum. G. Schramm has concurred with this view until recently; we disagree.

In 1271 the name of the river is *Onpoy*, in 1299, *Ompey*, *Ompay* and *Ompay* also in 1400. The - *ly* - ending of Ompoly gains ground in the 18th 19th century as a result of the explanation by the period's scientists that the word derives from *Apulum*. We believe that the name of Roman Ampelum would, at best, emerge as (early Hungarian) *Ampel*. This is not the only reason why the two names cannot be linked. Originally Ompoly was not the name of a river but of some land (1271: *Onpoy terra*, 1299: *terrae Ompey, nemus Ompey*). This would be the possessive case of the Hungarian (personal) name of *Omp* (cf. *Ompud*), which means "Ompé's", [something which] belongs to Omp. This is a common Hungarian construction of place names, the name of the river was a secondary derivative, thus, Ompoly is not of Roman origin.

It has also been assumed that *Abrud* is of Roman legacy because of *obrud*, a presumed Dacian word meaning ´gold´. The previous names of *Abrud* are: 1271: *Obruth*; 1320: *Obrudbania*, 1366 - *Obrugh*; 1366-70: *Obrugh*. - The varying writings of the last sound, d - gh (=Hungarian gy) th (=ty) possibly ch (= c or cs), suggests that an attempt was made to produce a sound for which there was no Hungarian equivalent. It might have been South-Slavic (Serbian). If so, then the word's derivation must have been closer to *obritji*, from So. Slav *obrići*. This, in turn, comes from *obrъ* ´dry allen leaves and parched grass´, also a personal name, affixed with the patronym - *itjo* ('the successors of' Obrъ). The original name of a locality and a nearby brook is *Zlatna* (*Zalatna*), as shown by its German name, *Gross-Schlatten*. *Abrud*, then, cannot be said to be a legacy of old.

On the territory of former Dacia there is no geographical designation which would have preserved names from the Roman era is any shape or form. This indicates the same as was explained above: after the evacuation of Dacia no Latin groups remained who could have passed on the place names to other peoples. Moreover, the names of rivers in the Transylvanian basin are of a relatively recent origin, which indicates frequent migratory population exchanges. Thus, even if some Romanized provincials remained in post-271 Dacia, they have later disappeared without a trace. The same fate befell Pannonian provincials who were resettled during the Hun era, - they disappeared without a trace. We need to note, though, that they must have spoken a Latin which was similar to pre-Dalmatian but that would not have been a direct link to the origin of Rumanians.

The history of Roman Dacia makes it clear that we cannot speak about the Romanization of the Dacians in the province and, therefore, we cannot promulgate Daco-Roman continuity. Nowadays we frequently encounter the totally illogical premise - that Dacians outside the border (of the province) also became Romanized. There are two separate civilizations within and outside the frontiers of the Empire and this difference is not wiped out by Roman export-goods. (To cite a distant example: Northern Barbarians who resettled in China became Chinese after a while, — but not those who lived outside China.) In Dacia, we cannot talk about a foothold of Romanism and, after Aurelian withdrew, we have no evidence that provincials continued to live in the territory. We do not dispute that there could have been individuals who remained in the province but we have no proof to sustain this theory; not even in regard to those who lived outside the law. What we know of the Latin spoken in Dacia implies that the language must have been similar to what was spoken in 2nd century Pannonia and Dalmatia and that, in the 3rd century, there was a strong Greek influence in the Province. Therefore, the Rumanian language does not originate in Dacian Latin; had it survived, modern Rumanian would not be its successor. There were only a few Latin-speaking provincials who settled here during the time of Hun rule. The paucity of their numbers would have prevented them from determining later linguistic processes. Besides, the language had characteristics which set it apart from the innings of Rumanian.

In short, our data do not uphold Daco-Roman continuity, it does not support the survival in Dacia of Latin-speaking nationality groups, either. The absence of geographical designations provides an irrefutable argument in support of the position we hold.

Footnotes:

(1) *Alföldi, A.,* "Dacians and Romans in Transylvania". (*Századok,* 1940 p. 166)

(2) *A. Mócsy* - Roman names as resources for social history. Budapest, 1985, p. 54-56. Cf. *Acta Arch. Hung.* 36 (1984) 212.

(3) *K. Horedt – Siebenbürgen in spätrömischer Zeit.* Bukarest 1982. 55.

(4) *K. Horedt – Siebenbürgen in spätrömischer Zeit.* Bukarest 1982. 55.

(5) *D. Protase:* Die Dakish-Römische Bevölkerung nördlich der Donau in der Periode von Aurelian bis zu den Slaven (7 Jh.) im Lichte der aktuellen Dokumente, in: Die Völker Südosteuropas im 6 bis 8 Jahrhundert. *Südosteuropa Jahrbuch* Bd. 17. München.

Chapter IV
Dacia after the Romans –
Dacia before the Rumanians.

The territory of Dacia did not turn into a wasteland following Roman withdrawal. We saw that its eastern areas were settled by Karps. By the mid-13th century, Aurelian made a short-lived attempt to restore the borders of the Province but it is unlikely that he would have disrupted these settlements. After he relinquished the Sucidava-Porolissum route (Celei - Mojgrád), it facilitated the further expansion of the Karps and created an opportunity for an influx of nationality groups, which had been living on the northern and western borders of the Province. Their immigration began after 271; a grave in Radnót attests to that. It has a large urn, typical of the Hungarian Great Plains Region, which held a medal portraying Empress Severina (271-275); it must have been interred subsequent to that date. The settlers had a culture characteristic of the Great Plains and of "Barbarians from the Imperial era". Examples of this culture could be observed at settlements from (Batos, Sinfalva) and in cemeteries (Maroscsapó). In addition to Karps and 'Great Plains Barbarians' German populations appear from the north-eastern parts of the Carpathian Basin, (Kisbács, Sepsibesenyő), as well as a small group (Magyarszovát, Csernáton, Kisekemező) which is different: they do not use cremation. In the meantime, the Karps occupy Oltenia (the former Dacia Inferior) (Locuşteni, Reşca, Fărcaşele).

This archeological mosaic conforms to the deductions we can make on the basis of contemporary sources. Some time after 291 Mamertinus makes a speech lauding Emperor Maximian (285-308).

He says that the Tervingi - who belong to the Goths - and the Taifals allied in attacking the Vandals and the Gepidae. (*Tervingi, pars alia Gothorum, adiuncta manu Taifalorum, adversum Vandalos Gipedesque concurrunt* - Genethl. Max. 17, 1). Ever since the Markomann wars, the Vandals have lived along the northern borders of Dacia, i.e. the north-eastern area of the Carpathian Basin and the upper reaches of the Dniester river. However, on the basis of other data, in this instance "Vandals" really must have been Victovals who lived close to the Upper Tisza (Theiss) and in the valley of the Someş rivers. In 248, the Taifali and Goths take part in the devastation of the Empire's Black-Sea area; other sources place them at the Danube-delta. Tervingi are the western group of the Goths. Their name (forest dwellers) suggests that we look for their habitat in the vicinity of the Carpathians (within Gothic archeological context). In credible sources it is here that the Gepidae appear for the first time. Iordanes also writes about this (the Fastida-Ostrogoth war) and tells us that the Gepidae are locked in by mountains and forests. They must surely have been living in the Carpathian Basin (Iord. Get. XVII). In other words, all the nations who participate in this war have lived along the border of Roman Dacia and around 290 AD, at least the Victovals and the Gepidae in the territory of former Dacia. This is one of the reasons why this war cannot be placed northeast of the Carpathians, R. Harhoiu's contention notwithstanding. Eutropius writes in 360 that Dacia in inhabited by Taifali, Victohali and Gothic Tervingi (Eutr. Brev. 8, 2, 2 - *nunc Taifali, Victohali et Tervingi habent*). Excepting the Gepidae, all of them are peoples which participated in the war of 290 (or pre-290). In connection with this war, Iordanes writes that the Gepidae suffered defeat and withdrew: (Regrettably, only this much can be used of Jordanes story. The royal name of *Fastida* is based on Latin *fastidium* (haughty, demanding) (Fastida *fuerat elationis erectus* - Jord. Get. XVII. 100): "Fastiva was bloated with arrogance". Thus, neither the town of Galtis nor the Auha river can be used to pinpoint more closely the location of the war - for all we know, it may have been near the Black Sea!). It is apparent that the war was fought for the possession of Dacia; the victors managed to grab a large portion of it, while the Victovali probably only held on to the territory they already had. Indeed, from the end of the 3rd century, a new archeological culture emerges in former Dacia, for the time being only in Transylvania. This new culture has links with the Goths and Taifali who have settled there. What Rumanian research calls the Sfîntu Gheorghe culture and the (No. I) cemetery in Bratei, may be the remnants of these peoples. A replica exists of the trough-shaped graves of Bratei and the legacy of on-site cremation in (Dančeny, Etulija) Bessarabia, in the region where Taifali have presumably lived at an earlier time. One of the graves at Sfîntu Gheorghe-Eprestető can be linked to this legacy, while the other graves with similar relics could be linked to Goth Tervingi. As a result of the wars fought for the possession of Dacia, the Karps are leaving their homes in the region between the Prut river and the Carpathians and the area of their Dacian Conquests. Galerius leads a campaign against them between 295-297. As per Eusebius (Historia Ecclesiastica VIII. 17, 3.) he took up the title of *Carpicus Maximus* six times and, at some point, during this time the Karps resettled within the borders of the Empire. More correctly, they were being resettled; *Carporum natio translata Omnis in nostrum solum*, Aur. Vict. Caes. 39, 43; *Carporum gens universa Romania se tradidit*, Cons. Const. ad a. 295-MGH IX. 230). The Karps also leave their settlement in Oltenia (the late Dacia Inferior); they are most probably replaced by Goths (Almăj,Caracal). In spite of the emigration of the Karps which was due to the wars around 290, it is hard to believe that only Taifali, Tervingi and Victovali would have lived in the former Dacia. Written records also dispel this assumption. In 367 Emperor Valens starts out against the Goths from Daphne (in the Argyas-Danube delta). The Goths took refuge in *montes Serrorum.* "Serrus' mountains" appear in ancient references only once. However, as we learn of Sarmatians in this area at a later date, we presume the Serri may have been Sarmatians (the name corresponds to Avestic *sairima*). We already know of these Sarmatians from the campaign of Constanine in 358 AD. They must have populated a portion of Dacia, specifically its South-west area. We also think that the 4th century findings from Micia (Vecel) can be attributed to them. We believe that they do not relinquish this territory; after they suffer defeat in 376 from the Huns, Athanaric retreats to the hilly, mountainous Caucaland (*ad Caucalandensem locum*), chasing out the Sarmatians. *Montes Serrorum* and mountainous *Caucaland* must refer to the Southern part of Transylvania.

From written references and from other evidence, we can gain a thorough understanding of the inhabitants of Dacia after 271. In the late Roman province there are no Romans - Latin-speaking Romans. We do not claim that no such individuals could have existed there; as the result of the Barbarians' forays masses of prisoners were abducted from the Empire. We do know, however, that on Dacian territory there were no Latin-speaking groups which constituted a community and which would have maintained contact with each other. There was no ethnic group characterized by Romanism. No evidence to the contrary is presented in written records or through archeological finds. If K. Horedt is prepared to use the Daco-Roman adjective, based on archeological finds post-dating 271, his error is in not noticing how much of the same culture the Barbarians (from the vicinity of Rome) acquired. Yet, a great deal of material originating from the European borders of the Empire, from the mouth of the Danube to the estuary of the Rhine has become accessible. We no longer have to rely on calculated guesses - in most instances we also have evidence. It is a fact that, after 271, there are Barbarians in Dacia and that there is no trace of a Roman way of life and of Latin speakers.

When the Huns appear on the scene, they become a determining factor in the history of Europe. The Huns chased out the western Goths, and later defeat the Romans at Hadrianapolis (Aug. 9, 378). The ethnic and political landscape of the erstwhile Dacia changes during this period, and the same holds true for large sections of the Roman Empire. After 376 the Huns settle in along the Lower-Danube. They take possession of Oltenia (the late Dacia Inferior), together with Muntenia. This is not only nominal rule; around 400, and at the start of the 5th century this becomes the central seat of Hun power. Numerous findings of cauldrons (in Sucidava, Desa, Hinova, Hotărani, 'Oltenia') and a richly appointed grave in Coşoveni attest to this. There is a population-shift in other parts of Dacia, as well. During the last quarter of the 4th century, the Ostrogoths - presumably Arianus Christians - (Marosszentanna culture) reach Transylvania. The Huns also resettle here Pannonian provincials at the start of the 5th century (Gyulafehérvár, Kolozsvár). In this period, the knowledge of the Latin language may have been considerable in the territories of former

Dacia Apulensis and Porolissensis. In the Christianization of the Goths a large role was played by those prisoners from the Roman Empire, whom they took around 260, during the time of their Middle-Eastern campaign. However, the majority of these enslaved people spoke Greek or some Middle-Eastern language, as demonstrated by the list of Goth saints (Sabas, Sansalas, Arpyla, etc.). According to Auxentius of Durostorum, the Goth Bishop, Vulfila (311-384) preached in Greek, Latin and Gothic. This however, cannot imply that he preached in Latin north of the Danube, because the Gothi minores, the people of Ulfila, settled in the Empire in 348. Among the Goths the sermons were preached in Gothic, as suggested by Vulfila's translation of the Bible into Gothic. The inscription on the hanging lamp in Beretfalva was actually written in Latin (*Ego Zenovius votum posui* - "I, Zenovius made the donation"- but its nearest likeness bears a Greek inscription and Zenovius also has a Greek name. Greek has as great a role in Christian conversion as does Latin. The whole period was characterized by polyglot nationalities. Priskos, in the court of Attila, writes about the Scythians - who were Attila's subjects - that they were a mixed population, speaking Gothic and Hun. Those, who associated with Romans also spoke Latin. In the middle of the 5th century, this was expected of the Huns, who ruled all of Pannonia by the mid-5th century and was especially true at Attila´s court, located somewhere between the Danube and the Tisza (Theiss) rivers, opposite Aquincum. (Numerous kettles found in the area also indicate the location). It is noteworthy that Priskos makes no mention of Latinized people beyond the Roman Empire. Among the Scythians only those speak Latin who have more contact with the Empire. This is what Priskos meant by "Romans". The rule of the Huns was a fatal blow to the Romanism of the provinces along the Danube. The critical event was not so much the period (432-434) when Pannonia fell to the Huns. There, the provincials were able to live in relative security albeit under changed conditions. It was the aftermath of the campaign of 447. The Huns razed the territory along the southern banks of the Danube, from Singidunum (Belgrade) to Nova (Sviştov, Bulgaria); some 200 km-s or a five days' walk. Naissos (Niş) became the Roman frontier-town. A wasteland was created along the frontier. All of Dacia Ripensis and the northern area of Moesia Superior became a no-man's land. Romanism, which flourished in the Danubian territory was wiped out, except for small traces in Pannonia and, in a few towns along the Danube in Moesia (which was primarily Greek). The areas which the Huns razed came under Roman rule temporarily one hundred years later, during the reign of Justinian. With respect to Daco-Roman continuity, these circumstances are significant also in terms of the Rumanian language. The ancestors of the speakers of the Rumanian language participated in the changes of late Latin (4th-7th Centuries), which do not appear even in the relatively isolated Sard dialect. This could only be possible if the assumed Latin language in Dacia had been in uninterrupted contact with Latin spoken on the Balkan peninsula. There was no opportunity for such contact between 447-551. Therefore, had the languages survived which were spoken by those who stayed behind after the fall of Dacia - or of Pannonian provincials, resettled here during Hun rule - this would now be very different from contemporary Rumanian. It is beside the point that neither Dacian, nor Pannonian Latin could have been a predecessor of Rumanian - as we have seen earlier. The relationship of Romanism to the local population in this era is characterized by an object which came to light in Vecel. It was a ring made out of an inscribed/fibula which originally bore a Latin inscription, *(Quartine vivas)* — an example of a behavior entirely different from Roman mentality.

Attila died in 453. The alliance of his sons is defeated at the battle of Nedao (the name of the Danube, distorted in a Goth epos to Denao, Dõnaws), which was won by the Gepidae and their allies. The Ostrogoths were in alliance with Attila's sons. They leave the battlefield in defeat and, thus, once again a complete population - exchange takes place on the territory of Dacia within a short time. The Ostrogoth settle in Pannonia in 456 (for 17 years only), when they leave we assume Pannonian provincials are leaving with them. We have no subsequent information about them. Dacia is taken by the victorious Gepidae. There can be no question about their possession of the northern part of the province (including the former Napocensis and Porolissensis). The family of Ardaric, King of the Gepidae, establishes a burial ground along the Someş river, at Apahida near Cluj, after the Goths are routed (Jord. Get 264). As victors and as heirs of the Hun power, the Gepidae are granted "peace" by the Imperium Romanum, i.e., the eastern Roman Empire and the annual payments due to an ally. A relic of these events was found in Ardaric's grave (I. grave in Apahida), a gold fibula. This brooch clasped a paludamentum (military cape) - a gift from the Roman Emperor. Ardaric's gold rings are also imperial gifts, one of them inscribed with the abbreviation: O M H A R V S (*Optimus Maximus Hunnorum Ardaricus Rex Votum Solvit)*.... "Ardaric, the mightiest king of the Huns, is honoring his vow"). According to Iordanes, the Gepidae occupy all of Dacia (*Nam Gepidi Hunnorum sibi sedes viribus vindicantes totius Daciae fines velut victores potiti*, Jord. Get. L, 264).

Numerous archeological sites attest to this in the northern part of the province (Cege, Mezőszopor, Marosnagylak, Kissink, Magyarkapus etc.). Our picture of the erstwhile Dacia Inferior or Malvensis (Oltenia), is less clear. However, as some of the Huns who were defeated by the Gepidae settled on the opposite side, in Dacia Ripensis, in the territory bordering the Vit, Lom and Isker rivers, it is conceivable that Oltenia was left as a barren borderland. The northern part of Moesia was overrun by a mixed and scattered population. Iordanes tells us about Mundo, a descendant of Attila. (For reasons of chronology: it was more likely his father, Giesmos). This 'Mundo' brought robbers (*scamarae*) and vagabonds to this barren and uninhabited area from the vicinity and ruled as their King. (Iord. Get. 301). This "kingdom" of Mundo's allies itself with the Gepidae or the Ostrogoths - depending on the political situation - until 529, at which time Mundo offers his services to Emperor Justinian. During this period, (prior to 535) an attempt is made to reestablish Roman sovereignty along the Danube and we can find Roman towns along its left bank (Litterata-Lederata, Recidiva-Arcidava). Conceivably, Oltenia may have been under the rule of Giesmos and Mundo. Mundo had a close relationship with the Herul people who settled in 512 in Dacia Ripensis and the western part of Moesia Inferior. Justinian resettled them in 535 in the vicinity of Singidunum (Belgrade), at the time of the reestablishment of Roman power in the area. The above reflects the ambiguous situation of Oltenia during the second half of the 5th century. At the beginning of the 6th this may also be the reason for the absence of archeological material in the region.

While their Kingdom stood, the Gepidae have most certainly had possession of Oltenia, and more than that. Going back to Cassiodorus, Iordanes wrote (Iord. Get. 33-34) that 'in the western part of Scythia lives the Gepida nation, surrounded by big and noted rivers. The Tisza (Patthissos-Theis) flows along its N-NW part, the mighty Danube along the South and the Flutausis river intersects it from the east. Beyond, there is Dacia protected by steep mountains which frame it wreath - like. - *In quo Scythia prima ab occidente gens residet Gepidarum, que magnis opinatisque ambitur fluminibus, nam Tisia per aquilonem eius chorumque discurrit; ab africo vero magnus ipse Danubius, ab eo Flutausis secat.... introrsus illis Dacia est, ad coronae speciem arduis Alpibus emunita.* This description reveals that Gepida-land extended beyond the Carpathians up to the Danube and the Flutausis rivers. The latter is frequently identified as the Olt, as a truncated version of Aluta. Iordanus' text tells us, however, that this river is to be found beyond the Carpathians. This is also what Schuchardt and Daicoviciu declare. In various manuscripts the river also appears as *Flutaus, Flutausi, Flutasi* and we assume this is the Alanian name of the Prut river. Flut-av reflects customary Alanian usage, *av* means 'water' (and 'river').

Gepida dominance continues to spread. They occupy the majority of towns in Aurelian Dacia (Ripensis and Mediterranea) (Procopius, De bello gotico III. 33, 8). This occurs after 535 and is probably related to Mundo's death in 536. The Gepidae gained as allies the Heruls who had been resettled in the vicinity of Singidunum. They also took possession of the northern area of Moesia Superior, which they held until 551. Between 473-504 and 536-567, the Gepidae also ruled the territory between the Drava and Sava rivers, (in between it was under the Goths of Italy) the possibility exists that Latin-speaking groups would enter the Gepida Kingdom, the former Dacia. This deserves serious consideration. Gepidae occupy an area which is under the hegemony of the archbishopric of the Justiniana Prima, founded in 535. It encompasses the provinces of Dacia Mediterranea and Ripensis, Moesia Prima, Dardania, Praevalitana, Macedonia Secunda and Pannonia Secunda. M. Friedwagner sees the possibility of the emergence of a new neo-Latin language within the archbishopric; the Gepidae occupied an area of this very region. In the charter of the archbishopric, we note the expectation that " both banks of the Danube would be populated with our citizens and that we would again rule over Viminacium, Recidiva and Litterata which are beyond the Danube. "(... *ut utraque ripa Danubii iam nostris civitatibus frequentaretur, et tam Viminacium quam Recidiva et Litterata, quae trans Danubium sunt, nostrae iterum dicioni subactae sint'*... Cod. Iust. Nov. XI.).

All of this remains an expectation. At best, we might conclude that this was the central seat of power which Mundo relinquished. The Gepida-occupation resulted in a further southern shift of Romanism from the central portion of the Balkan Peninsula. Friedwagner may be correct in assuming that the founding of the archbishopric (in the context of Gepida campaign thrusts) started the development of the Rumanian language.

We also possess archeological evidence pertaining to the expansion of Gepida power south of the Danube (Arčar, Iatrus, etc.). It is more surprising that no such evidence comes to light in the area between the Lower-Danube, the Carpathians and the Prut. Except for one shard from Şimnic there is no trace of the characteristic Gepida relics from the Great Plains region and from Transylvania. We know of an Ipoteşti-Cîndeşti culture in the region; even Rumanian researchers link it to the Transylvanian Gepida culture. The object which came to light (ceramics, lanterns and metal objects) also reflect this connection, - in addition to evidence of local characteristics. To illustrate: a bronze strap-end found at the site of the Ipoteşti-Cîndeşti culture's site at Soldat Ghivan, has an exact duplicate in the Gepida cemetery at Tiszaderzs; a similar object was found at Marosveresmart and in a Pécs (Hungary) cemetery from Avar times (public cemetery - Pécs). Pieces unearthed in Caričin Grad (Iustiniana Prima) and Kizlev (at the Dnieper) attest to a more distant relationship. We are led to this region by additional characteristics of this archeological material. In 594, a Christian Gepida guides the Byzantines who are ready to attack the Slavs inhabiting the Ialomiţa (Ilivakia) region. In the Ipoteşti-Cîndeşti culture there definitely are traces suggesting a Christian presence; we can assume that in a wider context, the peoples of this culture can be considered Gepidae. They cannot be assumed to be Slavs; with their objects-relics we are familiar. The assertion that the peoples of this culture are "Roman" (i.e. Neo-Latin), because they show Dacian traditions and Byzantine connections (!) is obviously false.

The post-Hun, Gepida era is characterized by the retreat of Romanism along the Danube; South of the Danube in particular. We do not deny that Latin speakers may have entered Gepida territory in former Dacia. They may have come as prisoners or as merchants etc., but Gepida archeological findings of bent-legged fibulae or iron pins are no evidence of their legacy. Regarding the Romans of the Balkan peninsula and their alleged contact with Dacia: the fact that Moesia

Superior and the areas along the Danube of Dacia Aureliana were, between 447 and 551 AD, wastelands or dominated by Barbarian peoples, excludes a continuous connection during the late Latin period between the north and the south. In a language which developed along separate lines for 100 years, we cannot search for the characteristics of Balkan-Latin, - yet, these do exist in the Rumanian language.

In the vicinity of former Dacia, the expansion of east-European populations dominates during the period which follows the Gepida Kingdom. In 567 the Avar-Langobard alliance defeats the Gepidae. Thereafter, for 350 years this was a territory which is known as Avaria, land of the Avars, - up to the early 9th century. However, we do not note significant changes in the former Roman province at this time. Although early Avar findings make their appearance here by the end of the 6th century (Korond, Erzsébetváros), long-time Gepida settlers have stayed put. Cemeteries of the Avar-age up to the 7th century bear such evidence - Mezőbánd, Marosveresmart. There are numerous findings in Oltenia - the former Dacia Inferior - of the Ipoteşti-Cîndeşti culture which seem to date from the post-Avar occupation (Făcăi, Fărcaşul de Sus, etc.). As the same time, the Slavs make an appearance in Wallachia's eastern and Transylvania's south-east. region. We have no archaeological data on the Slavs from the territory of former Dacia prior to the middle of the 7th century (Nagyekemező). However, thereafter they will become long-term, continuous settlers of the hilly, mountainous region. Ethnic interrelationships of the era are revealed to us by written records and through archeological finds. A geographer from Ravenna describes Dacia in 800, using data from Iordanes as well as more ancient references. He writes that "Dacia which is now known as Gepidia, is populated by the Huns ....". *Datia ..... que modo Gipidia ascribuntur; in qua nunc Unorum gens habitare dinoscitur'* - An. Rav. I, II). He goes on saying: "Dacia, also called Gepidia, is now inhabited by Huns who are also called Avars".. *Datia .... que et Gipidie apellatur, ubi modo Uni, qui et Avari inhabitant'* - An. Rav. IV. 14). This agrees with archeological data which substantiate the settlement of the peoples of the Avar Empire on the territory of the former Dacia. We have evidence as to the identity of those peoples. In 600 the Byzantines initiated a campaign in the area of the Tisza river. During this foray they destroy three Gepida villages and take 3000 Avars prisoner: 800 Slavs (according to the 'Historia' of Theophylaktos Simokatta the number was 8000) 3000 Gepidae (none, according to the above source) and 2000 Barbarians (6200 as per T. S.). Independent sources validate this picture, augmenting it with Bulgarians. We might add that, in this age, Huns and Avars were considered to be eastern nomads, Bulgarians included. The 'Barbarians' showing up on the roster of prisoners cannot be identified as Bulgarian; they are the 'byproduct' of the final tally of prisoners taken. But then, we cannot turn them into anything else, either. To see them as "ancient Rumanians" would exceed the limits of any hypothesis.

There are some changes in ethnic inter-relationships in Avar times; as we understand them, these changes result in the strengthening of the Turkish element from the east. When Byzantine frontier-defenses collapse along the Danube in 602, these events help to eradicate the last remnants of Romanism which had managed to survive in a few towns of the territory, most of which have become Hellenized. Let us note that there existed groups speaking late-Latin within the Avar Empire, - but not in Dacia. This has been supported by archeological evidence from the vicinity of Keszthely, Hungary. In addition, we have the legacy of place-names in Trans-Danubia's western and south-western area (of Hungary) - Zala, Zöbern, Lafnitz, Rába - (names of rivers). We can include in this group those Romans who were made captive by the Avars in course of their Balkan campaigns and who repatriated to Byzantine territory in the 630's. However, many of them were Greek. The defenders of Sirmium also prayed to God in Greek when the Avars occupied the town in 582. The Avar occupation of the Carpathian basin ends - for a long time to come - free contact between territories lying north and South of the Danube (military campaigns and the repatriation of prisoners of war do not count as 'natural connections'). The process is also strengthened by the immigration of Bulgarians and the establishment of their statehood in the northern part of (contemporary) Bulgaria in 681.

The territory connects the northern and southern banks of the Danube but creates a final separation between the territories of the eastern Roman Empire (originally: Imperium Romanum) and "Barbarian" Europe. It is at this time that the Roman Empire becomes Byzantium, and is obligated to acknowledge the 'de facto' emergence of another power within its borders. The period between 567-795 (or to 803, when the Avar empire actually ceases to exist) brings about the complete liquidation of Romanism along the Danube. For the beginning of the epoch G. Schramm also concurs with this view and substantiates the retreat of Romanism from the whole of the Balkan Peninsula to merely its Southern tip.

In 811, following the collapse of Avar hegemony in the Carpathian basin the former Dacia comes under Bulgarian rule (Dacia Inferior -

Oltenia - was already theirs) and will remain so until the time of the Hungarian conquest of the territory. The conditions in existence among different folk groups - as we knew them - underwent a change in response to the determined and aggressive resettlement policy of the Bulgarians and the transformation generated by their institutions. The Bulgarian Krum Khan resettles 12,000 men and their families (different sources quote different figures) across the Danube (εἰς Βουλγαρίαν ἐκεῖδεν τοῦ Ἴστρου) after he takes Hadriananpolis in 813. This comes to 40,000 people - according to the source with the highest quote. Even without this reference, we could ascertain from archeological evidence that ethnic groups from Bulgaria - south of the Danube - migrated to Wallachia and Transylvania. The bi-ritual cemetery at Bratei is a relic of these times, and so is its replica in Oltenia (Izvoru, Obîrşia, etc.). This cemetery reflects the coexistence of the old-time population and the large number of Slavs who migrated to this region or were resettled here from the Danube delta. (The former were identified by their characteristic 'avar' graves.) The migration also points to a N.W. shift (from S. E.) of the population and also of these ethnic groups. Along with the Slavs, who are resettling here, Bulgarians also arrive: the Onogundurs (Maroskarna, Kézdipolyán) who still speak Turkish at the time, a so-called Bulgarian-Turkish. In the 820's a sizable Slav group arrives from eastern Europe. They settle along the Szamos River. These were originally western Slavs (Abodrits) and were later known as Predenecent peoples (Szilágynagyfalu, Szamosfalva, Apahida). Their name comes from the Donyec river. A significant ethnic mix has taken place in the former Dacia. The remaining population of the Avar Empire, Bulgarians and different Slav groups intermingle in the former Dacia, and here we can enumerate three groups: those already here, those who were resettled from the vicinity of the Danube-delta and the Abodrits. It also is possible that ancient Rumanian groups - from the Southern part of the Balkan peninsula - were among them. They might come with those who were resettled by the Bulgarians, or simply as a result of opportunities for travel and movement within territory under Bulgarian rule. K. Horedt and L. Makkai assume that Rumanians migrated and settled northward in the 9th century. They engaged in transhumance between the Danube and the Carpathians. These assumptions are well-intentioned but lack substantiation. Completely so in the case of Makkai whose starting point is the Latin identity of the cities along the Danube during Iustinian's reign but such settlements did not occur. At any rate such settlers would not have become shepherds; we also know that transhumance is bound to a given locale, where summer and winter grazing areas are interchangeable. Thus, more distant settlements are not logical. Horedt refers to Hungarian sources, Kézai and Anonymus. He misinterpreted Kézai who acknowledged Szekler presence in the Carpathian Basin prior to the Hungarian conquest, but he also stated that they settled in Transylvania only after the conquest (SHR I. 162-163). This is important, inasmuch as Horedt ties Rumanian presence in the region during the 9th century to Kézai's comment that the Szeklers and the Rumanians (*blacki*) lived together in the alpine region. Anonymus is harder to explain. Not only because of the anecdotal narrative of the 13th century chronicler but because his unsubstantiated statements spawned a large volume of literature. Many researchers have viewed his work as an accurate source for the 9th century. Anonymus claims to have knowledge of Rumanians (*Blaci*) along the Szamos river at the time of the Hungarian conquest in 896. However, he also claimed to know of Czechs in Nyitra, Bulgarians in Zemplén, Greeks in Titel and Belgrad, Kumans in the Bánság, Germans (*Romani*) in Veszprém, Hungary. Contemporary sources - i.e. close to the time of the Conquest - assure us that *none of these* peoples were in the area to which Anonymus attributes them, not even the Germans and the Bulgarians. How did this 13th century chronicler come to identify these groups as inhabitants of the area at the time of the Conquest? According to J. Deér, (and I. Z. Tóth, Gy. Győrffy and L. Makkai agree): the writer "populated" these areas with nationalities who were neighbors of 13th century Hungary. We would like to modify Deér's premise with the observations that Anonymus only selected nationalities with whom Hungarians had waged war. Russians, Poles, and Serbs were not included. In other words if Anonymus lists the *Blaci* (Rumanians) as 9th century inhabitants of the Carpathian Basin that could only mean that, in the 13th century they were not a significant population in that region. Credible sources substantiate this - in the mid 13th century they only know of Vlachs (Rumanians) beyond the Carpathians.

During the period of Bulgarian rule in the 9th century we are therefore unable to verify that groups of Rumanians would have entered the former Dacia from the Southern region of the Balkan peninsula. Some findings were made in a Wallachian settlement (Bucov) which had Glagolite and Cyrillic letters and so-called Murfatlar symbols. It seems to be without foundation to attribute these to (rural) Rumanian writings, when we know that these symbols were being used by the Bulgarians at the time. Today we already know that the Murfatlar writing came into being in 893, or very soon thereafter. It was the by-product of anti-Greek measures taken by Simeon, and (legible) inscriptions were, therefore, written in the Bulgar-Turkish of the Danube region. One cannot take a 10th century vessel from Dobrudja (Capidava) and identify thereon the 'Rumanian name' of *Petre* - read left to right - when all the inscriptions on the object are written right to left and the above is meant to be read as *ertep*. The word means 'I write' in (Danubian) Bulgaro-Turkish. An ethnic identification of archeological finds is frequently difficult to make, and when this happens with the *sole aim* of showing Rumanian origins then we must disqualify both hypothesis and results. Verifiable data have not established the resettlements of ancient Rumanians from the Balkan Peninsula to the former Dacia; the groups resettled by Krum from Hadrianapolis did not stay either. Given the first opportunity - after 25 years - they returned to their original home, with Byzantine (and Hungarian) military assistance. Other groups which were made to resettle there may have had similar histories.

At the time of conquest of this territory in 895, Hungarians found Danubian Bulgaro-Turks, eastern and Southern Slavs in the former Dacia. The tribal population of the late Avar empire may have dominated the region's southern area, Oltenia. (Izvorul, etc.) The defeat of Bulgarians enabled the Hungarians to occupy Dacia's Transylvanian area in the late 9th and early 10th Centuries. Their cemeteries date back to the first half of the 10th century on Zápolya-St. in Kolozsvár (Cluj), and in Marosgombás. Early Hungarian chronicles attest to the occupation of Transylvania, which was among the first such areas in the Carpathian Basin. We learn that "they reached the borders of Hungary, i.e. of Transylvania" (a.k.a. Erdély) *deveniunt in confinium regni Hungarie scilicet in Erdely*, SRH I. 286.). Apparently, Anonymus was unaware of this reference. After the fighting for the new land died down, the allied Kavars settled in Transylvania. Place-names in the area do not reflect the names of the conquering tribes, and the *only places where these can be absent* in conquered territory would be those where the allied Kavars lived. Transylvanian cemeteries dating from the period of the Hungarian Conquest indicate a burial ritual (stones under the head) which differed from those in Hungary, and this implies that we must view this population as unique in the Carpathian basin of the 10th century. As additional verification, we can point to the inscription in the Kazar style and language about a process of construction in Alsószentmihályfalva, near Torda. The Kavars were Kazars and the inscription has probably come from their ruler, the "*gyula*". In the first half of the 10th century this was the site of his headquarters. The oldest Transylvanian fortress, Tordavár (Várfalva), was built here, but transferred in the middle of the century to (today's) Alba Iulia.) A characteristic of the period: the ruler transfers his seat of power from one Roman center (Potaissa) to another Roman site (of ruins): Apulum. In 952, the then ruler - or "*gyula*" - accepts Christianity in Constantinople and is assigned a bishop (Hierotheos) who erects in Gyulafehérvár (Alba Iulia) the first house of worship, known as the "round church". It is unlikely that Hierotheos would have come by himself. We do not know who accompanied him but we do know that, at this time, a segment of the local population came from the Southern territories of the Balkan Peninsula. An eastern-rite Christian cemetery in (Csombord near Nagyenyed) is the counterpart of others from the turn of the 9th-10th Centuries found in today's South-Bulgaria south of the Balkan mountains; the inhabitants of Csombord must have immigrated from there. This population might have been Rumanian, -

or there could have been Rumanians among them. They came from that portion of the Balkan Peninsula which has written evidence of the existence of Rumanians there. However, Csombord is too far removed from the Barcaság in the Carpathian Basin, where Rumanians appeared between 1202-1209. They must have been there earlier, though: (the land which was given to the Cistercian monastery at Kerc was taken from them). Also, the period from the second half of the 10th to the end of the 12th century is too long a time to establish a connection between the Rumanians of the 10th century and latter-day ones. In addition, those words in the Hungarian language which are of Bulgaro-Slav origin (*rozsda*-rust; *mostoha*-stepparent; *mesgye*-lane) are too numerous to infer a connection other than a direct Bulgaro-Hungarian one. As this Bulgaro-Slav language initially was only in usage South of the Balkan mountains, the presence of their words in the Hungarian language suggests a settlement of Bulgarians in the territory. Some of the words, which became part of Hungarian usage (*pap*-priest, *kereszt*-cross) have a religious connotation. These we can attribute to Christian conversions taking place in eastern territories such as the baptism of the 'Gyula' (Chieftain). Therefore, the newcomers from Csombord must have been Bulgaro-Slavs but we wish to repeat: the arrivals could have included Rumanians. This can neither be proven, nor disproved.

In 1003, St. Stephen, King of Hungary goes to war against the Supreme Chief (Gyula) Prokuj (who was his uncle) and occupies his land. Transylvania becomes an integral part of Hungary of the Middle Ages, but the separate development of Transylvania during the preceding 100 years left its mark. The suzerain lord of the territory retains the inherited title of Vajda (voivode), originating in the 10th century, as were the Supreme Chiefs - including the Gyula - in earlier times. Populating this voivodship, which suffers repeated forays from eastern nomads - the Petchenegs, Uzes and the Kumans - continues to be difficult. There is no other territory within Hungary in the Middle Ages with such a large portion of the colonized population: the Saxons, the Szeklers and - temporarily - even the German Order of Knights (Knights Templar). It almost resembled Trajans' forced resettlement of his veterans into Dacia. This diverse group of settlers is augmented at the end of the 12th century by Rumanians as frontier guards along the Southern Carpathians. The number settling in the Transylvanian Basin is small, and in 1290 the Hungarian King, András III, intends to gather all Rumanians on royal property but three years later he relinquishes the plan.

The above illustrated that we cannot ascertain a legacy of Romanism in Dacia subsequent to the cessation of Roman hegemony. There are no communities left - large or small - where Latin is spoken. By the end of the 3rd century, the new settlers drove out even the Karps; the population has completely changed in the province. The same thing happens one hundred years later, after 375; with the arrival of the Huns, the earlier inhabitants leave the territory. They are replaced by Ostrogoths, resettled by the Huns (or they might have come on their own). Following the Battle of Nedao in 454 a third population-exchange takes place. The Ostrogoths move to Pannonia and Dacia is occupied by the Gepidae. Only from this time on can we consider any continuity in the region; the presence of the Gepidae in the Carpathian Basin is recognized for a long time, up to the 9th century. We do not know what effect the Hungarian conquest had on the ethnic relations in the region. Archeological data is sparse but we cannot exclude the possibility that once again it brought about a population displacement in Dacia.

These historical events reveal that, in this territory, we cannot assume the existence of Roman - Rumanian continuity - or up to the end of the 5th century, that of any other peoples. This may be clear by now. With regard to additional references: rivers, which do not leave Transylvania do not bear names of ancient origin. The name of smaller rivers have Hungarian or Slavic origins. The largest among them, the Küküllő has a name of Turkish origin. As it cannot have derived from Bulgaro- Turkish, Petcheneg or Cumanian, the process of elimination leaves the Kavars who could have named the river *Küküllő*, which means Kökényes in Hungarian or *Tîrnava* in Rumanian (which is a word of Slavic origin). This bears witness to the likelihood of population movements in wake of the Hungarian Conquest. On Dacian territory we may assume to have witnessed four such migrations, i.e. population exchanges. Romanism could only be a recurrence in this region, as indeed happened 900 years later when Rumanians made their presence known on the borders of the former Roman Province.

Chapter V
Origin of the Rumanians

1. Linguistic Data

Neo-Latin languages are the outgrowth of homogenous or nearly uniform, Latin which was spoken in the Roman Empire. The following illustrates the chronological development of the Rumanian language:

1st-2nd to 3rd-4th- centuries —	Latin spoken in the period of the empire
4th to 6th century —	Eastern Latin
7th to 11th century —	Proto- or Common Rumanian
12th to 15th century —	Old Rumanian
16th to 20th century —	Rumanian

The chronology is, naturally, approximate and characterized by differences of opinion. For instance A. Rosetti tends to place Eastern Latin, i.e., the development of a specific variety of Latin spoken in Italy, Dalmatia, and the Danube Region, in the mid-3rd century. There is no consensus on terminology either. The period of Eastern Latin is, considering the entirety of the Romance languages, the Proto-Romance period. In Hungarian, that becomes confusing, because ´proto-román´ may signify both ´Proto-Romance´ and ´Proto-Rumanian´. To circumvent this ambiguity, we will use the designation ´Romanica´ (Romance) instead of ´Neolatin´.

Protoromance, the basis of the vowel system of the Neo-Latin languages, has a vowel-system which differs from the Latin of the Roman Empire, as follows:

latin		ă	ā	ĕ	ē	ĭ	ī	ŏ	ō	ŭ	ū

$$latin \quad ă\ ā \quad ĕ\ ē \quad ĭ\ ī \quad ŏ\ ō \quad ŭ\ ū$$

$$\diagdown\diagup$$

$$preromanica \quad a \quad ę \quad e^1 \quad ị \quad i \quad o^2 \quad o^1 \quad ụ \quad u$$

$$\diagdown\diagup \qquad\qquad \diagdown\diagup$$

$$e^1 \qquad\qquad o^1$$

What we see here is that instead of the contrast between long and short vowels in Latin, in Protoromance, the open (ę, o²,) and closed (e¹, o¹.) vowels are opposing each other. These changes penetrate Eastern Latin's Eastern Zone; in Rumanian ō and ŭ do not merge. Example: *gŭla* 'throte', Dr. (this abbreviation refers to Danubian Rumanian and not Daco-Rumanian or Northern-Rumanian) Ar., Mr. *gură*, Istr. *gurę*, but Ital. *gola*, Sp., Port. *gola*. The adopted words - from Latin to Albanian also reflect this format: Lat. *fŭrca*=villa, Dr. *furcă*, Alb. *furkë*, but Ital. *forca*, etc. In this particular case the Dalmatian language presents a dual profile. Here, the differentation between ō and ŭ as in Rumanian - appears only in the original closed syllable. Lat. *bŭcca* 'face' Dr. *bucă*, Dalm. *buka*, but Ital. *bocca*, etc. The relationship of this variable system to Latin is as follows:

$$latin \quad ă\ ā \quad ĕ\ ē \quad ī\ ī \quad ō\ ō \quad ŭ\ ū$$

$$\diagdown\diagup \qquad\qquad \diagdown\diagup \quad \diagdown\diagup$$

$$preromanica \quad a \quad ę \quad e^1 \quad ị \quad i \quad o \quad u$$

$$\diagdown\diagup$$

$$e^1$$

Naturally, there are exceptions to the rule: Lat. *autŭmnus* - fall; Dr. Ar. Mr. *toamnā*, Istr. *tomnę*. Historically, this means that the changes in Latin of the 2nd and 3rd centuries have begun to affect that Latin which subsequently became the precursor of Rumanian. The change $ĭ, ē > e^1$ preceded the $ō, ŭ > o^1$ changes; the former dates back to the 3rd century, the latter to the 4th. In this respect, it is noteworthy that the Latin loanwords in the Albanian language show the same changes as does Rumanian. However, the Rumanian language contains all the changes which occurred in Latin during the 4th-6th centuries, while, for example, in Dalmatian, - *k* - remains, if followed by a long - *e* -. (Lat, *cēna* - ′dinner, feast′; Dr. *cină*, Dalm. *kaina*; Rum. *c + e, i = ts*). None of this means that Protoromance on the basis of Rumanian did not develop from the Latin spoken in the Empire. J. Herman has provided an explanation of this phenomenon: the $ō, ŭ > o^1$ change did not spread Eastward beyond the Western border of Moesia Superior; there are no data indicating this change in the region East of a straight line drawn from Singidunum (Belgrade) towards the south. This shows that the ancestors of the Rumanians and the Albanians must have been living east of this line in the 4th (and 5th-6th) centuries.

In Rumanian, the following phenomena originate from the changes that occurred in the 2nd and 3rd centuries:

$ĭ > e^1$: Lat. *magister* > *maester* >Dr. *măiestru* 'master';

v> b: Lat. *alveus* > *albeus* >Dr. *albie* 'trough';

- *ti* + vowel: *t* becomes affricative: Lat. *tertium*> *tersiu*, 'third', Dr. *(an) țărț* "2 years back";

- *tl- > cl*: Lat. *vetulus* > *veclus* 'old' > Dr. *vechi;*

-pt- > *t*: Lat. *septembris* > *setembre* 'September', cf. Lat. *baptizare* 'baptize' > Dr. *boteza;*

- Drop of *-r, -s,* and *-t* at words end: Lat. *frater* 'brother', Dr. *frate*

Sound changes by assimilation:

e > *a*: Lat. *passer(e) passar* 'sparrow, bird' > Dr. *pasăre;*

i > *a*: *silvaticus* > *salvaticus,* 'wild' > Dr. *sălbatic;*

o > *e* dissimilation: *rotundus* > *retundus* 'round' > old Dr. *rătund;*

v - disappears between vowels: Lat. *avunculus* > *aunculo* 'uncle' > Dr. *unchi.*

In addition to these phonetic changes, also changes in morphology appeared: neutral nouns became masculine, in the 3rd declination the substitution of the nominative singular by the root of the declined forms, connecting adverbs with prepositions etc. These changes of the 2nd and 3rd centuries in the Latin on which Rumanian is based are identical with the changes in the Latin from which the other Romance languages developed.

The changes which occurred in *4th-6th centuries* in Protoromance are more numerous:

The short, stressed Latin *ĕ* becomes a diphthong. This alteration consistently appears in Rumanian, Dalmatian and certain Rhetoroman dialects; in Spanish, Italian and French, only in open syllables. This is basically not the case in Provancale, Sardinian, Catalan and Portuguese.

Lat. *petra* 'stone', Dr. *piatră* (< *pieatră* < *pietra*), Dalm. *pitra*, Ital. *pietra*, Engad. *peidra*, Friaul *piere*, Fr. *pierre*, Prov. *peira*, Cat. *pedra*, Sp. *piedra*, Port. *pedra*.

Lat. *ferrum* 'iron', Dr. *fier*, Dalm. *fiar*, Ital. *ferro*, Sard *ferru*. Engad. *fier*, Friaul *fir*, Fr. *fer*, Prov.,- Catal. *ferre*, Sp. *hierro*, Port. *ferro*.

The assibilation of *di-* occurred in the 5th century:

Lat. *radius* ´ray´ Dr. *rază*, Dalm. *ruoz* 'thunder', Italian *raggio*, Sard *rayu*, Engadin *raz*, Friaul *rai* (but *raza* ´hand of the watch´), O.Fr. *rai*, Sp *rayo* etc. Preceding stressed *o, u*, in Rumanian there is no - *z* - but - *ğ* -, just as *-ti-* changes to - *č* - in this situation.

The uniform development of Protoromance is characterized by the phonetic formation of *ce, ci (ke, ki)*. The palatalization of *ki* + vowel begins in the 2nd and 3rd centuries; it is beginning to be interchanged with the *ti* + vowel-group (which palatalized in the same manner). Palatalization of *ke* was still not generalized by the 5th century. P. Skok's assumption that the palatalization of *k* and *g* in the development of Rumanian would have occurred in the 7th-8th centuries deserves consideration in view of Albanian and Dalmatian usage.

Lat. *civitas* "city", Dr. *cetate*, Dalm. *čituot*, Italian *città*, Engad. *čited*, Fr. *cité*, Prov., Catalan *ciutat*, Sp. *ciudad*, Port. *cidade*, Alb. *qytet*.

Lat. *cera* "wax", Dr. *ceră*, Dalm. *kaira*, Italian *cera*, Sard *kera*, Eng. *čaira*, Friauli *sere*, Fr. *cire*, Prov., Catal. Sp., Port. *cera*.

Lat. *crux* "cross", Dr. *cruce*, Dalm. *krauk*, Italian *croce*, Sard *ruge*, Engad. *kruš*, Friauli *kros*, Fr. *croix*, Prov. *crotz*, Cat. *creu*, Alb. *kryk*.

These changes are the same in Rumanian as in Italian and Western Neo-Latin languages. Rumanian parallels Rhetoromance, but is partly different from Dalmatian, and significantly so, when we look at Latin characteristics in Albanian. In Albanian we find a palatalized -*q* - (=*k´*) in place of the Latin - ki - (*qytet.< civitate, shoq < socius*), and -

ke - is replaced by the unpalatalized - *k* -. Latin loanwords in Albanian cannot be separated from the same derivation in the Rumanian language; this suggests an early - and short - relationship between the two (4th, 5th cent.) and that this connection must have been intensive.

The modification of the tonal system is accompanied by formative changes, as well conjugated verbs which denote continuing action were defined by the application of *habeo: ... episcopum ... invitatum habes* "You invited the bishop" becomes (Dr.) *ai invitat pe episcop'*. This will be the customary usage in Neo-Latin languages but it should be noted that in Arumun and in Oltenian dialects the plusquamperfectum was retained. Use of the genitive case instead of the dative case becomes frequent: *dedit nomen illorum* "named them" (gave them a name), but the Rumanian language retained the singular dative case in relation to feminine substantives which belong to the 1st and 3rd declinations. Examples of the use of the genitive case instead of the dative appear in the 7th century, it must be noted however, that, on the Balkan Peninsula, this might have occurred earlier, given the Greek influence. The vocabulary also reveals new elements: (*primo vere* > *prima vere*, 'spring', Italian *primavera*, Dr. *primăvară*). The change of meaning of Lat. *hostis* "enemy", became wide-spread (Dr. *oaste*, Old Italian *oste*, Engad: *oast*, etc. "army". This modification could have occurred only when the forces of the Roman Empire consisted of Barbarians, the former enemy; thus, not prior to the 5th century. E. Löfstedt established that substantiation of altered meaning is on record as of the 6th century. At the same time, this vocabulary parallels Italian and Rhetoromance (especially Friauli). It suggests that the Latin-speaking groups of the Balkan Peninsula had close contact with Italians until at least 600 AD. Of the Rhetoromance links certain phrases stand out: the preservation of the Lat. *albus* "white", Dr. *alb*, Dalm. *yualb*, Engad. *alf*, Port. *alvo*. Even more so, the permanence of *basilika*, "church", Dr. *biserică*, Dalm. *basalka*, Engad. *baselgia*, O. venetian *baselega*, Veltellina *bazelga*, "reformed church", Alb. *bazilikë*. During the 6th and 7th centuries this term was replaced by *ecclesia* (*kishë* in Alb.) The retention of *basilika* can be traced to the ecclesiastical Latin of the end of the 4th, beginning of the 5th centuries. On one hand, this portrays the chronology of the relationship of Balkan Romanism to its Western counterpart, on the other hand, it reflects upon the early separation of the ancestors of Albanians and Rumanians. We also find that the close relationship of the antecedents of the Rumanian language with Western Romanica - up to 600 - excludes the possibility of the development of the Rumanian language on former Dacian territory; there was no opportunity for this to happen.

There is a segment in the history of the Rumanian language which is inseparable from Albanian; - we have already seen evidence of this. There is a reciprocity between Albanian and Rumanian: each adopted words from the other but many characteristics of the syntax of the Rumanian language - its so-called 'Balkanism' - are ascribed to Albanian. The tonal system in Rumanian has undergone change vis a vis Latin. A parallel of the modification can be found in the Albanian language.

Unstressed Lat. *a* > Rum. *ă*, Alb. *ë*. These sounds are identical, although, there is a slight variation in their formation (as in Bulg. *ă*). In all Neo-Latin languages we can observe a variation in unstressed vowel-articulation, especially in Spanish, Portuguese and Southern

Italian dialects (although, some of this is present in all languages). Thus, the question arose whether the Rumanian-Albanian variances should be viewed as having developed independently from each other. Our data do not support such a theory.

In both Albanian and Rumanian, this sound (*ă, ë*) developed from unstressed a:

Lat. *familia* "family" > Dr. *femeie* "woman", Ar. *fămeae*, Mr. *fumeal´ă*, Alb. *fëmijë*.

Lat. *camisia* "shirt" > Dr. *cămaşă* , Alb. *këmishë*.

Lat. *parens, parenten* "father"> Dr. *părinte*, Alb. *përint*.

In Albanian, as well as Rumanian the a before nasals (*m, n*) becomes *ă, ë*:

Lat. *canis* "dog" > Dr. *cîine*, Alb. *qën, qen*

Lat. *sanctus* "holy" > Dr. *sînt, sîn*, Ar. *sînt*, Alb. *shënt, shën*.

In Common Rumanian *î* was a variant of *ă*. In Rumanian and Albanian - under certain circumstances - this sound might develop also from other sounds (*i, e, o, u*).

As seen earlier, both Rumanian and Albanian keep the Latin *ŭ*; in other Neo-Latin languages this became *ō* (with partial exception in Dalmatian: Dr. *furcă*, Alb. *furkë*, "fork"). The consonant combination of - *kt* - and - *ks* is very characteristic in Rumanian. The other Neo-Latin languages show here assimilation (Lat. *lac, lacte* "milk", Italian *latte* (also in Rumanian where - *k* - is part of an unstressed syllable; Lat. *maxilla* "jaw", Dr. *măsea*); or the change of - *k* - from a tectal into an affricat sound or its loss by way of the - *i* - (Lat. *directus* "straight" Dalm. *drat*, Fr. *droit*, Port. *dereito*, in Romanian, - *kt* - and - *ks* - give way to - *pt* - and - *ps* -.

Lat. *pectus* "breast", Dr. *piept*;

Lat. *directus* "straight", Dr. *drept*, Meglenorum. *dirept*;

Lat. *lac, lacte* "milk", Dr. *lapte*;

Lat. *lucta* "fight", Dr. *luptă*, etc.;

Lat. *coxa* "hip", Dr. *coapsă*.

Similar changes occur partly also in Albanian:

Lat. *lucta* "fight", Alb. *luftë*,

Lat. *dictare* "to point", Alb. *dëfton*, Geg. *diftój* "to show", etc.

Lat *coxa* "hip", Alb. *kofshë, koshë*,

Lat. *laxa* "skin", Alb. *lafshë*, lash (different as per Barič)

Lat. *mataxa* "raw silk," "string", Alb. *mendafshë*, etc.

The equivalent of the Rumanian - *pt* - sound goup is - *ft* - in Albanian and that of *ps*, - *fsh*. This demonstrates that Albanian Latinisms had been dependent on Rumanian. However, these sound groups have also other variants in Albanian:

Lat. *directus* "straight", Alb. *dreite*

Lat. *tractare* "handle", Alb. *traitoj* "to spice"

Lat. *fructus* "fruit", Alb. *fryt* (<*fryit*).

The two alternants in Albanian are said to be the result of tonal and stress-phenomena. Example: Latin - *ct* - (after - *a* - and high vowels) would be - *it* - in Albanian and - *ft* - if the sonant was different. This appears to be implausible if we look at the previous examples of Lat. *mataxa* > Alb. *mëndafshë*; Lat. *fructus* > Alb. *fryit*. H. Barič demonstrated that the - *it* - substitutions for - *ct* - are of Dalmatian origin (Lat. *fructus*, Dalm. Veglia *fróit*). However, the situation is more complex in Dalmatian. In the Veglia dialect we find *guapto* in lieu of the

Lat. *octo* (D.r. *opt*) and in Raguzan there is *kopsa* for *coxa*. Barič posits that Dalmatian *guapto* was effected by *sapto* ´seven´ and that the Raguzan *kopsa* was borrowed from Rumanian. We concur with the latter assumption (in Dalmatian we would expect **kuapsa*) but his explanation of *guapto* does not fit. If the sound changes *ct.> - xt-> -it (i with a ^ under it)* existed in early Dalmatian, then the equivalent of the Latin *octo* should look like **yuito* in Dalmatian. Yet, this development would differ so greatly from the developmental links in *septem > sapto* that we must exclude the existence of an analogous process. Yet, Barič does draw some noteworthy conclusions which would suggest a transitional dialect between the earliest Dalmatian and Rumanian languages during the Pre- or Proto-Romance period. While we have no substantiating data about its phonemics, we can hypothesize that the Latin - *ct* - and - *ks* evolved in disparate ways. We should not assume that the Roman influence has two strata in Albanian with one of these dating back to an earlier Albanian-Protoromace symbiosis, and the other to a later period during which there was contact with the Romanism which existed along the shores of the Adriatic. In Albanian one cannot make a chronological differentiation between the two strata. A more likely explanation would posit that those who spoke early Albanian lived with early Rumanian speakers or with those who spoke the assumed extinct transitional dialect. This would point to a Protoromance which preceded Rumanian and which was more distant from its Dalmatian version.

Latin - *lv* - and - *rv* - undergo similar changes in Rumanian and Albanian. (Lat. *salvare* ´to save, to rescue´ Alb. *shëlbuem*; Lat. *silvaticus* "wild game", Dr. *sălbatic*; Lat. *servire* "to serve", Ar. *şerbi*,

Alb. *shërbenj*). Other similarities between the two languages include the *n>r* alternation (rhotacism): Lat. *minutus* "minute", Dr. *mărunt*, but Ar. *minut*; Southern Alb. Tosk *zëri* "sound" but Albanian *geg zâni*, etc.) Rhotacism was widespread in Danubian Rumanian (today only among the *Moț*-es); [Rumanians living in the Munții Apuseni - Transylvanian Alps - transl.) and exists also in Istrorumanian. In Albanian, it occurs only in its Southern dialect. We have no obvious explanation for this phenomenon, but it does point to a connection between the ancestors of Danubian Rumanians and the Istrorumanians with the forebears of Albanians who spoke a southern, i.e. Tosk, dialect. It is certain that in both cases, we have to do with two different *n* - sounds.

Morphology points to yet another area of similarity between Rumanian and Albanian, including syntactic changes. The most conspicuous of these is the postponed article: Dr. *cal* "horse", *calul* "the horse"; *fată* "girl", *fata* "the girl" Alb. *zog* "'bird", *zogu* "the bird"; *vajzë*, "girl", *vajza* "the girl". In Bulgarian, this development (*voda* "water", *vodata* "the water") is of later origin. It cannot be found in texts of the 11th century, and becomes widely used only in the 17th century. The postponed article exists in the Scandinavian languages, in Armenian, in North-Russian dialects and in other languages, as well. In Rumanian, it developed from the Vulgar Latin demonstrative pronoun (*homo ille*, etc.), but cannot be separated from Albanian, as the pronoun-structure is identical in both languages, such as the use of dual articles: Dr. *omul cel bun*, Alb. *njeriu i mirë*, "the good person", etc. The postponed article in Bulgarian can scarcely derive from any other source than Rumanian.

Similarities are also apparent in the objective case of personal pronouns, the indefinite pronoun, as well as in word-formation. The most striking among these pertains to the ordinal numbers between ten and twenty: Dr. *unsprezece, doisprezece* "eleven, twelve", etc. Alb. *një-mbë-dhjetë, dy-mbë-dhjetë,* ʹeleven, twelveʹ etc. This formative exists in Slavic languages too, but there we do not find an *unus-supra-decem* structure. Rumanian does not follow the Latin formative and must have taken it from a foreign language. This could have been none other than Albanian.

The two languages are also alike in their use of substantive constructions rather than the infinitive. It is particularly important that the meaning of some words of Latin origin underwent the same type of change in Rumanian as in Albanian:

Lat. *conventus* "gathering, meeting"; Dr. *cuvînt,* Alb. *kuvënd* "speech"; -

Lat. *draco* "dragon"; Dr. *drac,* Alb. dreq "*devil*"; -

Lat. *falx* "sickle"; Dr. *falcă,* Alb. *fëlqinë,* "jaw" –

Lat. *horreo* ʹI shudder (with horror)ʹ; Dr. *urăsc,* Alb. *urrej* "I hate"; -

Lat. *mergo* "I sink"; Dr. *merg* "I go", Alb. *mërgonj* " I remove";

Lat *palus, paludem. (palude)* "swamp"; Dr. *pădure,* Alb. *pyll* forest

Lat. *sella* "chair"; Dr. *şale* "waist"; Alb, *shalë,* "thigh, leg". –

Lat. *sessus* "session"; Dr. *şes,* Alb. *shesh* "plains"

Lat. *veteranus* "veteran"; Dr. *bătrîn,* Alb. *vjetër* "old".

The precursor of Albanian (words) was the same Balkan Protoromance from which the Rumanian language originates. On the one hand, we know that the Dalmatian *palus* preserved its original meaning. On the other hand, we have an attestation of the change of meaning of *mergo*: a tomb inscription from Lǎžen, Bulgaria reads: *immargeban ... in quartum decimumque annum* ´I went away (I did) at the age of 14´. Thus, these Latin loanwords of Albanian derive from the same language to which we attribute the origins of Rumanian.

There is a singular connection between Dr. *sat* (*fsat* in the 16th cent.) and the Albanian *fshat* ´village´. The word comes from the Lat. *fossatum* "ditch" (original meaning: ´military encampment surrounded by a rampart´) but the loss of the vowel in the first syllable indicates an Albanian origin. We might also say it has been re-borrowed from Albanian within the context of the mutual relationship between the two languages.

This close relationship is indicated also by a number of words shared by Rumanian and Albanian, whose origin is not known. There are some 100 of these and the largest group (25) pertains to shepherding. Ten words have to do with nature, ten with animals and 12 with plants. Only four words apply to parts of the body. A few examples:

Alb. *avull*, Dr. *abure* "steam, mist", Alb. *rragalë*, "hut", Dr. *argea* "weaver's room, vault, cellar", Alb. *batsë, baç* "head-shephard"; Dr. *baci*, Alb. *bollë*, "large serpent", *bullar* "water-snake"; Dr. *balaur* "dragon", Alb. *baigë, bagelë*, "animal droppings"; Dr. *baligǎ*, Alb. *baltë*, "swamp, clay"; Dr. *baltǎ*, Alb. *bredh* "pinetree"; Dr. *brad*, Alb. *brushtullë* "burdock"; Dr. *brusture*, Alb. *buzë*, "lip"; Dr. *buzǎ* , Alb. *kësullë*, "kerchief"; Dr. *cǎciulǎ*, Alb. *këpushë*, "tick"; Dr. *cǎpuşǎ*, Alb. *katund* "village"; Dr. *cǎtun* "farm"; Alb. *dash* "sheep", Dr. *daş* "lamb"; Alb. *dru* "tree"; Dr. *druete* "tree trunk"; Alb. *therimmë*, "wood shavings, shards"; Dr. *fǎrîmǎ* "fragment, piece"; Alb. *gjemp* "thorn"; Dr. *ghimpe*, Alb.

gropë, "hole"; Dr. *groapă*, Alb. *mal* "mountain"; Dr. *mal* "shore"; Alb. *modhullë*, "pea"; Dr. *mazăre*, Alb. *përrua* "brook"; Dr. *pîrîu*, Alb. *rëndës* "gizzard"; Dr. *rînză*, Alb. *shkrump* "carbonized, charred"; Dr. *scrum* "ash"; Alb. *thumbullë*, "button, knot"; Dr. *sîmbure* "seed"; Alb. *shtrungë*, "milking compartment", Dr. *strungă*, Alb. *shut* "hornless"; Dr. *şut, ciut*, Alb. *thark* "sheep pen"; Dr. *ţarc*, Alb. *vatrë*, "hearth", Dr. *vatră*, etc.

These are considered the "autochthonous" words of the Rumanian language. Even though there are cases in which a borrowing from Albanian is possible (e.g. *ghimpe*), this is excluded in most cases because there are no regular sound correspondences (for example, Alb. *th* may correspond to Dr. *f, s, ţ*). The possibility exists that Albanian as well as Rumanian could have borrowed these words from a third or a fourth language. The total number of these ´autochthonous´words - (not all of which exist also in Albanian) would, according to I. I. Russu, be 161; but this number can be disputed. The majority of these words can be found in the Albanian language and it may be pointed out that they strengthen the close Albanian-Rumanian connections described above.

There was earlier mention of an Albanian-Rumanian co-existence in the 4th-6th centuries. The question is, where did this take place? Contemporary Albanians who do not live in Albania proper, live in the Southwestern part of Serbia (in Kosovo and adjacent Serbian territory, the Western region of Macedonia and the southern area of Crna Gora), and in the North-West corner of Greece. However, Albanians are not indigenous to this territory, not-withstanding the opinion of Albanian linguists. Old Illyrian place names came to them second-hand, Latin place names have Old-Dalmatian characteristics. Albanians could not have lived along the coast for very long; their word-stock - pertaining to the sea and to fishing - has come from different languages, Slavic included. The language lacks words from ancient - Greek and this suggests that their settlement in these parts came later. The earliest mention of their presence in these parts dates from the 9th century.

The foregoing has shown us that we must not neglect the connection between Albanian and Dacian; in spite of incomplete records we can see the inter-relationship of the two languages. Identical phonetic changes and common words in the two languages suggest stronger connections than records reveal. However, it is likely that we would find in contemporary Albanian the ideal linguistic mix. Not too long ago, G. Meyer described it as a "semi-Romanized Balkan tongue" (*halbromanisierte Balkansprache*). There is only one explanation for the four versions of the Idg. *s-* (at the beginning of the word) in Albanian (*gj, sh, h, th*): in some of these words the initial *s-* is not the continuation of the ancient Idg. sound. (Since Latin *s* corresponds to Albanian *sh*, this is hardly questionable.) Geographic names suggest that (one of) the antecedents of Albanian must be sought in the Carpathian region. Only Albanian - (or a closely related language) - can explain the -š sound in the name of the rivers Temes, Maros, Szamos in replacement of the original Idg. -*s*. We can probably include the *Körös* river, but we lack early data. Traces of an Albanian, Tracian and Dacian sound change can be discovered in the name of the River Temes - an - *m* - replacing the original - *b* -. In view of existing linguistic evidence we can hardly doubt that the language(s) spoken during antiquity in the region of the Southern and

Eastern Carpathians must have been forerunners of Albanian and that (one of these languages) must have been Dacian. More concisely: what we call Daco-Geta languages - for want of more complete records.

This premise has a highly visible — although controversial — piece of evidence: the name of the river Szeret. The following variants are extant: *Tiarantos* (Herodotus); *Hierasos* (Ptolemy), *Gerasus* (Ammianus Marcellinus), *Seretos*, *Sarat* (Konstantinos Porphyregennetos), Hung. *Szeret*, Dr. *Siret*. It would be wrong to separate these names from each other as has been done of late (also, by G. Schramm). This is because all can be explained from the Albanian variations (*gj, th, h*) of Idg. *s-*. *Tiarantos* could reflect a secondary transmission of *Θarant-*, and the same process is operative with *Hierasos* and *Gerasus* vs. *Jeras-*, *Gjeras-*. The root is Idg. *sru-*, *sreu-* "it flows, flowing". The endings are not clear. The - *nt* - in *Tirantos* is probably denoting a present participle (flowing); we see a modified version of in Seretos. The other variants may have been created from the assimilated version of *-nt-* (*-tt-*), enlarged with *-yo-* (*serant-yo*). Thus, the different versions of the name of the river are interconnected; we can attribute the differences to linguistic variations, dialects and separate allusions to the upper and/or lower section of the river. The opinion of those who disagree with the premise that a correlation exists seems to be unsubstantiated. Yet, a connection between the various names of the river can only be posited if we assume the existence of an Albanian - like language in the area. Coupled with established records, this linguistic clue traces the Albanian language and the forebears of the Albanians to the beginning of the 1st cent. in the vicinity of the river. Supplemental data also permit us to believe that the predecessor of Albanian was Dacian, — more exactly, a close relative of Dacian. When a language, such as this, becomes Romanized to the extent we have seen here, the population must have lived for an extended period in a Latin-speaking region. What's more, a sizeable segment of the population must have been speaking Latin. Nevertheless, some believe that Romanization could - did - take place among peoples residing beyond the frontiers of the Empire. How that works is illustrated by the Latinism of Gothic and Western German languages: these provide a culturally graphic but linguistically shallow view. This access to a Latin linguistic environment is conceivable only within the Roman Empire. Many of those, who spoke a language related to Dacian lived within the Empire (but one cannot definitively include the Getae and Moesi because the Daco-Getan place names in their territory can also be attributed to later settlements). We also know - have observed - that the Romans have evacuated large populations from the left bank of the Danube (such as the resettlement projects of Aelius Catus, Plautius Silvanus). The majority of the people involved must have been speaking a language similar to Getan or Dacian. However, these relocations took place too early for the displaced - and dispersed - populations to have retained linguistic unity in a Latin and Greek environment (Plautius Silvanus relocated large populations from the left bank of the Lower-Danube in the 60's).

We know of only one Dacian speaking, Dacian-related ethnic group along the Lower-Danube which was relocated to the Roman Empire as a national entity: the Karps. A. Alföldi has been claiming for a long time that Dacia has been given up by the Romans as a result of attacks by the Karps: today we have archeological evidence attesting to Karp settlements in the abandoned former territories of the Province (Septér, Mezőszopor, Obrázsa). Prior to the official relinquishment of the Province, this settlement must have been impacted by strong Roman influence; this we can determine from Roman objects in Karp cemeteries. Once Dacia had been given up, the situation changed. The Karps had been enjoying an actual - or perceived - sense of security (guaranteed by the Romans) but in 295-297 Galerius leads a campaign against them, as a result of which the Karps are relocated within the Roman Empire. (Galerius) *Carporum ... gens ... devicta in Romanum solum translate est* (Irod. Rom. 299), *Carporum natio translate omnis in nostrum solum* (Aur. Vict. Caes. 39, 43), *Carporum gens universa in Romania se tradidit* (Cons. Const. ad a 295 - MGH IX. 230). Thus, various sources corroborate that the Karps were resettled within the Roman Empire in 295 (296 or 297?). We know that Galerius takes up the title of *Carpicus Maximus* six times (i.e. he defeated the Karps six times) but, thereafter, we hear no more about them. Although, Constantin the Great is *Carpicus Maximus* in 318-319, we believe, this title was bestowed on him for a successful campaign conducted against territories which had been former Karp settlements. We also believe that it is wrong to identify, on the basis of Zosimos (*Historia nova* IV, 34, 6), the *Karpodakai* with the Karps; the word is an acronym, made up of Carpathian and Dacian.

Some of the relocated Karps settled in Pannonia, others in Moesia Inferior, the province bordered by the Lower Danube. In Pannonia they left traces in the vicinity of Sopianae (as per Ammianus Marcellinus); Karp graves were found on Heténypuszta (Hungary) and in 368, they were mentioned as living in a settlement - *vicus Carporum* - in Moesia Inferior (Amm. Marc. 27, 5, 5). It may not require special emphasis that people settled "en bloc" within the Roman Empire at the end of the 3rd century, has greater opportunity to retain its national identity and its language than indigenous ethnic groups from the provinces. A majority among the latter must have been speaking - by then - the Empire's common and understandable language: Latin (or Greek in the East). Of the diverse groups of people speaking Dacian, the Karps were the ones with the opportunity to preserve their nationality within the Roman Empire. We can rest assured that they survived, and that the Albanians were their descendants. Albanians call themselves *shqip,* from Greek *skythés* (plural: *skythai*). In Latin: *scythes/scytha. Shqip* (Albanian) - if traced from *Scupi, Skopje, Shkup* - contradicts all phonetic laws (but this is how P. Skok saw it.) Balkan-Latin pronounces - *f* - instead of Greek δ , this we see on an inscription in Salona, where the Greek *Athenodóros* was written as *Afenodorus* (CIL III. 9178). In certain cases, the Rumanian equivalent of Alb. "*th*" (Greek Θ) is also -"*f*" and the same is the case with Arumun, which has fallen under strong Greek influence. In Balkan Latin (which - in view of Salona - includes Dalmatian Latin) Greek *skythés* must have been (gens) *scifa.* In this word the *f > p* change can be explained both in Albanian and Balkan Latin (Dr. *luptă* , Alb. *luftë,* Greek - although not significant - *Astivos,* Lat. **Astifus,* Alb. *Shtip).* In other words: the name by which contemporary Albanians call themselves, can be traced to the designation ´*Skytha*´; this was the name of a people living on the Northern shores of the Black Sea and the lower Danube; they were called by this name by the Romans as early as the beginning of the 1st century (Greek influence). This was also the name of Karps who migrated from Scythia (and probably of others as well). The Karps adopted this name in course of their cohabitation with Latin speakers and, as time went on, they took it as their own,- as present day Albanians. Since "Scythian" was used to describe only peoples living outside the Empire - along the Lower-Danube or in the vicinity of the Black Sea, - the ancestors of the Albanians must have migrated to the Empire from other parts. As we try to determine where they had lived together with Latin speaking peoples, our records suggest Pannonia and Moesia Inferior. We will, however, exclude Pannonia as a possibility in view of linguistic considerations which we will later enumerate. The idea of Albanian relocation from the left bank of the Danube has surfaced earlier. V. Pârvan thought so; he viewed the Albanians as Dacians. A. Philippide was another exceptional Rumanian researcher. He took the Albanians to be Pannonians - (I. I. Russu also considered this possibility, as his later writings reveal). As we observe the history of Balkan peoples prior to Roman occupation/expansion, it is unlikely that they could have retained their national identity and their language, but it is noteworthy that the Karps - with a 300 year leeway - survived as a people. This is of some significance in looking at the possible Romanization - within 150 years - of those Dacian natives who may have survived.

Based on the above observations, we can pinpoint the territory as Moesia Inferior where Albanians and Rumanians lived together between the Balkan-Mountains and the Danube, - at least in the 4th century. This coincides with data we have provided earlier about the Latin antecedents of the Rumanian language: its locus had to be east of a straight line south of Belgrade but, perhaps even further east than we presume. An additional dialect may have existed between this and its Dalmatian predecessor. This hypothetical - and temporary - dialect can only be placed in Moesia Superior (i.e. Dacia Ripensis and Mediterranea after 271). East of that territory, we are only left with Moesia Inferior - where Karps also left their mark in place-names. Taking note of Albanian, we find an explanation for the Bulgarian version of the river *Jantra* (which was known in antiquity as *Iatrus*) ; a nasal tone is being incorporated which is characteristic of Albanian (for example Lat. *mataxa*> Alb. *mendafshë*, etc). At the end of the 4th and through the 5th centuries - between the lower Danube and the Balkan-Mountains - those who spoke Latin and the descendents of resettled Karps fled South. The former locale of the ancestors of Albanians, can be determined through place names. *Niš* - in contemporary Serbian, instead of Latin Naissus, Naisus - can only be explained by Albanian mediation, and on the basis of the Dalmatian *a>e* change (Lat. *casa*> Dalm. *kesa* etc.) from a presumed late-Latin *Neisus*. Another place-name which was borrowed by Slavic via Albanian is Serbian *Štip* (Greek *Astibos*, Lat. *Astibo*). The *s* > *š* sound change and the omission of the unstressed *a-* at the beginning of a word (Lat. *amicus* > Alb. *mik*, etc.) can only be explained by Albanian. The word the Albanians adopted may have been *Astifus* in popular Latin. Thus, Albanians found refuge during the 5th century in the Morava-Vardar valley, from the region of the lower-Danube. This is where they had been living - until migrating Slavs settled here - perhaps in the 7th century; and it was there they came into connection with the Protoromance ancestor of Dalmatian.

Following the 6th century, the ancestors of the four contemporary Rumanian dialects (Danubian Rumanian, Arumun, Meglenorumanian, Istrorumanian) must have lived together in a narrow enclave. This could not have been in the Vardar-Morava Valley, in the immediate vicinity of Albanians living in occupied territory, nor could it be in the area between the lower-Danube and the Balkan-Mountains. In the latter event, there would have been many more words of Old-Slavonic derivation in Rumanian (such as *sută*, '100'; *stînă* -'sheepfold, pen') - but there are only a few of these. This period is characterized by linguistic changes noticeable in all four of the Rumanian dialects. The changes occurred during the post-Albanian and the pre-South-Slavic or Bulgarian period, i.e. after the 5th and prior to the 9th centuries. Included among linguistic changes is another modification of the sound system. Protorumanian changes unstressed Latin a to ă . Stressed - e - and - o - become diphthongs when followed by an a *(ă)* or e (Lat. *cera* - wax, Dr. *ceară* Ar. *țeară* , Istrorum. *čåra*; Lat. *mors, mortem* - 'death', Dr. Ar. Mr. *moarte*, Istr. *mortę*); *an* and *am* become *în, îm* (Lat. *manus* - hand, Dr. *mînă*; Lat. angelus - 'angel', Dr. *înger*; Lat. *campus* - meadow, Dr. *cîmp*). It is characteristic of the period that - *l* - becomes - *r* - (Lat. *filum* - 'thread', Dr. *fir*; Lat. *gula* - throat, Dr. *gură*; Lat. *sol* - sun, Dr. *soare*); *d, t, n, l,* and *s* preceding the original Latin *ī* and ĕ > *ie*, were palatized as a result of which a whole series of new sounds came into being [*dz (>z), t, n', l', ș*]. It is conceivable that the preservation of the masculine vocative (such as *bărbate*!) in Protorumanian occurred in this period, or in the following one. This is attributed to Slavic influence, as is the appearance of *h* in the sound system.

This period of the Rumanian language: the (6th) - 7th-8th centuries, is characterized by the development of the specifically Rumanian characteristics, with a very weak Slavic influence. In this period were transferred many of the words pertaining to religion of

Greek origin, those which, because of their sound pattern cannot have been borrowed later (Gr. *agiasma* "holy water", Dr. *agheasmă*; Gr. *akhathistos* "prayer", Dr. *acatist*; Gr. *kalogeros* "monk", Dr. *călugăr*). In all likelihood, the following were also borrowed during this period: Dr. *jur* "vicinity, area" (Gr. *gyros* 'circle'), Dr. *drum* "road" (Gr. *dromos* "running, field"), Dr. *stur* 'black-beard, cinder, icicle" (Gr. *stylos* "column"), etc. probably dates from the onset of this period which means that, during this era, Protorumanians drew nearer to the area where Greek was spoken. In other words, they migrated South, which would explain the dearth of Old Slavic words in Rumanian dialects. (It is worth noting that in both Rumanian and Albanian the presence of early, i.e. ancient Greek words is problematical. To be sure, there are many parallels in this respect between Rumanian and Albanian. Gr. *brotakhos*, Alb. *bretëk*, Dr. *broatec* "frog", etc. The same explanation might apply to Alb. *mokën*, *mokër*, Gr. *makhana* ´machine´ but the Alb. "millstone" may be an adapted Karp word from Pontus-Greek. This assessment will be validated if we hypothesize that the majority of Protorumanians ended up South of the Haemus (Balkan) Mountains. Another reference (also noted by th. Capidan) comes from the Arumun who have known since Antiquity, the names of Thessaloniké, Elasson (in Thessalia) and the Aóos river in Epirus: *Sărună*, *Lăsun*, *Băiasa* (although we may have a different explanation for the latter). On the basis of their sound pattern *(-l- > -r-, -on > -un)*, these place names must have existed in Arumanian from the 6th century on; thus, the speakers of Protorumanian in the 7th and 8th centuries must have been living in the vicinity of these territories, i.e., also in these territories. This actually means that the Rumanian language came into being from Latin spoken in that part of the Roman Empire where Greek was spoken.

This is also the territory to which the Slavic loanwords of Protorumanian, i.e. Common Rumanian, link us. Next to a negligible number of Old-Slavic words, we can identify a large number of Bulgarian - Slavic words which found their way into Rumanian. E. Scărlătoiu counts 307 "South-Slavic" words in Arumun; most of these also exist in the other Rumanian dialects. These words encompass the whole material and spiritual culture, referring to the following categories: 87 pertaining to material culture, 18 to agriculture and animal husbandry, 46 or 49 - cultivated plants, etc. (The different figures come from Scărlătoiu). As Rumanians integrated these words into their own language, the Old-Slavic ě became *ia, ea* (Dr. *mreană,* Ar. *mreană,* Mr. *mreancă* < Old Slavic *mrĕna* 'barbel', Dr. Ar. *hrean*<O.Sl. *hrĕnß* "horseradish", etc.) Ancient Slavic *tj, ktj, dj* changed to *şt, jd* (Dr. *maşteră* <Bulg. *mašteha* "stepmother"; Dr. *peşteră* Ar. *piştireaуă,* Mr. *peaştiră* <O. Sl. *peştera* 'cave' etc.). These sound patterns are Bulgarian, i.e. Lithurgical Slavic or Old Slavic. The dividing line between Ancient Slavic *tj, ktj, dj* and Bulgarian *št, žd* goes today (i.e., before the First World War, which changed the borders) through Vidin and Lake Ochrid. In antiquity, however, the situation was different. Even today, in the vicinity of Sofia Ancient Slavic ě is still being pronounced in the Serbian manner: *e* and not *ja* - as in other parts of Bulgaria. Our sources indicate that this Bulgarian - type Slavic existed originally only South of the Balkan-Mountains. Let us refer to Bulgarian *Arčar* (*Ratiaria* in antiquity) in which Latin *ti* turns into the *č* , (thus, Old Slavic *tj* changed to *ć* or *č,* not to *şt* as in Bulgarian). The early Transylvanian place names of Slavic origin have "Protoserbian"

characteristics: *Szelicse* and not *Szeliste* (see the remarks pertaining to the word: *Abrud*), as noted by J. Kniezsa. This leads us to the conclusion that contemporary (literary) Bulgarian - Slavic was originally spoken only South of the Balkan-Mountains; - the territory where ě, e, and *ja*, respectively, is pronounced may be closer to the original status of the language. The spread of 'Southernmost' Slavic may be explained by the strong influence of liturgical Slavic.

Linguistic data attest to the beginnings of the Rumanian language - during the time of the Empire - in Moesia Inferior. This is where Latin speakers co-habited with the Karps (forebears of Albanians), in the 4th-5th centuries. From here, during the Great Migration, they moved South of the Balkan-Mountain into territory where Greek was spoken. This is where Common Rumanian developed in the 7th-8th centuries, and where it lived on through a period of Bulgarian-Slavic influence in the 9th-10th (and 11th) centuries. Many of the well-known Balkanisms of the Rumanian language can be traced to exposure to Greek which may have started in Moesia Inferior and may have become even more prevalent in the area between the Balkan-Mountains and the Aegean Sea. We do not know what role the Latin spoken in Moesia Superior (i.e. in the two Aurelian Daciae and in Dardania) may have played in the development of Common Rumanian. A. Mócsy attempted to isolate the unique characteristics of Latin spoken in Moesia Superior but the attempt was futile. However, we know that Common Romanian did not preserve Latin ŭ (lat. *autŭmnus*, Dr., Ar., Mr. *toamnă*, Istr. *tomnę*) and that suggests that Balkan Latin's middle-dialect (the transitional dialect) also played a part in the development of the Rumanian language.

2. Data from topography and history: the testimony of the written sources.

The following sources will also provide data which are not specific to Rumanians only, since these people - known as *Vlah* - appear in written records fairly late; our earliest sources point to the end of the 10th century. However, there is circumstantial evidence pertaining to their presence in various areas of the Balkan Peninsula.

A reference to their early history lies in the poetic inscription of a grave in Lăžen (see above), part of which reads:

Ipso immargebam caro florente marito in quartum decimumque annum ... 'I died at the age of 14, in the flowering of my precious manhood'.

The meaning of the Latin *mergo* is "I sink," while *in-mergo* could be translated as "I dip, I dive". Yet, C. Daicoviciu is right in translating the text as "*Mergeam în (pe) anul al 14-lea*", i.e., "I departed at the age of 14." In this case we can pinpoint the locale of the change from Lat. *mergo* "I sink > Dr. *merge* "goes, departs", Alb. *mërgonj* "I remove". The finding was made along the river Asamus, today Osăm, Southwest of Novae (Svištov) in Moesia Inferior. The process which led to the formation of the Rumanian language may have begun here. Indications of this process may be seen not only in the change of meaning in *mergo*; in *immargebam* the *a* in place of *e* may be an error but, more likely, it points to a very early *a* > *ă* alteration (Alb. *mërgonj*). We find support for the hypothesis that the locus of the formation of the Rumanian language was in Moesia Inferior from the continued use of local place names: (*Almus-Lom, Ciabrus-Cibrica, Augusta-Ogosta, Oescus-Iskar, Utus-Vit, Asamus-Osăm, Jatrus-Jantra*). This adoption /

preservation of place names resembles the Pannonian experience which, however, does not mean that the Latin language continued to survive in these parts.

In chronological order, the next period which provides us with data is 553-555. We have Prokopios's writings describing the building program of Justinian (Peri ktismatón). It is common knowledge that this work lists a great many fortifications which have Latin names. These also include names with characteristics of the type of Latin from which the Rumanian language subsequently developed. First, among them is *Skumbro*, located in the Remesiana area (Bela Palanka, Serbia) (Procopius, De Aedificiis IV, 4). In antiquity, Vitoša was known as *Scombrus mons*; this was the site of Prokopius' *Skumbro* fortification. This name cannot be seperated from *Scombrus*. However, in Rumanian, Latin ŏ, ō changes before *n, m* + consonant to *u* . (Lat. *bonus* ´good´, D. r. *bun*, etc.). Instead of *Scombrus* (as a place name, ablativus case) *Scumbro* stands out, with its characteristic Rumanian sound change. Along the Istros (Danube), in Moesia, we find the place name *Gemellomuntes*. We do not know where this "twin peak" was situated, but - according to Beševliev - it would be the *Kalvomuntis*, located between Marcianopolis and Anchialos. At any rate, we must look for it in the Balkan Mountain range. *Muntes* reflects a late Latin form in contrast to the traditional Latin *montes* (cf. D.r. *munte, munţi*). Although according to the sound changes in Rumanian, one would expect *munţi*, rather than *muntes* (Italian *monti* is a similar *per analogiam* popular Latin construction of the plural), but this does not alter the fact that *on* + consonant changes in Rumanian (and in Rhetoromance) to *un*. Accordingly, *Gemellomuntes* is a Protoromance form which can be viewed as preceding Common Rumanian. In addition to this location, Prokopios lists *Asilva* (= *Ad silvam*) and *Fossaton* (*Fossatum*), (Procopius, *De aedificiis* IV., 11).

Our next reference has less substantiation. In the province of Haemimons of the Hadrianapolis District (Balkan Mountains), we find a fortress by the name of *Tzitaetus*. A. Philippide assumes the name might come from the Lat. *civitas vetus*, but we may also consider a misspelled *Tzitateus* (>*Tzitaetus*). *Tzitateus* might be a Latinized *citate* ´cultivated´, from *citate-us*, which is the equivalent of the D.r. *cetate* "castle" (Lat. *civitas*, *civitatem*). Here, too, we find the type of Protoromance which preceded Common Rumanian.

A map will reflect that the Rumanian - sounding locations listed by Prokopius can be found in the Balkan Mountain-region and, - in the case of Haeminons - in its Southern area. We should add that in the surroundings of the above mentioned names, two fortifications named *Fossaton* appear (cf. Lat. *fossatum*, Dr. *sat*, Alb. *fshat*, "fortification, village".

It is safe to conclude that a late-Latin language was spoken in the Balkan Mountains and its Southern slopes which was the precursor of Rumanian; this occurred during the first half of the 6th century - probably during the reign od Justinian: 527-567. This must have been the environment and the period which marks the linguistic evolution of Latin to Rumanian, i.e. Protorumanian. This mountain range must have contributed to the development of nomadic sheepherding. At the time, this was practiced by isolated Thracian groups but later it became a characteristic manner of sheepherding for Rumanians. Incidentally, even several hundred years later, the Arumun herded their sheep from Greece to the pasture land of the Balkan Mountain-range. Not surprisingly, for this type of sheepherding there are old Slavic words in the Rumanian language (*stînă*, ´sheepfold, pen´, *stăpîn* ´farmer/master´, etc.). The ancestors of the Rumanians may have met here the remnants of various Balkan groups which maintained a similar lifestyle. The Bessus comes to mind about whom we have references dating back to the 6th century and whose language must have supplied those "autochtone" Rumanian words which have no equivalent in Albanian.

Some decades later, we find another reference to the ancestors of the Rumanians at the Southern end of the Balkan Mountain-range. In the war of 587-588, which followed an Avar raid, Komentiolos - a Byzantine commander - leads his armies from Marcianopolis to the Eastern Balkan Mountains, in the vicinity of the Kamčija river. As Theophylaktos Simokatta writes in Historia II, 15, 3-9:

'They took off from the Haimos toward Kalvomuntis and Lividurgon ... they notice the kagan .... whose tents were put up some four miles away .... multitudes of his peoples spread over Thracia. Komentiolos ... ordered them to go to Astike ... However, fate ruled otherwise ... a pack animal threw off his burden ... those behind him called to his master and told him to turn around and take care of his animal ... this upset the orderliness of the march ... Many echoed the sentence - as they heard it ... they kept yelling about retreat and told each other in their mother tongue (ἐπιχωρίω γλώττη) to turn around: "*torna, torna ...* " (Translated into Hungarian by S. Szádeczky-Kardoss - T. Olajos). We find a similar story in the writings of Theophanes Confessor (Chronographia); his text quotes "*torna, torna phrater*" ("a pack animal divested itself of its burden whereupon another man spoke to the animal's owner in his native tongue (πατρώα φωνή: "*torna,*

torna frater". The story clearly indicates that the loss of order among the marchers was caused by someone speaking in a "native tongue" (ἐπιχωρίω γλώττη) calling on the one ahead of him to turn around; some soldiers thought a command was given to retreat. (In the Byzantine Army the language of command was Latin: *cede, sta, move, transforma*, etc.). D.r. *turna* means today ´to pour, to pour out; to cast´ but, earlier, it also meant ´to turn around´. Undoubtedly, Latin was the language of the soldier who created chaos; a Latin spoken in the area. It is also certain that it carried the seeds of Protorumanian; Komentiolos' army marches from the Balkan Mountain region toward *Kalvomuntis* (´bald mountain´) the sound pattern of this name indicate antecedents of the Rumanian language. To be sure, *muntis* is the ablative plural of *monti* - a frequent occurrence in place-names; and *on > un* is also characteristic of Rumanian tonal. This place name has a Rumanian - more accurately: Protorumanian - character in both regarding its sound pattern and its structure, and there can be no doubt that the inhabitants of this region were Protorumanians. This region is the Southern part of the Balkan-Mountains. Although according to V. Beševliev, Kalvomuntis lies on the road leading from Marcianapolis to Ankhialos, this is most improbable (at best, Gemellomuntes could have been located thereabouts), because Komentiolos' army is moving from the Balkan-Mountain region toward Astiké, which lies between Plovdiv and Drinapole. Therefore, Kalvomuntis must be located South of the Balkan Mountain-ridge, as also corroborated by other parts of the narrative to which we referred.

At the beginning of the Protorumanian era, around 600, the ancestors of the Rumanians lived South of the Eastern Balkan Mountain region - in and around today's Bulgaria. Because of the

Protorumanian characteristics of *Kelvomuntis*, this era began most probably in the mid-sixth century, around 550.

For the next few centuries, we have only sporadic and unvalidated information pertaining to Protorumanian places of residence. An anonymous writer of the 7th century, whose notes were preserved in the monastery of Kastamonitu (on the island of Athos) is writing about the era of the destruction of paintings (717-843). According to his notations, in the 8th century, Bulgaria was occupied by the *Rhékinos,* the *Blakhorékhinos* and the *Sagudateos.* Advancing further, they took possession of Macedonia and reached *Athos*, the holy mountain, where they were baptized by the monks. Given the late date of the reference we cannot vouch for its accuracy but, it is likely, that the author relied on earlier sources. Earliest note of the Sagudateos - Saguditae - at the Southern region of the Balkan Peninsula is taken at the beginning of the 7th century in connection with "The miracles of Saint Demetrius" (recorded in Thessalonika). In the Kastamonitu text, we find a reference to *Blakhorékhinos*; in accordance with the characteristics of such compound words, it refers to Vlaks who live at the Rhékios-river. Accordingly, we are told of Vlahs who were found in the 7th century along the Rhékios river, flowing East of Thessalonika. In light of other pertinent data we have this is by no means impossible. The Greek word *Blakhos,* - of Southern Slavic origin, designates Rumanians. The *Volcae* were a Celt tribe. Their German name, *Walho-*, was originally the name used for Celts in the Roman Empire; later it designated Romans. Eventually, it became the name by which Neo-Latin peoples were known. When the word reached the Slavs it had the latter meaning. They used it for

Italians and Rumanians (Bulg. *Vlah,* Serbo-Croat *Vlah* 'Rumanian', Hung. *Oláh,* Kaj-Croat. *Vlah,* Slovenian *Vlah, Lah,* Czech *Vlach,* Pol. *Wlóch* 'Italian', cf. Hung. *olasz* 'Italian'.

There are placenames in northern Greece (*Sărună, Lăsun, Flărina,* etc) which have been preserved since the time of antiquity. These, as well as other data, help to establish the presence of Protorumanians in the Southern region of the Balkan Peninsula during the 7th and 8th centuries.

We have already noted that the Rumanian language contains few words of Old-Slavic origin, and lacks entirely Bulgaro-Turkish words. The North-East region of today's Bulgaria was occupied in 681 by the Bulgarians of Asparukh; their subsequent expansion into other territories does not alter the fact that their home base remained to the North of the Balkan Mountains. The absence of words from their language in Protorumanian suggests that the latter must have lived quite a ways South of the Balkan Mountains. An additional indication: in the Rumanian language no trace is left of the Latin name of the Danube, which was *Danuvius.* If this had been inherited, it should be today in Rumanian **Dînui,* yet the Danube is called *Dunăre* in Rumanian. Although there are those who assume a Dacian *Donaris* (from this, *Dunăre* could really result), from which it would originate, this name is not recorded in the sources. We have evidence that the original inhabitants of the lower-Danubian region (including the Dacians) called this river by the name *Istros.* Even if the ancestors of the Rumanians had been in contact with the Dacians, their language should have retained the Latin name of the river.

Contemporary names for the Danube (*Donau, Dunav, Dunaj, Duna*) eventually lead us to the Gothic *Dōnaws*, which was mentioned around 400 as *Dunawis* (Pseudo-Caesarius Nazianzus). Iordanes recorded *Nedao*, which is the same name: *Denaw- Donaw*, with metathesis. From Gothic *Donaw-*, Slavic *Dunavĭ* developed regularly. Yet, in most Slavic languages - Bulgarian and Serbian excepted - *Dunaj (Dunajĭ)* became universal. Geography connects it to the Bulgaro-Turkish *Dunag;* Turkish and Bulgaro-Turkish words do not usually end in -v ; thus the - γ - ending. In the Petcheneg and Cuman languages the word became *Dunaj.* This is the root Rumanian *Dunăre*, since - in that language - j frequently turns into r: e.g. Hung. *tolvaj* > Dr. *tîlhar;* Hung. *melegágy* "hotbed">Dr. *melegar,* Dr. *are* "he/she has" cf. <*aït, aiure(a)*< *alīubī* "elsewhere"; *speria* < *expavēre* "to scare", etc. Presumably, Dr. *maşteră* < Bulg. *mašteha* belong to this group.

We presume that Rumanian *Dunăre* is of Cuman origin (an analogous fit among nouns ending in -*ea*). As such, it cannot possibly pre-date the 12th century. The Latin name of the Danube became extinct in Rumanian which suggests that the ancestors of the Rumanians, the Protorumanians, must have lived quite a distance from the Danube because even those who did not live close to great rivers, usually knew their name. We can safely assume that Protorumanians were staying far from the Danube also at the time of their Southern-Slavic contacts in the 9th, 10th and 11th centuries; otherwise their language would have borrowed the Bulgarian version of the Danube: *Dunav.* This again implies that the ancestral home of the Protorumanians must have been in the Southern area of the Balkan Peninsula; which also is in accordance with the records in Kastamonitu.

A certain reference from the 9th century also pinpoints the vicinity of Thessalonike. It is common knowledge that an apostle of Slavs, Konstantin-Cyrill, created the Glagolitic alphabet, wherein he used for the f - sound - (which the Slav language lacked) the Greek φ and θ. However, in the Greek language, θ never was used for the f sound. But it was used for this sound in Balkan Latin just as - th - in Arumun sounds as - f . Therefore, it is safe to assume that, when Konstantin developed the Glagolitic alphabet, he considered the Protorumanian dialect from the area of Saloniki (his home base). Consequently, many Rumanians must have been living in the Thessalonike-region in the 9th century.

The first mention of Vlahs (Rumanians) is from 976. In his *Synopsis Historiarum*, Ioannes Skylitzes writes that David, brother of Samuel, who later became Tsar of the Bulgarians, was murdered by a "Vlah coachmen" (*Blakhoi hoditai*) between Kastoria, Prespa and *Kalas drys* ('Beautiful Oaks'). This event is to have taken place in the area where the borders of contemporary Macedonia, Albania, and Greece converge. At this time, Vlahs could be found in large numbers in Northern Greece. In 980 the Byzantine Emperor, Basileios II. named one Nikulitzas to be the "arkhon" of the Vlahs who lived in the Hellas (administrative area) - thema, the seat of which was Larissa. In 1020 the Emperor establishes an archbishopric at Ohrida (the Moldavian and Muntenian church remains under its jurisdiction until 1767!) which will have jurisdiction over the Vlahs of "all Bulgaria". At this time Bulgaria was under Byzantine domination. Skopje was the seat of the territory. Its major towns were: Strumitza, Prilep, Prizren, Ohrida, Kastoria, Štip, Niš and Serdica. Today, these can be found in Serbia's

Southern and Bulgaria's Western region. Given the data at our disposal it is unlikely that Vlahs would have inhabited the Northern districts (themas) of Bulgaria at the time (10th century). Nevertheless, as they were free to roam, they could well have migrated Northward: the Byzantine Empire's expansion on the Balkan Peninsula, created conditions favourable to exploration. In 1095, a Vlah named Pudilos (Slavic *Budilo*) reported to emperor Alexios Komnenos, who was camping near Ankhialos that the Cumans crossed the Danube; these Cumans were guided by Vlachs across the Balkan Mountain passes. Thus, Vlachs can be found by the end of the 11th century on the Northern slopes of this mountain range.

The speedy Northward expansion of Rumanians is noted by Kekaumenos (Strategicon) in the 11th century. His chronicle is often cited as one of the pieces of evidence substantiating the Rumanians' Dacian origin. This Byzantine official wrote (translated to Hungarian by M. Gyóni): "the race of the Vlachs is an altogether unreliable and corrupt group ... they fell into captivity after Emperor Trajan defeated and vanquished them; even their emperor was slaughtered. His name was Dekebalos and the Romans exhibited his head on a spear in the center of the town. These people are the so-called Dacians and Bessos. Earlier, they had been living near the Danube and Saos rivers, which we now know as the Savas, where the Serbs live in a fortified and inaccessible location. Relying on this haven, they pretended friendship for the Romans and submissiveness toward their late emperors, but they went off from their fortifications to plunder Roman provinces. Therefore, the Romans took umbrage and, as I said before, set out to destroy them. Thus, they left the area they inhabited and spread all over Epeiros and Macedonia, but the majority settled in Hellas."

Kekaumenos does, indeed link Vlachs and Dacians to events which occurred in 1066, and links them also to the Bessus, (Bessos) a Dacian tribe living in the Balkan Mountains. However, he does not know where the Dacian country was; he places them in the vicinity of the Sava river. This linkage cannot be attributed to Kekaumenos describing the Aurelian Dacian provinces south of the Danube because these were East of the habitation of Serbs at the time. Nor can it be assumed that the Thessalian Arumun would have retained traditions from origins pointing to the Dacia located on the right banks of the Danube - (so states A. Mócsy in his latest writings). Kekaumenos links Vlachs, Dacians and Bessi in accordance with the Byzantine custom of giving names used in antiquity to contemporary peoples. But why would specifically Vlachs from the Larissa region be identified with Dacians and the Bessi? It is easier to find an explanation for identification with the latter. Kekaumenos records that Thessalian Vlachs tended their sheep in the mountains of Bulgaria between April and September; this is the earliest written record of transhumant sheepherding, and it was known that the Bessi lived in the mountain region of Bulgaria in ancient times. The identification with the Dacians must have been for different reasons. We assume this had to do with Vlach shepherds who, by then, reached Serbian-inhabited areas near the Sava river. (One of the routes of nomadic sheepherding leads from Thessaly by way of Skopje to Serb-inhabited territory along the Ibar river.) This group of people could not be linked to the Bessi; another source of identification had to be found. Kekaumenos chose Dacians. In all probability the similarity between

Blakhoi and *Dakai* (in contemporary Greek pronounciation) had to do something with it. This done, the only thing left for Kekaumenos to do was, to share all the negative information about Dacians which he interpreted in the context of his limited education. According to him, the Vlachs reached Serbia by the second half of the 11th century in the same manner as they moved north of the Balkan Mountains during this period.

Thereafter, we hear of them in the vicinity of the Danube with increasing frequency. In 1164, they capture Kommenos Andronikos near Halics, (where he is trying to flee) in the Danube delta. Their settlements in the Balkan Mountains become gradually permanent. In his "Historia" Niketas Kloniates notes (in relation to the events of the establishment of the II. Bulgarian Tsardom in 1185) that Isaakios Angelos II. enraged the Barbarians residing in the Balkan Mountains with tax levies; these were the people "who had been called the Mys at an earlier time but now they are known as Vlachs". We know that, between Braničevo and Niš, Greeks, Bulgarians, Serbs and Vlachs attack the crusaders of Frederick Barbarossa in 1189. Also, from 1198-99, to the middle of the 15th century, the official documents of Serb Kings repeatedly refer to the Vlachs living in their country; and there still are many placenames of Rumanian origin in the territory of the Serbian kingdom.

All this does not imply that in those days the Vlachs of the Balkan peninsula were purely Rumanians. True, the Vlachs serving in the Byzantine army are described as the descendents of early settlers from Italy; so says Ioannes Kinnamos, as he writes about the 1167 campaign of the Byzantine Emperor, Manuel, against the Hungarian king, Géza II. However, at the turn of the 11th century, Anna Komnéné claims that all those who maintain a nomadic lifestyle are called *Vlachs* in everyday language. The majority of personal names they used during the period were also Slavic. Nevertheless, some differentiation must have existed among the Vlachs, which is borne out by the comment of Presbyter Diocleatis (Regnum Slavorum) around 1160-1170. He writes that "Bulgarians occupied the entire province of the Latin-s; once upon a time, they were called Romans, but now they are known as Morovlachs i.e. Black Vlachs". (However, it is most likely that, in this case, they refer to "Byzantine Vlachs": *Morovlachi* derives by metathesis from the original *Rhomaioblakhoi*).

Our data make it clear that the framework for the northward migration of Vlachs was created by the Byzantine recapture of the Balkan Peninsula up to the Danube; part of their pasture-land shifted to the southern portion of the Carpathians. This was the result of conditions for the Bulgarian-Vlach-Cuman coexistence in the 2nd Bulgarian Tsardom (which was established in 1185-86). From there on, their appearance within the Carpathian Basin was only a matter of time. However, in the 13th century only small groupings, sporadic settlements were to be found within the Kingdom of Hungary, as revealed by the decree from 1290 of the King of Hungary, András III (see above). The story of the Vlachs' extensive migration into the area is part of the history of later centuries and parallels the period when they disappeared from Serbian territory. Some settled on the Istrian Peninsula.

Historical data indicate that the Latin-speaking population fleeing Moesia Inferior became "Rumanian" in Northern Greece, South of the Balkan Mountain-range, on the banks of the Aegean Sea. Starting with the 11th century, there is a Northward migration in groups of ever-

216

increasing size. As a result of this migration, the unified Rumanian language is divided into four dialects towards 1200 AD; the historical data are in accordance with the conclusions drawn from the study of the Rumanian language.

Notes:

  [1] - denotes the letter *e* or *o* with a dot under it

  [2] - denotes the letter *o* with a right curling tail under it similar to *Ĭ*

(These symbols could not be created by any Font set at the editor's disposal)

Chapter VI

Dacians, Romans, Rumanians

It may not be necessary to reiterate all the conclusions we reached on the basis of the evidence examined in previous chapters. We only have "negative" data pertaining to the Romanization of the multi-ethnic, multi-lingual indigenous population of the Dacian Kingdom. Therefore, we cannot even hypothetically discuss Daco-Roman continuity. Our sources also revealed that the Latin spoken in Dacia could not have been the forerunner of the Rumanian language but it could well have been the basis of Dalmatian. Yet, historical data preclude this possibility. Of course, we do not claim that no single Dacian Roman could have become part of Rumanian ethnogeny, but a Sarmatian or Germanic individual could have done the same thing. Specific cases can be examined historically but they will prove the exception, rather than the rule.

As we could see, there were frequent population exchanges within the territory of the former Dacian Kingdom, or Roman Province in the 270's, 370's, 450's and probably, something similar occurred in the 890's. Yet, these movements do not support the survival of an earlier population, even if we were to assume that this might be the case. There is no ground for such assumptions. The geographical designations of the former Dacia do not include a single Roman place name and, the Rumanians who settled here in the Middle Ages, adopted the overwhelming majority of their waterway and place-names from Hungarians, Slavs and even Saxons (excepting a few insignificant waterways and names of villages which were late settlements). This could not have come about, had they been continuous residents of the region from Roman times. One can try to refute the evidence reflected by place names (such as claiming "they were translated") but to translate the names of waterways and place names which have no meaning is not only not customary but also impossible.

Let us assume that - contrary to all data at our disposal - a Romanized population continued to exist on Dacian territory during the period of the Great Migrations, who would have been the ancestors of Rumanians. In this case, we would find in contemporary Rumanian a large number of words of Germanic (Gothic and Gepida) as well as of Turkish (Avar and Bulgarian, later Petcheneg and Cuman) words. Furthermore, these words would have to be present in at least as large numbers as those which the Rumanian language shares with Albanian. Yet, such are not found, which is illustrated by the unsuccessful attempts of K. Gamillscheg, who tried to show Old Germanic words in the Rumanian language. Especially striking is the absence of Cuman words; this suggests that Cumans were no longer present in large numbers in the territory by the time Rumanians arrived in significant numbers. This happened in the period following the Tartar invasion, thus the settlement of a substantive number of Rumanians north of the Danube can be traced to the second half of the 13th century.

We are left with negative data regarding the survival of Romanism in the former Roman territory of Dacia. However, a wide variety of data exists to substantiate how the ancestors of Rumanians evolved into a nation in the southern region of the Balkan Peninsula. We also ascertained that the ancestors of the Rumanians did have some links with Dacians; they did live together for some time with their tribal kin, the Karps, in the area between the lower-Danube and the Balkan Mountains. The Rumanian and Albanian languages constitute proof of this earlier intermingling. Latin-speaking Romans from Moesia Inferior who were the ancestors of Rumanians inhabited a territory, the original population of which spoke Geta: a language related to Dacian. Thus, a connection between Dacians and Rumanians does exist, but it is a tenuous connection. Therefore a link can be acknowledged but under no circumstances does this support Daco-Roman or Daco-Rumanian continuity. The humanistic theory of such continuity belongs to the history of science.

Nevertheless, we realize that this humanistic theory - and the sequels that followed - is not likely to be soon discarded. There will be those who will continue to consider Anonymus an authentic and reliable source. Likewise, credit will be given to the reference in Russian annals, pertaining to ancient history, wherein white Ugrians (*Ugri bělii*) chased the "Volochs" from the land of the Danubian Slavs. They will fail to note that this confusing story in Russian annals speaks of 'Norici' (*Norci*). These Norici are described as Slavs. It is true that these Slavs were attacked by the Voloch (Romans). If white Ugrians drove them away they must have been Huns, considering the modernized use of names employed by this source. From this same source we also hear of Hungarians (*Ugri*) chasing out Volochs at the time when they conquered the territory. We believe this assumption is based on the tendency to link a well-known event to a similar name. Analysts of historical data know of many such examples. Thus, the existence of Rumanians along the Danube during the period of the Hungarian Conquest was not mentioned by late-Russian chronicles.

Facts can be misrepresented through rationalization but they nevertheless remain facts. Even if we are reluctant to acknowledge them.

Bibliography and Comments

There are distinct difficulties related to research on a subject which has been neglected by the local scientific establishment during the past 40 years. (While Hungary was under Communist rule - translator). When the difficulty is compounded by limited resources, the outcome will be somewhat uneven. The recent publication (Budapest, 1986) of *Erdély Története* (The History of Transylvania) was of great assistance; in the first volume, there are several thematic references to the subject covered by this study. This enabled us to omit from this writing a detailed review of Dacia's history; *E. Tóth* provided a detailed summary of the subject in the History of Transylvania (although it lacks a more detailed description of Dacia Inferior, later Dacia Malvensis). Unfortunately, the same cannot be said with regard to source material pertaining to the Dacian Kingdom. On this subject, no comprehensive work has been done in Hungary since 1942 (*A. Alföldi*: Zur Geschichte des Karpatenbeckens im I. Jahrtausendes v. Chr. AECO VIII. 1942). In his later writings, Alföldi reiterated the views expressed in his major work of 1942. Subsequent studies left many questions unanswered, warranting a more detailed analysis of the Dacian Kingdom in this work. A great deal has been written about the period of the Great Migrations to which this work referred only insofar as it is related to the question of Daco-Roman continuity. We did take great care to describe the development of ethnic relations within Dacia.

Due to aforementioned reasons, this book does not include a review of the contemporary bibliography of the subject, as it would have to encompass Rumanian archeological and historical research and ethno-linguistics, as well. Readers with expertise in certain aspects of our study will have observed that we did not follow up on some hypotheses, such as E. Gamillscheg's theory regarding Rumanian "tribal territories". He uses dialectal manifestations to establish the continuum of Romanism where Rumanian is spoken today on the territory in the vicinity of the Danube. The flaws in this theory were pointed out at the time by *L. Gáldi* ("Zur frage des Rumänischen Kerngebiets in Siebenbürgen" AECO VIII. 1942). - We were unable to present a detailed analysis of the Blacks, or Volochs, who are mentioned in the gesta of Anonymous and in Russian annals, respectively. However, such a discussion seemed dispensable since these were not contemporary sources whose reports had already been subjected to research-scrutiny. Nevertheless, at some future time, we plan to re-examine that material, as well. We would also like to note that we did not report in detail on already established arguments disputing the theory of continuity, other than providing a summary in the section of the book which reports on existing research on the subject. Among these is the allegiance of Danubian Rumanians to the Orthodox Church - from late-Roman times on - this also establishes their long historical presence in the Byzantine Empire.

L. Tamás provided a significant overview of the theory of continuity from a perspective of the Middle Ages and the Renaissance . *"Romains, Romans et Roumains dans l'histoire de la Dacie Trajane"*

(Romans, Rumanians and Vlachs' in Trajan's Dacia) (Budapest, 1935 - AECO II. 1936). This work encompasses the whole subject and is the last comprehensive Hungarian work in this area. The value of L. Tamás's study is somewhat diminished by his excessive criticism of N. Drăganu's work (*N. Drăganu: Românii în veacurile IX-XIV pe baza toponimiei şi a onomasticei*, Bucureşti, 1933), which induces the author to some exaggerations. A. *Philippide* (Originea romînilor, I., Iaşi, 1925) provides an extensive overview of research done on the origins of Rumanians. *I.I. Russu* has reviewed the pertinent bibliography (*Etnogeneza românilor*, Bucureşti, 1981). Russu is prepared to make sharply-worded observations; calling Gergely Moldován "a Rumanian renegade" characterizes his viewpoint. (He describes Lajos Tamás "a Schwabian renegade"). Nowadays, such an approach sounds distinctly odd, even coming from Russu. His data reflect concerted effort, though. - A. *Armbuster* undertook to create a definitive study of the subject (*Romanitatea românilor*, Bucureşti, 1972). A partially revised sequel is: *La romanité des Roumains*; Bucureşti, 1977). This is a useful historiography but his conclusions are wrong because they do not follow from the facts exposed in the book. He claimed the awareness of Roman origin permeated Rumanian consciousness; this view was already challenged by C. Daicoviciu. - In addition to the above-mentioned works, there were many papers which aided this writer. Among Hungarian contributors we would like to mention L. Gáldi's numerous studies.

The chapter about the Dacians is novel in structure and concept; the reasons are simple. They include the realization that, in its study of the period, Rumanian historical analysis was focused on the concept of continuity. Consequently, there was a tendency to disregard self-evident historical conclusions (such as the relationship between Dacians and Iranian-speaking peoples - Scythians, Sarmatians - and what the consequences of such relationships might have been. The review and assessment of this period by Hungarians was not without error, either. This may have been due to Hungarian researchers' reliance on the work done by A. Alföldi, whose extensive studies on the subject were adopted without adequate familiarity with original references. The same also applies to the latest Hungarian treatise on the subject (A. Mócsy: "The Dacian Kingdom" (in: *History of Transylvania*, I. Budapest 1986) he paints with too broad a brush. - V. Párvan's Getica is a seminal work in its summary of source material pertaining to the period and so is *Istoria Romîniei* (Bucureşti, 1960) which lists sources not found in earlier works. In comparison, *I. H. Crişan* presents no new insights in: *Burebista şi epoca sa*, (Bucureşti 1977). Other studies were also published on the Age of Burebista, but they are mostly a collection of texts about Celts. On the other hand *H. Daicoviciu's* work: *Dacia de la Burebista la cucerirea romană* (Cluj, 1972) makes full use of all known sources, - but without breaking new ground-except on minor points. A. Mócsy provides a useful guide to the early history of the Dacians, utilizing Patsch's hindsight, but offering little that is new in *Die Vorgeschichte Obermösiens im hellenistisch - römischen Zeitalter* (The history of Upper-Moesia in the Greek-Roman period). The same can be said about most of the latest literature on the subject (C. Patsch, M. Macrea).

Fortunately, this writer has been exploring this period for decades; a condensed version of the chapter on pre-history is included in Vol. I. of the History of Transylvania under the heading "Prehistory of Transylvania". *A. Vulpe's* work presents a basically similar outlook - although differing in parts - in Die Geto-Daker, Geschichte eines Jahrtausends vor Burebista (Dacia 31, 1987). This is already a response to certain data presented in the History of Transylvania. Also noted: *V. Dumitrescu-A. Vulpe: Dacia înainte de Dromihete* (Bucureşti, 1988). - Some of our research on early Dacia and the Burebista or Boirebistas-age exists in manuscript form. This unpublished work on the Carpathian Basin prior to Roman occupation is known and used in Hungary as an integral part of the literature pertaining to this period. Our paper on the Prehistory of Transylvania has evolved from the above material.

Research of the period has failed to note that the Kingdom of Dacia came about as the result of an organized military establishment and independently of ethnic factors. *G. Widengren* develops the "Männerbund" concept in: "Le symbolisme de la ceinture." *Iranica Antiqua* 8, 1968. In addition, *A. Alföldi* writes about this in his work on the Carpathian Basin (mentioned earlier) and in "The Age of Rome; Budapest in Antiquity" (*History of Budapest*, I. - Budapest 1942). This theme recurs also in other papers, the subject of which is Dacia but he fails to see the essential issue. Boirebistas is connected to the Bastarnae not only by his name but also due to a certain sequential logic. This is not negated by the circumstance that his Kingdom was established in a territory where Dacian was spoken - or a language akin to Dacian. The language of the Bastarnae is not known today, nor can it be reconstructed but we can ascertain that it had nothing to do with Dacian. Notwithstanding the differences in comparative structure and size, an apt analogy may be the Kingdom of the Franks - who ruled over the Gauls. Our text may not have sufficiently established that Boirebistas must have been an "allied soldier" in the army of Eupatór Mithridates. This may explain a great deal about Dacian governmental infrastructure, including the foreign sounding - Armenian? - name of the capital.

C. *Daicoviciu* developed a review of the period under study based on a large volume of source material ("Dakien and Rom in der Prinzipatzeit" from *Aufstieg und Niedergang der römischen Welt*, II; 6 - Berlin-New York 1977). His previous works should not be neglected, either; of special interest is *Dacica* (Cluj, 1969), a collection of his more significant works.

Although written in 1893-4 (Vienna) *W. Tomaschek's: Die alten Thraker* I-II (Ancient Thracians) is still a useful reference on the Dacian language, and other circumstances. His *Les restes de la langue dace* (Muséon, Louvain 1883) is a seminal work. - *D. Dečev* collected much of the source material in *Die thrakischen Sprachreste* (Vienna, 1957). *Xarakteristika na trakijskija ezik - Charakteristik der thrakischen Sprache*, (Sofia, 1952) in which he shows, for the first time, the AMTA features in the Thracian language. Another work of his deals with Dacian plant-names: *Die dakischen Pflanzennamen* (Godišnik Sofijskija universitet, istor - filol. fakultet. XXIV, I. 1929). *I. I. Russu* also explores the Dacian language: *Limba traco-dacilor* (Bucureşti, 1959) - *Die Sprache der Thraco-Daker* (Bucureşti, 1969).

Regrettably, his work reflects the (old) viewpoint, according to which the Dacian and Thracian languages are connected. Much of Russu's etymology is quite improbable, yet he tends to be very critical toward other researchers' work. The *Introduction to the History of the Indo-European Languages* is the last detailed study done by *V. Georgiev* (Sofia, 1981). It encompasses his earlier findings, which appeared in: *Trakijskijat ezik* and "Albanisch, Dakisch- Mysisch und Rumänisch" (*Linguistique Balkanique* 2, 1960). - *C. Poghirc* developed a thorough study in: *Considerations linguistiques sur l'ethnogenèse palèobalkanique* (RÉSEE XIV - 2, 1976) and his other papers are also noteworthy. - *J. Hubschmid* extols the same theories as Georgiev in "Substrate in Balkansprachen" (in: *Kultur Südosteuropas, ihre Geschichte und ihre Ausdruckformen* (Culture of Southeastern-Europe, her history and modes of expression, *Südosteuropa-Schriften* 6, 1964). - I did not know how to assess *G. Reichenkron's* collected articles: *Das Dakische (rekonstruiert aus dem Rumänischen)* (Heidelberg, 1966), (i.e. The Dacian language - reconstructed from Rumanian) - this title reflects his methodology. Reichenkron - who was E. Gamillscheg's pupil - assumes that the Rumanians are the successors of the Dacians. When he encounters Rumanian words of unknown etymology, he attempts to create Dacian words through the use of reconstructed radicals. It seems unnecessary to provide examples.

C. *Váczy* contributed a detailed analysis of Dacian plant-names: "Nomenclatura dacică a plantelar la Dioscorides şi Pseudo-Apuleius" (*Acta Musei Napocensis* V-VI; VIII-IX, 1968-72), with an extensive bibliography. The significance of this work is that it corrects earlier, erroneous plant definitions; it has only limited applicability in linguistics.

V. Georgiev and his followers share my theory about the Dacian language. Yet, even though every one has been treating linguistic material pertaining to the Dacian language as one unit, I strongly believe that we have clear evidence of several languages. This is also more logical historically, since on Dacian territory there were also a large number of Celts. Other groups have also lived there but their identification is more difficult.

We cannot list all Indo-Germanistic works and papers which we consulted as this book was being written but, we do want to single out *P. Kretschmer's* still valid study: *Einleitung in die Geschichte der griechishen Sprache.* Göttingen, 1896) (Introduction to the history of the Greek Language). - The literature of Daco-Albanian relations (and references to the Albanians' more original, Northern residence) includes several noteworthy works. In 1925 *J. Melich* published (in Budapest): *Hungary at the time of the Conquest*, where he wrote that the names of *Abrud* and *Ompoly* may have been transferred into Hungarian directly from Dacian. Because of these and other words, *G. Schramm* shares this hypothesis (*Eroberer und Eingesessene* - Conquerors and Inhabitants - Stuttgart, 1981). Both exclude from this category the names of the *Szamos, Kőrös, Maros*, and *Temes* rivers. However, Niš has prompted *N. Jokl* (*Real- lexikon der Vorgeschichte*, I. Albaner) to identify the $s < š$ change as Albanian. If so, then we should be able to draw the same conclusion about the above - mentioned rivers; G. Schramm also pointed this out. - Note also: *H. Barić: Lingvističke studije* (Sarajevo, 1954). *I. Popović*: "Bemerkungen über die vorslavischen Ortsnamen in Serbien" (*Zeitschrift für slavische Philologie*, 28, 1960). *Geschichte der Serbokroatischen Sprache* (Wiesbaden, 1960), "Quel était le peuple pannonien" ... (*Zbornik radova Vizantinoloskog instituta* 7, 1969), *L. A. Gindin*: "K kronologii i karaktyeru slavjanyizacii Karpato-balkanskovo prosztransztva", in: *Formirovanyije rannyefeodalnich szlavjanszkih narodnosztyej* (Moscow, 1981). At the same time, the Dacian etymology of *Abrud* and *Ompoly* are open to question but - alongside Popović and Gindin we would find it difficult to conclude that, in the territory, there would have been Slav presence in the 5th Century.

The above mentioned works provide information about the material culture of Dacians; *K. Pink* explored coin mintage: *Die Münzprägung der Ostkelten und Ihrer Nachbarn* (Diss Pann II. 15, Budapest, 1939). So did *C. Preda*: *Monedele geto-dacilor* (Bucureşti, 1973). *I. Glodariu* described commercial practices: *Relaţii comerciale ale Daciei cu lumea elenistică şi romană* (Cluj-Napoca 1974) = Dacian Trade with the Hellenistic and Roman World - (BAR Suppl. 8. Oxford 1976). While we cannot enumerate all papers and monographs written on the subject, special mention is due to *M. Babeş*: "Descoperirile funerare şi semnificaţia lar în contextul geto-dace clasice", (*SCIVA* 39, 1988). At long last we get a comprehensive look at Dacian burial customs, although most of the questions still remain unanswered.

We are better informed about the Roman period. In the *History of Transylvania*, Vol. I., *E. Tóth* provides an overview of the whole bibliography of the period, which should suffice as reference.

Nevertheless, *P. Király's* work on the history of the Roman Province, and of the Dacian Wars continues to be of value: *Dacia Provincia Augusti* (Nagybecskerek, Hungary - 1893). Another significant work is *C. Daicoviciu's: Siebenbürgen im Altertum* (Transylvania in Antiquity) (Bukarest, 1943). Of great importance are *A. Alföldi's* papers "Dacians and Romans in Transylvania" (Budapest, *Századok*, 1940) = Daci e romani in Transilvania, "Zu den Schicksalen Siebenbürgens im Altertum"; (Transylvania's Destiny in Antiquity) (Budapest, 1944); "Keletmagyarország a Római Korban" (Eastern Hungary in Roman Times) (published in Budapest, 1943 in *Magyarok és románok* (Hungarians and Rumanians - edited by *J. Deér - L. Gáldi.*) - Our references to Trajan's Column came from *C. Cichorius: Die Reliefs der Traianssäule* (Berlin, 1896). In "Der Forschungsstand zur Kontinuität der bodenständigen Bevölkerung im römischen Dazien (2-3. Jh.)" (The Status of Research on the Continuity of the Autochthonous Population in Roman Dacia in the 2nd-3rd Centuries, *D. Protase* offers a detailed analysis of the hypothesis of Dacian continuity (published in Berlin-New York, 1977 in *Aufstieg und Niedergang der Römischer Welt* (The Rise and Fall of Rome). He also wrote: *Autohtonii în Dacia* (Bucureşti, 1980) and: *Problema continuităţii în Dacia în lumina arheologiei şi numismaticii* (Bucureşti, 1966). The latter work occupies itself also with the period which follows the relinquishment of the province. We believe, the survival of the native population was put into the proper light by the examples given in the text. A summary of written records was provided by *I. I. Russu: Daco-geţii în imperiul roman* (Bucureşti, 1980). He also summarized the inscriptive material of "regio Ans.": "Materiale epigrafice în muzeul raional Dej". *Activitatea Muzeelor* (Cluj, 1956). *I. Mitrofan* developed a study of the Dacian castrum of Vármező: *Castrul roman de la Buciumi* (Cluj, 1972), etc. and a summary: "Aşezare ale populaţiei autohtone în Dacia Superioară" (*Acta Musei Napocensis* IX, 1972). Romanism in the Danubian Region was explored by *D. Tudor: Oltenia romană* (Bucureşti, 1978). His work contains data of the whole region and continues to be a valuable source. We refer to *R. Syme* on Roman rule in Muntenia and the "Hunt-papyrus" in The Lower Danube under Traian (*JRS* 49, 1959) and in other papers.

Dacian family names are an important link in the matter of continuity. *A. Kerényi* provided the first summary of this subject: "A dáciai szemêlynevek" (Dacian Family Names) (*Diss. Pann.* I. 9, Budapest, 1941). *A. Alföldi* provided an analysis of this material in: "Zu den Schicksalen Siebenbürgens", idem. These names - as well as additional ones - were also reviewed by *I. I. Russu*: "L'Onomastique de la Dacie romaine", in *Onomastique Latine*, Paris, 1977. *L. Balla* added exhaustive studies to the subject: "De la romanisation de la Dacie" (*Acta Classica Debreceniensis* XIV. 1978) and "Recusantes provinciales in Dacia" (*Oikumene* I., Budapest, 1976). He also explored the population-history of Roman Dacia: *Tanulmányok Erdély Történetéről* (The History of Transylvania - Studies); Debrecen, 1988; therein he also refers to papers which we are not describing here. Balla also recognizes the orientalization of the Province at the turn of the 2nd and 3rd Centuries. - *A. Mócsy* attempted a novel system of the analysis of family names: "Lateinische Cognomina als Geschichtsquelle: Zwei Typen der provinzialrömischen Kultur", *Acta Archaeologica* 36, 1984 (Latin family names as historical sources -

Two Types of Roman Provincial Culture); also Budapest, 1985. Dacian names of plants are used here for the first time in assessing linguistic manifestations in the Province; applicable references are to be found in this text. A. *Mócsy* also explores Romanization in general: *Gesellschaft und Romanisation in der Römischer Provinz Moesia Superior* (Budapest, 1970), and so does E. *Tóth* in *The History of Transylvania*, Volume I.

H. *Mihăescu* wrote about the language of inscriptions in: *La langue latine dans le Sud-est de l'Europe* (Bucureşti-Paris, 1978). About regional differences in Vulgar Latin, A. Tovar's work is noteworthy: "Das Vulgärlatein in den Provinzen", which was published in: *Die Sprachen im Römischen Reich der Kaiserzeit* (Languages in the Roman Empire), Köln, 1980. Including his previous works, J. *Herman* contributed to a study of the development of Romance languages: *Új eredmények, új kérdések a román nyelvek kialakulási folyamatának vizsgálatában.* (New results and new questions in the developmental assessment of the Romance languages), Budapest, 1985. These works do not provide material about Dacia, because there are no inscriptions to study from the mid-3rd Century on. Yet, this is the very period in which differentiation becomes an issue.

N. *Gostar* writes about perceived Dacian indigenous cults: Cultele autohtone în Dacia Romană (*Anuarul Institutului de Istorie şi Arheologie*, Iaşi II. 1956) but fails to take into account that there are no data which would substantiate identification with earlier indigenous cults.

A. *Alföldi* provides the most thorough account of the evacuation of the Province: "*A gót mozgalom és Dácia feladása*" (Gothic activity and relinquishment of Dacia). (*EPhK* 53-54, 1929-30) and further analysis of data in subsequent studies. - *G. Bichir* summarized the bibliography pertaining to the Karps in: "Carpii în istoriografia română şi străină" (*SCIV* 22, 1971), and in *Cultura carpică* (Bucureşti, 1973). He describes the Barbarians in Wallachia in: *Geto-dacii din Muntenia în epoca romană* (Bucureşti, 1984). This work contains the inscription on a bowl from Socetu: *Aurelius Silvanus fecit pataelam bonam*: the text in this form, and the lettering suggest contemporary fabrication.

D. Protase summarized the data on continuity in his works cited above, his latest work on the subject was: "Die dakisch-römische Bevölkerung nördlich der Donau in der Periode von Aurelian bis zu den Slawen (7th cent.) im Lichte der aktuellen Dokumente" (The Daco-Roman population north of the Danube from the period of Aurelian up to the 7th Century). The study appeared in: *Die Völker Südosteuropas im 6. bis 8. Jahrhundert* (*Südosteuropa Jahrbuch* 17, Berlin 1987). (Published in: Southeast-European Peoples in the 6th-8th Cent.) Protase's extreme viewpoint becomes quite apparent in comparison to other, not altogether unbiased works such as *K. Horedt's*: *Siebenbürgen in spätrömischer Zeit* (Bucureşti, 1982) and *O. Toropu's*: *Romanitatea tîrzie şi strāromânii în Dacia Traiană sud-Carpatică* (Craiova, 1976); as well as *D. Tudor's* above-mentioned *Oltenia romană*. A critical analysis by *E. Tóth* of Horedts's work is to be found in *Acta Archaeologica*, 1985: "Zur frühen Völkerwanderungszeit von Siebenbürgen" (The early period of peoples' migration in Transylvania.) The above works have at least some material basis in contrast to *L. Bârzu's*: *Continuitatea creaţiei materiale şi spirituale a poporului român pe teritoriul fostei Daciei*

(Bucureşti, 1979). (Continuity of the material and spiritual culture of the Rumanian people within the territory of former Dacia). Two other works in this category are: C.C. Giurescus': *Formarea poporului român* (Bucureşti, 1971) and *N. Stoicescu's*: *Continuitatea românilor* (Bucureşti, 1980).

In my research of the most important source materials on Dacia's history I made use of the best available editions: *Eutropii breviarium ab urbe condita*. Recognovit *C. Santini* (*Teubneriana*, Leipzig, 1979). It appears clearly from Santini's Foreword that Paulus Diaconus' text must be given preference over other interpretations.

K. Horedt provided the most detailed study of material elements of the early Great Migration-period. *I. Bona's* voluble account of the same period can be found in *The History of Transylvania*, Vol. I: "Dáciától Erdőelvéig. A népvándorlás kora Erdélyben" (From Dacia to Erdőelve: The era of the Great Migration in Transylvania.) *K. Horedt* reviews the later relics of the period in a more object-related manner *Siebenbürgen im Frühmittelalter* (Bonn, 1986) (Transylvania in the early Middle Ages). The present writer's critical review of the latter appeared in: *Danubian Historical Studies*, 1, 4, 1987. *R. Harhoiu* criticized Bona's outline: "Die Beziehungen Zwischen Romanen und Barbaren in Siebenbürgen in der Sicht einer ungarischen Geschichte Transilvaniens" (*Dacia* XXXI, 1987) (Relations between Romans and Barbarians in Transylvania from the perspective of Hungarian history of Transylvania). Although, the critique is in some respects exaggerated, much of it is valid because the applicable chapter in the History of Transylvania overrepresents the historical significance of material data. *G. Vékony* provides a short survey of this historical period, based on all accessible source material: "A dák-római kontinuitáselmélet a középkori Erdély történetének tükrében" (*Életünk*, 1988/3-Szombathely) = The Theory of Daco-Roman Continuity (NHQ XXIX, 110, 1988).

Horedt and Bóna have provided a detailed bibliography of the period. We will only list the most important references. *L. Bârzu* writes about the Baráthely (Bratei) cemetery: *Continuitatea populaţiei autohtone în Transilvania în secolele IV-V* (Bucureşti, 1973). *J. Bóna* already called attention to parallels between burials here and in Moldova in the History of Transylvania, Vol. I. (Second edition). See also *I.A. Rafalovics: Dancseny. Mogilnyik cernahovskoy kulturi III-IV. vv. n.e.* (Kisinyov- 1986). The cemetery at Etulija in the Prut-delta has more in common with the cemetery at Bratei than the one cited by Bóna. Also: *T.A. Scserbakova's* "Mogilnyik pervih vekov nasej eri u s. Etulija" (in *Archeologicheskije isledovanyija v Moldavii* (1974-1976 g.g. (Kisinyov 1981). The topography of these cemeteries call for identification with the Taifals. 4th Century records must have been collated on the basis of data provided by *Horedt* (*Siebenbürgen...*, see above). Bona failed to consider this as he attributed to the 4th Century cemeteries like those of Marosszentanna in spite of chronological evidence to the contrary. All researchers - Bóna excepted - maintain that subsequent findings cannot be assigned to pre-mid 4th Century. Chronological data permit the assumption that cemeteries of the Marosszentanna-type date from the end of the 4th or beginning of the 5th Centuries. Therefore, these must be viewed as part of the legacy of Ostrogoths who were resettled here by the Huns, just as the Pannonians who were found in Cluj and Alba Iulia. The findings at

Alba Iulia were first reported by *K. Horedt*: Gräber des 4. und 11-12. Jahrhunderts aus Karlsburg; *Untersuchungen zur Frühgeschichte Siebenbürgens* (Bucharest, 1958) (4th, 11th and 12th Century graves in Karlsburg [Gyulafehérvár - Alba Iulia]). The latest report on the sarcophagi in Cluj came from *D. Protase*: "Observaţii privind inscripţia ´creştinată´ de la Napoca" (*SCIVA* 36, 1985). Protase asserts that the cross carved in the letter O has been made later, in spite of the testimony of the photograph of the relic, published in the article, which clearly indicates the contrary.

In view of the ethnic composition of the era of the Huns, one cannot assume a Slavic presence based on rhetor Priskos' words of *medos* ´bragget´, and *strava*, ´wake´, quoted by Iordanes. There were actually Alan dialects in which the Iranian *a>e* change is found, cf. Hung. *méreg*, ´poison´ Oset *marg*, Hung. *üveg*, Oset *avg* ´glass´. Thus, Priskos' *medos* could well be an Iranian word from the Carpathian Basin and Iordanes' *strava* is likely to be a "hapax legomenon". With reference to the Omharus-ring: the VS, which is in a separate line, clearly indicates that it is an abbreviation. We know of no such name for the period; we cannot attach any meaning to the word. Therefore, our explanation, or a similar one, is most plausible.

The latter phase of the Great Migration is amply covered by those works of Horedt and Bóna to which we have referred earlier. *O. Toropu* is one of the sources for the extra-Carpathian region (Romanitatea..., see above). Another source is *S. Dolinescu-Ferche*'s summary (citing earlier literature, as well): "La culture 'Ipoteşti- Ciurel- Cîndeşti' (V-VII siècles). La situation en Valachie" (*Dacia* XXVIII, 1984).

K. Horedt believes that Rumanians migrated "upward" (north) in the 9th Century - this theory would be hard to support. Findings from that period have lately become more numerous - as in the case of the Danubian-Bulgarian cemetery from Maroskarna. A monstrous example of the theory of continuity is *E. Zaharia's Populaţia românească în Transilvania în secolele VII-VIII* (Bucureşti, 1977): the author classifies an Obîrşia-type cemetery as Old-Rumanian through the simple device of attributing to Christianity graves which contain skeletal and cremated remains! (For reference to Obîrşia-type cemeteries see: *O. Toropu-O. Stoia*: "La nécropole préféodale d'Obîrşia- Olt", Dacia XVI., 1972). With their Avar and Danubian-Bulgar connections and Slavic cremation practices, Obîrşia-type cemeteries/graves bear witness to 9th Century Bulgarian rule. From this period, we have unequivocal data about Dacias' population - (or a segment thereof) in Annales regni Francorum ad a: 824: "*Praedenecenti .... contermini Bulgaris Daciam Danubio adiacentem incolunt*". In other words, during that period of time Danubian Dacia was inhabited by a Slavic people, the Praedecenti, also called Abodrits. Since written records from this period refer, besides the above population, to the Bulgarians, we can only attribute to the Abodrits the burial mounds of Nagyfalu-Szamosfalva, which were foreign to the region. (See also: *G. Vékony*: "Spätawarenzeitliche Messer mit Volutengriff" (in: *Urzeitliche und frühhistorische Besiedlung der Ostslovakei in Bezug zu den Nachbargebieten*, Nitra, 1986) (Settlements in Eastern Slovakia during antiquity and the early Middle Ages as they relate to adjacent lands.)

J. Deér writes about Vlachs mentioned by Anonymous in *Magyarok és Románok* I. (Budapest, 1943) (Hungarians and Rumanians). On the other hand, *Pascu's Voievodatul Transilvaniei* I. (Cluj, 1971) is a caricature of historical writing. Deér's analysis — augmented by this writer's modifications — offers an unequivocal interpretation of the above source. Studies referring to the Volochs mentioned in Russian annals include: *M. Gyóni:* Les Volochs des Annales primitives de Kiev (*Études slaves et roumaines* II. 1949) and *Gy. Kristó:* "Rómaiak és vlachok Nyesztornál és Anonymusnál", in: *Tanulmányok az Árpád-korról,* Budapest 1983 ("Romans and Vlachs as they appear in the works of Nyestor [Nestorius] and Anonymus", in Studies of the Árpád-period). At the time the Norici are identified as Slavs by the *Ipat'evskaja letopis,* the Volochs mentioned above can't possibly be considered Franks. They must be viewed as Romans - as confirmed also by I.V. Jagič.

In addition to the literature cited above, Dacia's settlements of the 10th Century were explored by *G. Vékony,* who wrote about runic inscriptions from the mid-Migration-period in the Carpathian Basin: *Későnépvándorláskori rovásfeliratok a Kárpátmedencében* (Szombathely, 1987). In the same study there is a short description of Murfatlar and Bulgarian inscriptions on a vessel from Capidava. The sitings of Murfatlar alphabet-markings on a vessel from Bucov (cf. *M. Comşa: Cultura materială veche românească,* Bucureşti, 1978) testify that the settlement's inhabitants were Bulgaro-Turkish and not Old-Rumanian.

Still considered a seminal study of the Rumanian language is *O. Densusianu's*: *Histoire de la langue Roumaine*, I-II (Paris, 1901, 1914, 1932), as well as *A. Philippide*: *Originea românilor*, I-II (Iaşi, 1923, 1925) which refutes the theory of continuity. *A. Rosetti's*: *Istoria limbii române* (Bucureşti, 1968) proved to be an invaluable reference to the Latin, Balkan and Slavic phases of Rumanian, each of which is subjected to thorough individual analysis. - *The Early History of the Rumanian Language* (Lake Bluff, 1977) by *A. Du Nay* was also written to be a general survey. He provides a detailed analysis of the theory of continuity and offers its rebuttal. [A thoroughly revised version was published in 1996: *The Origins of the Rumanians*, Matthias Corvinus Publishing, Toronto-Buffalo – editor's note.] In addition to the works mentioned above, the Albanian connection is explored by *H. Barič* in: *Albano-Rumänische Studien* (Sarajevo, 1919) and: "Albanisch, romanisch und Rumänisch" (Godišnjak I, 1975). *I.I. Russu's* Etnogeneza (cited earlier) analyzes all parallel words. The finding of territories where variants of Vulgar Latin in the Balkan peninsula were spoken is a new development, although such a division is indicated by the data provided by J. Herman, as well as the network of relationships between Albanian, Dalmatian and Rumanian.

The linguistic characteristics of Common Rumanian were surveyed by *E. Petrovici* ("Unitatea dialectală a limbii române", in: *Studii de dialectologie şi toponimie*, Bucureşti, 1970). Also: *M. Caragiu Marioţeanu et alii*: *Dialectologie Română* (Bucureşti, 1977). Regarding the Aromân dialect, important for the study of the history of the Rumanian language, see *T. Capidan*: *Aromânii. Dialectul aromân* (Bucureşti, 1932), and more recently: *A. G. Lazarou*: *L'aroumain et ses rapports avec le grec* (Thessaloniki, 1986); although well-informed, he asserts the Arumun are of Greek origin. Considering the theory of Daco-Roman continuity, this unique, but impossible theory is to some extent understandable.

The Slavic connection is explored by *A. Rosetti: Istoria limbii române* and "Les plus anciens mots slaves méridionaux du romain", in: *Mélanges lingistiques* (Bucureşti, 1977), as well as: *E. Scărlătoiu: Relaţii lingvistice ale aromânilor cu slavii de sud* (Bucureşti, 1980), and The Balkan Vlachs in the Light of Linguistic Studies (*RÉSEE* XVII., 1979). *A. Du Nay* also deals with these relationships in: *The Early History*, but his data are often to be checked because of the typographical errors.

There are many monographs of varying length which could be cited but most of the data they present are also to be found in the works we used as reference.

With respect to the origin of Rumanians *K. Sandfeld's: Linguistique balkanique* (Paris, 1930) is of key importance, as is *M. Friedwagner's*: Über die Sprache und Heimat der Rumänen in ihrer Frühzeit (*Zeitschrift für romanische Philologie* 54, 1934) = On the Early History of Rumanian language and Homeland (Journal of Romanistic Philology). Another suitable reference would be *G. Reichenkron*: Das Ostromanische (in: *Völker und Kulturen Südosteuropas* (Südosteuropa-Schriften, I. München 1959). His conception is similar to *Gamillscheg's* (*Romania Germanica* II. (Berlin-Leipzig, 1935) Zur rumänischen Frühgeschichte in: Die Kultur Südosteuropas. Ihre Geschichte und ihre Ausdruckformen (*Südosteuropa-Schriften* 6, Wiesbaden 1964). He assumes that some archaic aspects of certain dialects bear traces of surviving Daco-Romans: Using his analogy, we would place the Csangos of Moldova into the ancient Hungarian homeland on account of their linguistic archaisms.

B. *Gerov* surveyed the perimeters of Balkan-Latin: Die Lateinisch-griechische Sprachgrenze auf der Balkanhalbinsel, in: *Die Sprachen im Römischen Reich der Kaiserzeit* = (Languages spoken in Imperial Rome: Latin Greek linguistic frontiers on the Balkan Peninsula.) (Cologne, 1980). Interestingly, this border thrusts southward along the rivers Utus and Asamus; this is where the inscription came to light which includes the verb: *mergo* in its altered form, providing a (different) meaning which is characteristic of Rumanian and Albanian. See: *C. Daicoviciu*: A merge; Fossatum-sat (*Dacoromania* 5, 1927-1928). There is a detailed analysis of the place-names mentioned by Prokopios in the work of *A. Philippide*: (*Originea*) which we have already cited. *V. Bešerliev* responds to the topographical aspects of the issue: Zur Dentung der Kastellnamen in Procops Werk 'De aedificiis' (Amsterdam, 1970), Geografijata na Balgarija u vizantijskite avtori (*Izvestija na Narodnija Muzej Varna* 23 (38) 1987) = An Interpretation of Castle-names in Procop's Works.

The events of 587-588 - the "*torna, torna frater*" - glossa - have an extensive literature. The latest summary was compiled by *A.G. Lazarou* (*L'Aroumain*, see above) who has incorporated many earlier references. - We believe that *V. Beševliev* erred in the locale he assigned to the Kalvomuntii: Bemerkungen über die antiken Heerstrassen im Ostteil der Balkanhalbinsel (*Klio* 51,

1969) = Observations pertaining to military roads in the eastern region of the Balkan peninsula. Earlier literature on this subject includes *P. Hunfalvy's The history of Vlachs* (Az oláhok története) I. (Budapest, 1894), which is still a useful reference. Also, the frequently quoted *Originea* of *A. Philippide*. A Hungarian glossary of place-names was developed by *Szádeczky-S. Kardoss -T. Olajos*: Sources of Avar History (Az avar történelem forrásai) IV. 2 (*Archeológiai Értesítő*, 1980 = Archeological Bulletin).

For references to the Balkhorekhinos, see: *P. Uspenskij: Istorija Afona*, IV. (Petrograd, 1892, 311) and *A.G. Lazarou*. - We know that, in this form, the Slavic name for Rumanians could not have been incorporated into the Greek language due to reasons of native wordstock-patterns (which would have ordained *Balkhos* in lieu of Blakhorekhinos). Our data come from late sources and can be traced no further back than the 10th Century. Therefore, many questions remain unanswered but there is a great deal which remains beyond dispute. (see: *G. Schramm: Eroberer...*).

There is extended literature dealing with names for the Danube, and versions thereof. The latest may be *G. Schramm*: Der rumänische Name der Donau (*Dacoromania* 1, 1973) = The Rumanian name for the Danube. - His explanation for the name is a perceived secondary internal Rumanian development, - quite inconceivable. The name for the Danube - *Danuvius* - could have been lost by Romanism moving south of the Danube-region because they could not very well have been near the Danube as Attila created a no-man's land in an adjacent strip of land in 447. For another study of the history of the region, see *Szádeczky-*

S.Kardoss: Geschichte des Attila-Abkömmlings Mundo und ihre Chronologie bei Theophanes (*Acta Classica Debreceniensis* X-XI, 1974-75) Until now, no Turkish connection has been considered.

The data that follows has long been common knowledge. (History of Rumanians - edited by *L. Gáldi* and *L. Makkai*), as well as summaries by *A. Philippide* and *Lazarou*. Also, *G. Murnu: Studii istrice privitoare la trecutul românilor de peste Dunăre* (Bucureşti, 1984); *M. Gyóni:* A legrégibb vélemény a román nép eredetéről, Budapest, 1944. (The oldest view re. the origin of the Rumanians); La premiére mention historique des Vlaques des monts Balkans (*Acta Ant.* I, 1951-1952). L'évêché vlaque de l'archevêché bulgare d'Achris aux XI-XIV siecles (*Études slaves et roumaines*, I. 1984).

In his above-mentioned work, *M. Gyóni* writes in detail about Kekaumenos' narration, presents an erroneous view of the two branches of Rumanian ethnogenesis: *Folklór és etnográfia* 24 (Debrecen, 1986) and: A dunai balkán térség romanizációja = The Romanization of the Danubian-Balkan region (*Világtörténet*, 1987/3). Mócsy is to have discovered some Rumanian traditions - M. Gyóni offers a substantiated counter-claim.

One of the best segment-analyses of the Balkan history of the Rumanians was done by *A. Dragomir: Vlahii din nordul peninsulei balcanice în evul mediu* (Bucureşti, 1959). *L. Makkai* gives a detailed description of their northward trek in *The History of Transylvania* I. (Transylvania in the Hungarian Kingdom during the Middle Ages). Also: Two Books - Two Different Views on the Hypothesis of Daco-Roman Continuity in Transylvania (*Danubian Historical Studies* 1, 3, 1987). This northward settlement cannot be separated from the same type of migration of Southern-Slav groups speaking the *št*-type of Slavic; the forebears of contemporary Bulgarians arrive north of the Balkan-Mountains at the same time. - Rumanian penetration into the Carpathian-Basin during the 13th Century occurs in two phases. One precedes the Tartar (Mongolian) invasion (1214) when groups of considerable size turn up at the end of the 12th and the start of the 13th Centuries. Their presence is substantiated by their take-over of the Kerc region between 1202-1209 and their participation in the 1208 campaign of Joachim, Commander of Szeben. (see: *L. Makkai: Transylvania*). The Tartar invasion destroyed their settlements, as a result of which no large-scale Rumanian communities could be found in this region by the end of the 13th Century.

This settlement-history of the region has found an important source of reference in *J. Kniezsa's*: The place-names of Eastern-Hungary (in: *Hungarians and Rumanians*, I.); Names of Transylvania's rivers (in: *Yearbook, Transylvanian Scientific Institute*, 1942) and in *E. Moór's* : The Matter of Place-Names in Eastern Hungary (*Századok* [Centuries] 1945-46). The latest study on the name of the Küküllő river was done by *L. Ligeti: Turkic associations of the Hungarian language prior to the Conquest of Hungary and during the age of Árpád.* (Budapest, 1986). The latter assumes the name is of Avar origin but we believe it may have been *Kükül* its original form. This is underscored by the Saxon Version of *Kokel (Kockel)* and *cuculiense* as an adjective.

A final point of emphasis: we could only list a portion of the literature used as references; we did not identify the handbook-type references. For additional information, the reader may turn to the bibliographies listed in the reference works we have cited.

Abbreviations

Acta Ant.	Acta Antiqua Academiae Scientiarum Hungaricae
Acta Arch. Hung.	Acta Archeologica Academiae Scientiarum Hungaricae
AECO	Archivum Europae Centro-Orientalis
alb.	Albanian
Amm. Marc.	Ammiani Marcellini Rerum gestarum libri
An. Rav.	Anonymi Ravennatis Geographia
ar.	Arumum
Aur. Vict. Caes	Aurelius Victor, Ceasares
av.	Avestic
BAR	British Archeological Reports
bolg.	Bulgarian
Cass. Dio.	Cassici Dionis Historiarum Romanarum libri
CIL	Corpus Inscriptionum Latinarum
Cod. Just. Nov.	Codex Justiniani, Corpus Juris Civilis, Novella
Cons. Const.	Consularia Constantinopolitana
dalm.	Dalmatian
DissPann	Dissertaniones Pannonicae
dr.	Danubian Rumanian
EPhK	Universal Philological Journal (Egyetemi Philológiai Közlöny.)
Eutr. Brev.	Eutropius, Breviarium ab Urbe condita
fr.	French
Genethl. Max.	Mamertinus, Panegyricus genethliacus Maximiano Augusto dictus
gör.	Greek

Her.	Herodotos
idg.	Indo-Germanic
ILS	Inscriptiones Latinae Selectae
Iord. Get.	Jordanes, Getica
Iord. Rom.	Jordanes, Romana
ir.	Iranian
isztr.	Istro-Rumanian
JRS	The Journal of Roman Studies
kaj-horv.	Kajkavština-Croatian
Kat.	Catalan
közalném.	Lower-Middle German
lat.	Latin
lengy.	Polish
m.	Hungarian
MGH	Monumenta Germaniae Historica
mr.	Meglenorumanian
nyj.	dialect
litv.	Lithuanian
ném.	German
NHQ	New Hungarian Quaterly
óang.	Old English
ócornw.	Old Cornish
ófr.	Old French
ófn.	Old Upper German
óir	Old Iranian
ol.	Italian
óm.	Old Hungarian
óol.	Old Italian
óörm.	Old Armenian
or.	Russian
oszl.	Old Slavonic
örm.	Armenian
összl v.	Ancient Slavonic
port.	Portuguese
prov.	Provencale
RÉSEE	Revue des Études sud-est européenne
rétor	Rhetoroumanian
rom.	Rumanian
Ruf. Festus, Brev. -	Rufius Festus, Breviarium rerum gestarum populi romani
SCIV	Studii şi Cercetări de Istorie Veche

SCIVA	Studii şi Cercetări de Istorie Veche şi Arheologie
sp.	Spanish
SRH	Scriptores rerum Hungaricarum
Suid. Lex.	Suidae Lexicon
szerbhorv.	Serbo-Croatian
szl.	Slav
szlov.	Slovak
ved.	Vedic

Contents

Mrs. Etelka Alapi, Dr. Ferenc Androczi, Mr. Jeno Arros,
Mr.&Mrs. Otto Avvakumovits, Mr. George Babits,
Mrs. Terezia M. Bajnoczi, Mr. István S. Balogh, Prof. S. Balogh,
Mrs. Katalin Baranski, Mr. Julius Bartha, Mr. Lajos Bartha,
Mr. Lajos Bartha/MHRF, Mr. Oscar Bartha, Mr. Andrew Beelik,
Mr. Janos Beller, Mr. & Mrs. Miklos Bende, Mr. Julius Benko,
Mrs. Marta Berta, Mr. Francis Bessenyey, Mrs. Eva Bessenyey,
Mr. George Bethlendy, Mr. & Mrs. Zoltan Biro,
Mrs. Irene Bokrossy, Mr.& Mrs. Steven Borbas,
Mr. Denes D. Boronkay, Mr. Karoly Borossa, Dr. Gabor Both,
Mr. Géza Budai, Mr. Aladár Burgyán, The Corvin History Society,
Mt. & Mrs. Thomas Csathy, Mrs. Margaret Csendes,
Mr. Louis Csizmadi, Mr. Béla Csordas, Mr. Vilmos Der,
Dr. Levente L. Diosady, Dr. L.S. Domonkos, Mr. Emery G. Dora Jr.,
Mr. Ignac Eder, Mr. Frank Erdelyi, Mrs. Katalin Értavy M.D.,
Mr. Steven Farkas, Mr. Rudolf Faulhaber, Mr. Frank A. Fazakas,
Mr. Gyula Fazekas, Mr.&Mrs. Leslie Feher, Mr. Tibor Fekete,
Mr. Albert-Ella Fodor, Mr. Nicholas Fodor, Mr Peter G. Fratrits,
Mr.&Mrs. Louis Fulop, Mr. Frank Gal, Mr. &Mrs. Victor Gerley,
Mr. Sephen Gulyas, Mr. Zsigmond Gyenge, Mr. Leslie Gyorok,
103. Tollas T.Öcs.Cs., Dr. Bela Halasz, Mr. & Mrs. Leslie Hanula,
Mr. Attila Hethelyi, Mr. Vilmos Hevesi, Mr. Tibor Hidas
Micro Dental Laboratories/András Hites, György Hites
Dr. Laszlo Hites, Mr. Frank Horvath, Mr. Istvan Horvath,
Mr. István Huff, Ms. Margit Iklody, Mr. Laszlo Ivanyi,
Dr. L. Jakab, Mr. & Mrs. George Jalics, Dr. Nandor Jenofi,
Mrs. Erika Józsa, Ms. Margit Kaffka, Rev. Arpad De Kallos,
Rev. & Mrs. Szabolcs Kalman, Mr. Emil Kanitsch,
Mr. George Kékesi, Mr. &Mrs. George Kekessy,
Mrs. Susanne A. Kemenes, Mr. & Mrs. Martin Kertesz,
Mr. J. Kerti, Mr. Jozsef Kis, Mr.&Mrs. Antal Kiss,
Dr. Erno Kiss, Mr. Károly Kiss, Mrs. Elizabeth Klement,
Mr. T. Kokai-Kun, Mr. George Kolonits, Mr.&Mrs. S.J. Magyaródy
Dr. & Mrs. Laszlo Kontur, Mr. Edmond de Koos,
Mr. & Mrs. Istan Kosa, Mrs. Katalin Kovats, Mr. Steve Kucsma,
Mr. Steve Kun-Szabo, Dr. & Mrs. Frederick Ladanyi,
Mrs. Katherine Ladányi, Mr. Stephen Lakatos,
Mr.&Mrs. Zoltan Lamperth, Mr. Tibor Lantos, Mrs. Susan Legeza,
Mr. Imre B. Lendvai, Mr. & Mrs. Laszlo Lesko,

Mr. & Mrs. L. Levius, Mr. János Lónyay,
Mr. & Mrs. Laszlo Lonyay, Mrs. & Mrs. S. Lopert,
Mr. Laszlo Lovas, Mrs. Margaret Lovrics, Mr. Tamas Ludescher,
Dr. Sandor Magyar, Mrs. Maharajak Katalin, Mr. Ferenc Sidlo,
v. Leslie L. Majthenyi, Mr. John Máté, Mr. Nick Mates,
Ms. Gabriella Mauthner, Mrs. Margit Mentler,
Mr. Lorand H. Meray, Mr. Nicholas Mezes, Mr.&Mrs. J. S. Miko,
Dr. B. Millinkovich, Mr. Janos L.F. Molnar, Mr. Janos Molnar,
Mr. & Mrs. David Molnar, Ms. Ellen Muray-Botos,
Mr. Akos L. Nagy, Mr. Edward J. Nagy, Mrs. Ilonka Nagy,
Dr. Julius G. Nagy, Mr. Karoly Nagy Mr. & Mrs. Louis P. Nagy,
Mr. Louis I Nagy, Mr. E. A. Nemes, Mr. Nandor Nemeth,
Mrs. Helene I. Nemeti, Dr. & Dr. Laszlo Osvath, Dr. Zoltan Ovary,
Mr. John Pader, Mr. Antal Pak, Mr. Sandor PAL,
Mr. &Mrs. Gyula Palinay, Mr. Gabor Z. Pap, Mrs. Marta Papp,
Mr. Jozsef Pataki, Mr.& Mrs. Joseph Pataky, Ms. Csilla M. Patrin,
Mrs. M. Magdalena Pattantyus, Mr. Rudolph Pechy,
Dr. Marta Pereszlenyi-Pinter, Mrs. Joan Peter, Dr. Ervin Poka,
Mr. Zsigmond Piller-Tahy, Mr. Istvan Pinter, Mrs. Maria S. Roy,
Mr.&Mrs. Istan Prileszky, Dr. Kalman F. Protzner,
Mrs. Elisabeth Rath, Ms. Katherine Rekai, Dr. Thomas F. Ruzics,
San Antonio Hungarian Ass'n, Mrs. Elisabeth Sándorfy,
Mr.&Mrs. Gyula Say, Mrs. Frank Schippel, Mr. Erik Selmeczy,
Mr. Walter Schrenck-Szill, Mrs. Anna Seregelyes,
Mr. Marton Seregelyes, Mr. & Mrs. Lajos Simo, Mr. Zoltan Simon,
Mr. & Mrs. Jozsef Solymos, Mr. & Mrs. Frank Somoskoi,
Mr. Stephen Sothy, Mrs. Albina Suba, Mr. Victor R. Sumeghy,
Mr. Zoltan Szabados, Mr. Bela Szabó, Mr. L. Szamoskozi,
Dr. & Mrs. Bela Szandtner, Szappanos Andrew Z.,
Mr. Jozsef Szecsey, Mr. Erno Szelepcsenyi, Mrs. Helen Szendi,
Mr. Julius Szentkuti, Mr. Ferenc G. Szentmihályi,
Mr. Szojka K. Lorand, Mr. & Mrs. Laszlo Szoke, Rev. John Szücs,
Mr. János Tamás, Mr. Frank Tarcsay, M r. László Thomay,
Mrs. Elisabeth Tömöry, Mrs. Éva M. Tömöry, Mr. Stephen Török,
Mrs. Julia Tudos, Mr. Csaba Tusko, Mr. Marton M. Vagi,
Mr. & Mrs. Jozsef Vamosi, Mr. István Huff, Ms. Eva Varady,
Mrs. Lujza Varosy, Mr. Leslie Vegvari, Ms. Katalin Voros, ·
Mr. Mátyás Wild, Mr. Peter Zathureczky, Mr. W.G. Zeman,
Mr. Tibor Zoltai, Mrs. Margaret Zydron,

OUR MEMBERS, ASSOCIATES, VOLUNTEERS, ADVISERS, PATRONS and FRIENDS

Gráber Család, Makk Család, Alapi Etu, Bakos Istvan,
Bányai Ferenc, Bedi Balázs, Beodray Ferenc-Pirike, Telek József,
Bereczky Gyorgy, Bereczky Zoltán, Bessenyey-Barcza Éva,
Brenner Katalin, Buda Márta, Desy-Nagy Lajos-Erzsébet,
Dr. Agner László, Dr. Balogh Imre, Dr. Forgách Péter,
Erdödi Ágnes, Falk Viktor, Globits László, Horváth Mihály,
Huff Istvan, Jálics Iza, Kaffka Margit, Kálnoky Ernö, Kardos Geza,
Keddy Gyula, Kincses Ágnes, Kis Ferenc, Kovács Mária,
Kövári György, Kozmon Idi, Kulifay Sylvia, Lamperthné Cili,
Magyaródyné Rózsi, Matica Agnes. Megyesi Csilla, Molnár János,
Pogány Erzsi, Somogyi Vince, Szabó Kati, Szabolcsné Erzsébet,
Szaday Ibolya, Szappanos István, Tarnói Eva, Toldy Piroska,
Tömöry Éva, Tóth Hilda. Vámosi József-Margit, Zika Klári,
Dr. Kontur László, Felsöványi Ékos, Haverland Attila,
Zimányi Magda, Bozóki Barnabás, Bogsányi Dénes, Benke Tibor,
Dr.Szeitz Tibor,Hegedüs István, Jakab Ferenc, Dr. Lippai István,
Szalai Katalin,Szalai Joe, Marshall László, Dr. Gyulai Ferenc,
Tóth László, Udvardy Otto, Csukonyi Zoltán, Arató Nóra,
Nagy Zsuzsa, Kazal László, Sass Márton, Sisa István,
Nás-Kovács Beata, Prof. Simon András, Prof. Wagner Ferenc+,
Prof. Borsody István, Prof. Chászár Ede, Prof. Wojatsek Károly,
Prof. Várdy Béla, Prof. Ludányi András, Prof.Balogh Sándor,
Prof. Kazár Lajos+, Prof. Wass Albert+, Prof. Szendrey Tamás,
Prof. Boros-Kazai András, Prof. Makkai Ádám
(Names in the Hungarian order)